DATE DUE

DE 19 '01

DEMCO 38-296

Visions and Revisions

BERG EUROPEAN STUDIES SERIES

GENERAL EDITOR: Brian Nelson (Monash University, Melbourne)

ADVISORY BOARD: Michael Biddiss (University of Reading), John Flower (University of Exeter), Paul Michael Lützeler (Washington University, St. Louis), David Roberts (Monash University, Melbourne), Tony Judt (New York University), Walter Veit (Monash University, Melbourne)

Marko Pavlyshyn (ed.), *Glasnost in Context*

David Roberts and Philip Thomson (eds.), *The Modern German Historical Novel*

Brian Nelson (ed.), *Naturalism in the European Novel*

Brian Nelson, David Roberts, and Walter Veit (eds.), *The Idea of Europe*

Dieter Freundlieb and Wayne Hudson (eds.), *Reason and Its Other: Rationality in Modern German Philosophy and Culture*

VISIONS
AND
REVISIONS

Women in Italian Culture

edited by

MIRNA CICIONI &
NICOLE PRUNSTER

BERG
Providence / Oxford

?906, U.S.A.

© Mirna Cicioni and Nicole Prunster, 1993

A CIP catalogue record for this book is available from the British Library.

Library of Congress Cataloging-in-Publication Data

Visions and revisions : women in Italian culture / edited by Mirna
    Cicioni and Nicole Prunster.
        p.   cm. — (Berg European studies series)
    Includes bibliographical references and index.
    ISBN 0–85496–710–9
    1. Women in popular culture—Italy.   2. Women in literature.
3. Italian literature—History and criticism.   I. Cicioni, Mirna.
II. Prunster, Nicole.   III. Series.
HO 1638.V56 1993
305.4'0945—dc   2092–16782
                                                                        CIP

Printed in the United States by Edwards Brothers, Ann Arbor, MI.

In memoriam

Janet Longmore

(1949–1987)

Contents

Contents

Tradition and Transformation: Women in Society and the Movement Toward Liberation

Introduction

Women have performed a dual role throughout feminism's twenty-year history. In addition to being producers of gendered knowledge, women also have become a primary focus of critical attention in what may be considered one of the most significant cultural consequences of the feminist movement. As is well known, initial critiques of the representations of women in cultural (scientific, legal, literary, artistic) discourses were followed by critiques of the very theoretical foundations of these discourses. Academic scholarship throughout the world was inevitably influenced, to varying degrees, by these developments. This is no less true of research on Italy carried out in English-speaking countries.

Until recently, English-speaking scholars looking at Italian literature, history, society, and the arts concentrated mainly on men and their work, while Women's Studies scholars focused principally on France and England to the near exclusion of their neighbor, Italy (Rutter 1990: 565–66; De Lauretis 1990: 13). This imbalance is still discernible in two collections of essays, elaborated from conferences held in 1983 and 1984 in the United States, which examine the Middle Ages and the Renaissance from a feminist viewpoint (Rose 1986; Levin and Watson 1987). Of a total of twenty-four contributions, only three deal specifically with aspects of Italian culture. William Monter in "Women and the Italian Inquisitions" (Rose 1986: 73–83) identifies gender as a prime factor in the control of crimes during the Inquisition in Italy. Elissa Weaver in "Spiritual Fun: A Study of Sixteenth-Century Tuscan Convent Theater" (Rose 1986: 173–205) breaks new ground by discussing the contribution to sixteenth-century drama of Tuscan nuns, among literary history's "lost voices." Constance Jordan's essay "Boccaccio's In-Famous Women: Gender and Civic Virtue in the *De mulieribus claris*" (Levin and Watson 1987: 25–47) brings to light the ambiguities inherent in a text that purports to present models for women. Several more recent volumes by feminist scholars concentrating on eminent women writers of the sixteenth century have helped redress this imbalance: Marcella Diberti Leigh's study of the renowned poet and courtesan, Veronica Franco (1988), and Adriana Chemello's monograph on the life and work of Moderata Fonte (1988). Constance Jordan's *Renaissance Feminism* (1990), by examining sixteenth-century treatises on women in the context of contemporary political thought, adds further to the now growing body of literature and historical research on women in the Middle Ages and the Renaissance.

Developments in the position of women in contemporary Italian history have also stimulated research. A few book-length studies of Italian feminism have appeared in the United States (Birnbaum 1986; Hellman 1987) and in the United Kingdom (Bono and Kemp 1991). Historical and sociological research has focused on the problematic nature of the legal and social reforms of the 1970s and 1980s,[1] which have been termed compromises to satisfy some of the demands of the women's movement and the cautious conservatism of institutions such as political parties and movements, trade unions, and welfare agencies (Caldwell 1981; Ergas 1982; Saraceno 1984; Rutter 1990).

Recent literary criticism has been influenced by feminist theory in two main ways. The representations of women in the discourses of canonized male writers have been reexamined with a critical methodology that analyzes the author's discursive position, making connections between textuality and sexuality. Italian women writers such as Matilde Serao, Sibilla Aleramo, Natalia Ginzburg, Elsa Morante, and Dacia Maraini have been discovered, or rediscovered, and translated; this, implicitly or explicitly, has led to a questioning of the canon that, until then, had excluded them.[2] Since the late 1980s, attention has also

---

1. Divorce was introduced in 1970. Contraception was legalized in 1971 and abortion was legalized – in a very restricted fashion – in 1978. In 1975 the patriarchal family law of 1942 was replaced by a new law that granted women formal status almost equal to that of men within the family. In 1977 a Sex Discrimination and Equal Pay Act was passed, and in 1984 a national Equal Opportunity Commission was set up. A bill on domestic and sexual violence, first put forward in 1979, was debated and amended by four successive legislatures, and, as of June 1991, had not become law.

2. Among recent works by Italianists are Bruce Merry's collection of essays on Italian women writers (1990), Alan Bullock's monograph on Natalia Ginzburg (1991), and Ann Caesar's forthcoming translation of Matilde Serao's novel *The Conquest of Rome* (1991). See also the collection of essays edited by Barànski and Vinall (1991).

been directed at Italian feminist theory, particularly at the strand known as "the practice of sexual difference," which is influenced by both Adrienne Rich and Luce Irigaray.[3]

These theoretical approaches needed to be brought together in cross-cultural initiatives focusing specifically on women on the one hand, and on Italian Studies scholarship on the other. The first move in this direction was the International Symposium on Women in Italian Studies, which took place at York University, Toronto, in February 1987. The second was the conference "Women in Italian Culture," held at La Trobe University, Melbourne, between 30 June and 2 July 1989. Ada Testaferri, in her preface to a collection of some of the papers presented at the Canadian symposium, points out the presence of a variety of disciplines and critical approaches, although literary criticism remains the dominant research area (Testaferri 1989: 11). Similarly, the La Trobe conference, open to scholars in all disciplines, was remarkable for the breadth of its contributions. Participants from Italy, the United States, and Australia met in a profeminist spirit to discuss the impact of women on a wide range of disciplines: literature, sociology, history, art, and popular culture. This conference was the genesis of the present volume, which contains a selection of the most significant papers and an invited paper by the Italian historian Luisa Passerini, included to complement the section on women in contemporary Italy with an analysis of the origins of second-wave Italian feminism.

This volume is an attempt to offer Italianists recent research – from different national, theoretical, and political positions – into the literary and social processes through which "women" have been constructed in Italian culture since the Middle Ages. It is also an attempt to offer English-speaking readers a variety of perspectives on women as members of contemporary Italian society, as literary characters, artists, participants in historical change, agents of change in Italian popular culture. Areas absent from the present coverage include science, economics, cinema, education, language, and the changing relationship between women and the political system in Italy, all of which have generated much important feminist research in Italy in the past decade. One of the aims of this collection is to stimu-

3. This "theoretical practice" (Gross 1986: 202) is discussed in Cicioni (1989), De Lauretis (1990), Cicogna and De Lauretis (1990), Rutter (1990), and Bono and Kemp (1991).

late further interest, research, and publication in all these areas by English-speaking scholars.

The essays in this volume are presented in two sections: "Women and the Male Gaze: The Literary and Artistic Heritage" and "Tradition and Transformation: Women in Society and the Movement Toward Liberation." With one exception, the essays in the first group examine the representation of women in literature written by men that spans the centuries from the Middle Ages to recent times. These rereadings of such canonical texts as Dante's *Divine Comedy*, Counter-Reformation comedies, and the novels of two major contemporary writers, Cesare Pavese and Carlo Emilio Gadda, reveal conflicting and, at times, ambiguous images of women that are not always in accord with the prevailing view of the time.

Flavia Coassin and Diana Cavuoto adopt different critical approaches in examining two contrasting female figures from Dante's *Divine Comedy*, Matelda and Francesca. Coassin discusses Matelda (*Purgatorio* XXVIII–XXXIII), the sole personification of the *Comedy*, within the broader context of the "female muse" in the poetic discourses of men, connecting her to other images of the solitary maiden recurrent in the poetry of the *dolce stil novo* and to their mythical sources. Coassin notes that the presence of such idealized, archetypal female images as Matelda in an epoch renowned for its Mariolatry no less than for expressions of misogyny, points to a need for balance, for a restoration of harmony within the individual as well as society. Dante's portrayal of the historical Francesca da Rimini (*Inferno,* Canto V) is somewhat more contentious, as is suggested by the mixed critical response that it has engendered. Cavuoto in her essay "Francesca Revisited" takes issue with both Romantic and present-day critics who have seen Francesca as either passive and weak or morally reprehensible and thus deserving her fate. Cavuoto substantiates her view that Francesca serves a positive, didactic function by analyzing a text replete with literary references. For Cavuoto, then, the lovers' predilection for one type of literature – the courtly-chivalric romances of the day – is symptomatic of the narrowness of their perception of the human condition. At the hands of Dante the poet, Francesca's historical dimension is replaced with an enduring, emblematic one: her encounter with Dante the pilgrim is a learning experience with regard to his own attitude toward literature and human relationships.

Using as his initial point of reference Boccaccio's archetypal *De mulieribus claris*, the (problematic) model for subsequent authors of supposedly profemale treatises, including that discussed in his essay "Men Framing Women: Sabadino degli Arienti's *Gynevera de le clare donne* Reexamined," Stephen Kolsky argues that in Arienti's 1490 work the praise of women is actually a secondary concern, given that the treatise affords priority to other discourses, most notably the political discourse. The exemplary female subjects in the treatise are, for the most part, constructions fashioned to fill a political need. The no less exemplary female protagonists of Counter-Reformation comedy in Italy are likewise circumscribed by being male constructions having a specific (moral) purpose, as Nicole Prunster suggests in her essay on female protagonists in the late sixteenth-century Italian comedy. The increase in autonomy and independence of this new breed of heroine is tempered by a pronounced moral conservatism lacking in the majority of their predecessors in early erudite comedy. These female characters are intended to serve as an example to the women in courtly audiences in upholding a system of at times questionable patriarchal values, such as family honor.

Negative images of women may paradoxically be put to positive purpose, as Margaret Baker observes in her paper "The Women Characters of Carlo Emilio Gadda." The lower class characters of this northern Italian writer, with their broad range of (often bizarre) physical defects, are instruments of social criticism in that they clearly do not reflect the fitness and progress emphasized by the Fascist regime. Gadda's middle-class Lombard women, for the most part property owners and observed in greater detail than their women servants, are instead the objects of satire, since it was that class that had appointed itself protector of social values in Fascist Italy. Gadda's social dimension becomes the personal dimension of human relationships in Cesare Pavese's last novel, *La luna e i falò*, in which – as Walter Musolino lucidly shows – women are seen to have no redemptive function, but are instead testimony to the ultimate meaninglessness for the narrator (and for Pavese himself) of human involvements.

The only essay with a historical and semiotic, rather than literary, focus analyzes representations of women and men in photographs of the period during World War I, a time of enforced separation of the sexes and mass participation of women in a variety of extradomestic activities. Author Paola di Cori sees in these images evidence of a profound transformation in the cultural definition of the sexes wrought by the social upheaval of the war years.

Definitions by women themselves of their cultural and social identity, and the gradual and at times contradictory evolution of these definitions, are central to all the essays in the second section. The essays by Piera Carroli and Lucia Chiavola Birnbaum are complementary in that they recover and sum up two forms of collective women's culture in preindustrial Italian society. Birnbaum shows how the official, conservative image of the Virgin Mary as a model of feminine patience and submissiveness is challenged in some contemporary southern Italian Easter rituals, where for generations women have played a major role and Christian themes have fused with pagan ones, connecting the Madonna to powerful pre-Christian female symbols, such as sibyls and fertility goddesses. Carroli places nineteenth-century lullabies in the social context of peasant life in northern and central Italy, pointing out that they had two additional functions besides the obvious one of lulling babies to sleep. They were a means of acculturating female children to the harsh reality of women's subordination to men, and at the same time they allowed women to express their frustration and anger at motherhood and their position within marriage.

Carroli's conclusion regarding the position of women in the society she analyzes – that "the coexistence of two opposing forces must have produced the incentive to bring about change" – is confirmed by the conclusion reached by Franca Bimbi in her sociological essay. Bimbi examines the transformations of the mother's role over three generations of Northern Italian women, in the context of some of the social changes that have taken place in Italy since the end of World War I, such as a decline in fertility rates and women's greater access to education and paid employment. Motherhood is Bimbi's paradigm of social identity, because – as she demonstrates – its construction affects peasant, working-class, and middle-class women alike, and changes in this construction contribute to eroding the power of men throughout society.

The shifting balance of power and authority within the family presented by Bimbi, however, still coexists with enduring male privileges within and without the family. Tina Lagostena Bassi's scholarly and angry essay juxtaposes the growing awareness among women of their personal and collective rights as individuals with the cultural values and assumptions – all too often shared by the defendants, their lawyers, and the judges – evident in trials for domestic and sexual violence in the 1970s and 1980s.

Much of the social evolution described by Bimbi and the changes of the Italian legal system in the attitudes to women, however slow and contradictory, would not have been possible without the emergence of a strong women's movement. Luisa Passerini's important essay outlines the historical developments of "second-wave" feminism in Italy, tracing its origins to various social and cultural influences during the 1960s, which culminated in the political movements of 1968. Passerini emphasizes the complex interaction of concomitant factors such as the reevaluation of personal experiences (which she defines as a "feminization" of politics), the emergence of new forms of social relations, and the tension between egalitarianism and political hierarchies. Passerini also points out some of the continuities and discontinuities between the women's movement in the 1970s and the women's movement in the 1980s.

The discourses and the practice of feminism also have had a deep influence on women's literary and critical production. Dacia Maraini's novel *Lettere a Marina* is an extended examination, through a variety of metaphors – letters, food, opera, the sea – of female passivity and women's need to unlearn it. Pauline Dagnino's reading of it is derived from the Kristevan-inspired tendency within feminist literary criticism that looks at different ways in which female desire is discovered and inscribed in literary texts. Dagnino's analysis of the symbols in the novel stresses Maraini's emphasis on the positive, nurturing aspects of the mother-daughter relationship, denied and silenced by the rules of patriarchy and rediscovered by the writer of the letters through her recalling and reconstructing a variety of relationships between women.

Some of the essays in this collection are explicitly informed by feminist theory in that they show ways in which women are inscribed in a subordinate role by male literary, historical, and legal discourses, or reinterpret widely held notions, questioning conventional "knowledge" on the topics they examine. In other contributions traditional scholarly approaches are adopted to reveal some of the tensions within Italian culture with regard to women. With their diversity of intellectual perspectives and theoretical foundations, these essays point out ways in which gender is a determining factor in all areas of social and intellectual experience. For this reason they complement and broaden existing scholarship in English on women in Italian culture, and suggest possible directions for future scholarship.

Acknowledgments

We wish to thank the many individuals and institutions that contributed to the success of the conference with their expertise and with their financial support. We are also indebted to Marilyn Lake, Director of Women's Studies at La Trobe University, and Professor Brian Nelson of Monash University for their advice, to Flavia Coassin and Walter Musolino for their editorial assistance, to Marisa Stirpe for her generosity with her time and ideas, and to Consuelo Di Leo for preparing the manuscript. Finally we thank Katherine Hagedorn for her painstaking assistance and advice in editing the book.

MIRNA CICIONI AND NICOLE PRUNSTER
La Trobe University, 1992

Women and the Male Gaze

The Literary and Artistic Heritage

ONE

Matelda:
Poetic Image or Archetype?

FLAVIA COASSIN

A s their recurrence in different epochs and cultures shows,
archetypal images exercise a powerful influence on imagi-
native and expressive modes. This essay addresses the problem,
encountered by feminist critics and artists, of how to deal with
"positive" female archetypal images, of which Matelda (*Purgatory*
XXVIII–XXXIII)[1] is an expression. The analysis of the development of this image and of its interaction with an often contrasting social reality is expressive of the tensions and aspirations at
play within a nation's culture. As the longevity of these images
resides in their dynamism, women artists, rather than dispens-
ing with them, may find it a more fruitful strategy to transform
them by giving them new meanings.

Before the question contained in the title can be answered, it
is necessary to define its scope and objectives. The title "Matelda: Poetic Image or Archetype?" is not intended to suggest that
poetic image and archetype are mutually exclusive. What must
be determined is the kind of poetic image that Matelda is, given
that she is the only personification in the *Comedy*. All the other
characters have historical reality, indeed usually a very recent
one; that is, they are real historical characters, most of whom
lived in the twelfth and thirteenth centuries.

There ought to be little difficulty in accepting Matelda as a
personification in the *Comedy*, albeit the only one, insofar as the
literature of different ages is replete with personifications. It is
rather common practice to represent an idea or a virtue in the
guise of a young woman, as can be seen with Dante's own gentle Lady Philosophy of the *Convivio* or the many anonymous,

---

1. The quotations and references to Dante's works are from the F. Chiappelli
edition (1978). The English translations of Dante's *Purgatorio* are by T. Oakey,
from the Temple Classics edition (London, 1964).

3

ineffable women sung by medieval vernacular poets. The fact
remains that Matelda stands out for her unique function in the
poem and the reader is compelled to ask what she represents.
She, too, remains anonymous till the very end, and the fact that
at the last minute Beatrice unexpectedly calls her by name only
adds to the puzzlement of the reader.

Another question underlying the original one is why predominantly female images such as these should be used as personifications. The immediate and all-too-obvious answer is that
it is so because the poets responsible are usually male. Yet it is
doubtful that women poets would have favored male images.
Robert Graves said that while a male poet (a non-Apollonian
one) would write in honor of and be inspired by the Muse, a
woman would be either a representative of the Muse or, if she
were a poet, the Muse herself ([1961] 1984: 447). If history had
been written by women, could the Muse have been male? The
question is difficult to answer because it is hard to imagine,
such is the power of this ancient imagery.

The meaning of "archetype," the second term in the question, is no less contentious. It is outside the scope of this discussion to argue for or against its alleged prelinguistic existence,[2]
although it can, of course, be extralinguistic. The premise
adopted here is not that archetypes may be viewed as basic universal human truths (although Dante would maintain that this
is so) but rather that their universality stems from their being
"older" images that seem to hold meaning and to have strong
expressive capabilities for different people at different times, as
is shown by the presence of similar myths and mythological figures within different cultures and epochs.

An archetype, then, is a profound and complex image, the
origins of which go far back in human imagination and whose
major characteristic is a permanence within the many expressions it receives through the ages. Although this characteristic
lends it a universal quality, it does not make the image static; on
the contrary, the fact that some archetypal images are taken up
at various points in time and are given new meanings and interpretations consonant with existing interests and needs proves
their formidable dynamism. It also provides useful documentation for historical as well as literary criticism. When set within
the sociopolitical context, an analysis of both the kind of arche-

2. See Jung (1933: 467, 556, 560), Durand (1979: 27–28) and Lévi-Strauss
(1953, I: 230–234).

typal images that predominate in the culture of a particular time and the particular expression they receive can disclose much about the ideological and emotive forces present in that culture.

Medieval vernacular poetry is, for the most part, love poetry in which woman represents the "other," unattainable and often incomprehensible, but an "other" who is better and wiser, superior in status, virtue, and knowledge. She becomes then the catalyst in man's cultivation of all that is nobler in his "self," and from this position to her becoming a mediator between earth and heaven, between man and God, is but a small step.

It is common knowledge that women in the Middle Ages had no political or economic rights, let alone power; indeed they were "silent" both as muses and as people. Given the knowledge of the actual social status of women, should all that these poets have said be dismissed as mere lies? It is a fallacy to expect the real to mirror the ideal (or vice versa). Rather, it should be asked how these idealized images interact with such a social reality, what system of tensions and aspirations they reveal. What does it mean, for instance, that extreme expressions of misogyny should be manifest at the same time as the cult of Mary flourishes? The prevalence of the female element in the imagination and ideals of an epoch, after a long history of patriarchal values, points to a need for balance, a restoration of harmony within the individual as well as within society.

The strongest images of woman, transmitted through mythology and literature, are those of the great mother, the young maiden, and the witch or siren. The three are complementary aspects of the primordial image of woman as creator and destroyer; they are, in other words, personifications of the cycle of life. In Graves's words:

> As the new moon or spring she was girl; as the full moon or summer she was woman; as the old moon or winter she was hag. ([1961] 1984: 386)

Christianity does not do away with these images, but makes them its own. Mary combines the features of the archetypal mother goddess Cybele, whose cult had spread from Asia Minor to Greece and Rome where she had been associated with local deities, such as Rhea or Demeter. Like the Phrygian Cybele, Mary is worshiped as mother of God and men and queen of heaven. She also is depicted as both powerful mother and young virgin, and, again, she is not the sole instance of such

5

duality, for ancient mythology and religions abound with the figures of gods or kings who were born of a virgin and then sacrificed to save mankind.

In this category are also Matelda and Beatrice. Matelda is the young maiden who restores Dante to Beatrice (or his capacity for happiness), and the latter, no longer the young maiden of the *Vita Nuova*, becomes the cathartic mother who questions him and rekindles his strength. Dante calls her "mother": "Cosí la madre al figlio par superba" [So doth the mother seem stern to her child] (*Purgatory* XXX, 79). Thus Beatrice becomes an archetypal image in an episode with descriptive elements, as an analysis of the text reveals.

In Canto XXVII of *Purgatory*, having arrived at the Earthly Paradise, Virgil had declared Dante's will "free, upright and whole" ["libero dritto e sano è tuo arbitrio," 1.141] and therefore he was now able to follow his "pleasure": "lo tuo piacer omai prendi per duce" [now take thy pleasure for guide, 1.131] rather than his reason ("ingegno e arte," 1.130). In other words, Dante has reached integrity, his will being one with that of God, and can therefore trust his instincts, for they conform with the divine natural order. The return to paradise is expressed in terms of a return to nature, that is, the restoration of harmony. This state is externalized and expressed through the image of Matelda. In the eternal springtime of the dense forest, alive with the colors and fragrance of the vegetation and the sounds of the foliage and bird songs, on the other side of a stream of most clear waters, there appears a solitary woman who sings as she gathers flowers wherewith her path is painted. Dante calls the beautiful maiden who seems to him to be warmed by love's beams, begging her to come closer so that he may hear her song. She reminds him, he adds, of Persephone at the time her mother lost her and she the spring flowers. There follows what is perhaps the most memorable moment in the description: the slow turning of her body as if in a dance movement. Thus turning, flowers in her hand and at her feet, she slowly moves towards Dante allowing him to hear her song. As she stops at the stream she raises her eyes, which shine with so bright a light as could never be seen in Venus's eyes. The love and joy communicated by this light fill Dante with anguish as he is overwhelmed by the desire to reach her but knows he cannot. Matelda then explains the reason for her rejoicing and the nature of the place given by God to humanity. She adds a corollary: this place had been dreamed by the ancient poets who had sung of the golden age. Still singing as an enamored woman ("cantando come donna innamorata," *Purgatory* XXIX, 1) she moves, like a nymph, upstream. She reappears in Canto XXXI when Dante, regaining consciousness, finds himself immersed by her in the water; following this she leads him into the dance of the four beautiful maidens, usually identified with the four cardinal virtues, who define themselves as nymphs and stars as well as Beatrice's handmaidens.

This summary of the episode draws attention to its main elements, the most notable of which is the following: Matelda is a very strong visual image that the reader immediately recognizes: where has she been depicted before? It is important to note that, while she is a very strong visual image, Dante does not describe her appearance; the reader does not know what she looks like or what she is wearing. Nonetheless she is perceived as a visual reality because she externalizes an internal image that all readers have, and it is this internal personal image that is recognized. Dante also recognizes her yet he does not give her a name. Till the very end she is "la bella donna" [the beautiful woman] (*Purgatory* XXVIII, 43, 100; XXXI, 100; XXXII, 28; XXXIII, 121, 134) to distinguish her from Beatrice who is called "la donna mia" [my woman] (*Purgatory* XXXII, 122). And it is significant that he does not ask her who she is. By being reminded of Persephone, Dante communicates to the reader his awareness of her being a complex memory. For the reader, too, she is a complex literary as well as personal memory.

There are several similar images in medieval poetry, in particular Cavalcanti's "pasturella" [young shepherdess]: she, too, is a solitary young woman wandering in a wood and singing "as if in love." She also brings to mind several paintings, such as the Pompeian Flora; or the young heroines of epic poems down to Milton's depiction of Eve as a young maiden in *Paradise Lost*, or, more recently still, Keats's Belle Dame Sans Merci, who, very much like Cavalcanti's "pasturella," is found wandering in the "meads" and who looks at the poet "as she did love" and sings "a faery's song." Mythology and classical literature are full of beautiful solitary young maidens found in similar settings, who, like Persephone, were pursued by enamored gods. These maidens usually are saved through divine intervention, often that of the lunar goddess, by being transformed into some form of vegetation or water course (for example, Daphne and Arethusa, who

7

were transformed into a laurel tree and a spring, respectively).
The metamorphosis is, however, nothing more than a return to
their essential nature, as earth and water traditionally were seen
as female elements. The primordial image of woman consistently was associated with the forces and cycles of nature, and as
such the women who represented them could be invoked but
not possessed. If a man tries to possess them, they elude him.
Dante, too, experiences a strong desire to possess Matelda but
knows he cannot. He can become one with nature only by
restoring harmony within himself. As often happens in myth,
images of the mother or young maiden can stand for the benev-
olent life-giving natural forces that, when called upon, will help
to bring about a metamorphosis in man through the death of
the old self and the birth of the new. The choice of Persephone
serves to point out this apparent duality. Death is necessary for
the rebirth of the human spirit just as it is in the cyclic renewal
of nature. Matelda administers precisely this rite of passage
through the traditional element of water, and Dante's loss of
consciousness symbolizes the necessary death before resurrection. It is a restoration of harmony between internal forces and
those of nature and therefore divine order. Note how the experience is, in fact, related in naturalistic terms:

> Io ritornai dalla santissim'onda
> rifatto sí, come piante novelle
> rinnovellate di novella fronda
>   puro e disposto a salire alle stelle.
> (*Purgatory* XXXIII, 142–45)

> [I came back from the most holy waves, born again, even as new
> trees renewed with new foliage, pure and ready to mount to the
> stars.]

It should be noted also that all the references immediately
related to the figure of Matelda are mythological: Persephone,
Venus, nymphs; Beatrice herself is likened to Minerva (*Purgatory*
XXX, 68). The setting is not only biblical but universal and literary, be it the Parnassus of the golden age or the "locus
amoenus," the springtime garden of the more recent vernacular poets. These things point to Dante's belief in the divine
order impressed on all created things that can be perceived by
all rational human beings, and his belief that it is the same
absolute truths that are expressed, with varying degrees of
approximation, through equally universal images.

8

In retaining all the mythical, literary, and biblical references in the image of Matelda, Dante shows that he is aware (and wishes to make the reader aware) of the richness and complexity that this image has acquired through the ages. The function of this image is to form a diachronic system that unifies and resolves the synchronic cluster of conflicts and desires. It is not mere coincidence that the imagery and language used in the description of Matelda are so close to the ones used by Cavalcanti for his "pasturella." These deliberate similarities, like those between Matelda and the many other young maidens and "donne angelicate" of contemporary poetry as well, draw the attention of the reader to Dante's mode of interpreting common tendencies.

In contemporary poetry, concomitant with the image of woman as a superior and ennobling creature, the concept of love undergoes a process of spiritualization, which, however, often appears a forced superimposition on the original erotic theme. At the same time, the beauty of the woman seems to mirror an ideal of beauty to which these poets aspire: a beauty and love that unsettle, that dispense equally life and death, energy and suffering. It is a poetry of turmoil, of the search for the "new," marked by a constant questioning of the meaning of love, nobility, art.

Matelda is clearly in love, yet hers seems a love without object. Instead, her love and joy are her very mode of being. In Matelda the erotic element is perfectly fused with the other elements, not suppressed as the reader often feels it is in Beatrice, in whom there is a progression from the old to the new love, and in these cantos, the two are present at the same time.[3] In Matelda's case there is no such discourse, her love is spontaneous. It is not of the same spontaneity of the soul at birth when it is innocent but unaware; instead, her love has a purity regained through wisdom.

The prevalence of the unsettling female image in this poetry implies a time of incipient and welcome change, and marks the formation of a new human ideal that encompasses social as well as individual factors. In social terms it is equated with the aspiration to justice and peace, expressed through the upholding of artistic values. Historically, these values consistently have

3. There are explicit references to the "old" love: "antico amor" ["ancient love"], "antica fiamma" ["ancient flame"], "antica rete" ["the toils of old"] (*Purgatory* XXX, 39 and 48, and XXXII, 6, respectively).

been imagined as a return of the suppressed female principle. Virgil's words "Iam redit et Virgo, redeunt Saturnia regna" [the Virgin comes back to us, and the rule of Saturn is restored] are interpreted by Dante as the return of Astraea, the star-maiden symbolizing Justice who fled from earth at the end of the golden age (*Monarchia* I, xi: 1).[4] Wisdom, particularly wisdom related to civic affairs, was symbolized by the goddess Minerva (Athena). In the Scriptures, Solomon is said to have chosen Wisdom (Sapientia) as his beautiful bride. Dante's Beatrice assimilates the function of Minerva and, as with the biblical Sapientia, the four virtues are ordained as her handmaidens. Beatrice is also a representative of the mother image; she is greeted by the twenty-four elders with the same words used by the angel at the Annunciation to greet Mary:

> Benedetta túe
> nelle figlie d'Adamo, e benedette
> sieno in eterno le bellezze tue.
> (*Purgatory* XXIX, 85–87)

> [Blessed art thou among the daughters of Adam and blessed to all eternity be thy beauties.]

She functions in lieu of Mary as the new Eve, for it is she who sits at the foot of the tree, thus restoring its fruitfulness.

If Beatrice stands for the wisdom that assisted in the creation and regulates and orders all things, Matelda stands for nature: Persephone and her mother, Demeter, are one and the same. She also stands for the ideal of humanity at its best, not only as it was before the Fall but also as it could be now. Persephone-Demeter being both light and darkness, death and rebirth, express a duality that is not contradiction but harmony; so Matelda is simultaneously innocence and knowledge.

Dante discloses the meaning Matelda holds for him through the dialectics of desire and memory, activated at the crucial moment between paradise lost and paradise regained. Matelda's love is one with the rejoicing in the beauty of nature. It is Dante's belief that this aesthetic pleasure in the beauty and order of nature must perforce disclose the divine will and therefore human destiny, and consequently regulate all aspects of human conduct. There is ample evidence for this in the *Convivio* and *Monarchia* as well as in the *Comedy*.[5]

---

4. For a discussion on this theme see Singleton (1967), chapters XI and XII.

Pagan tradition, with its goddesses and myths, serves for Dante as confirmation, through the universality of images and dreams and aspirations, of Christian truths and values. To the impartial observer it all serves as confirmation of the universal appeal of certain images; their recurrence at particular times can be read as symptomatic of the preoccupations of those times. And it has been observed already that poets and thinkers always have expressed the aspiration of their times to the positive ideals of justice and harmony through images related to a renewal brought about by the intervention of woman, or by the restoration of the female principle. Finally, to the not so impartial observer, these man-made images reveal that the positive female principle charged with the creation of, among other things, art and civilization, has been rendered silent and anonymous. Anonymous and almost entirely silent are the women sung by medieval poets: if they have a name, it is often a name invented by the poet to evoke or represent something of himself or of his poetry. They also look alike: they all have long blond tresses and green eyes; in later compositions, physical descriptions are left out altogether. The female principle has been clearly dispossessed, either by being made a silent muse, an abstraction, or bluntly, as mythology attests, by rape.

It was stated earlier that women, too, find it difficult to resist some of these female images. This is so not only because they are powerful and strongly embedded in our culture; there are other historical reasons as well.

The women's movement has meant above all the identification of women with women, and this makes it all the more difficult to imagine being inspired by a male muse. One may object that men did not identify with the muse, nor did they identify with or indeed even understand the women they sung as superior creatures; to them they were incomprehensible, the "other." Perhaps the "other" that, for a woman, is man, is instead too "real," characterized as it is by the many social implications that, historically, have meant mainly aggression and

---

5. See, in particular, the following themes in the following sections:
  the universe as manifestation of God:
    Monarchia I, viii, 2; II, ii, 8
    Paradise I, 103–105; XX, 8
  beauty as knowledge and persuasion:
    Purgatory XIX, 61–66; XIV, 149
  human destiny:
    Convivio III, xv, 4; III, xiv, 1–3; III, ii, 7–9
    Monarchia I, ii.

oppression. Perhaps women do not yet have enough positive male images.[6] As women artists develop their own expressive means, however, they may choose not to dispense with these female images but instead to give them the life and substance of which they had been deprived by male monotheism.

6. An example of a positive male image is the "wise old man," which is appealing as a form of the inspiring muse, but which has become problematic as a paternal image bestowing approval/disapproval. Not that this image is intrinsically unacceptable but, at this point in time, before it is possible to embrace once more the positive value of the "paternal," it is necessary to divorce it from its negative "patriarchal" aspect.

TWO

Francesca Revisited

DIANA CAVUOTO

Canto V of *Inferno*,[1] in which Dante meets the souls of Paolo Malatesta and Francesca da Rimini, has long been a source of inspiration for poets, writers, and musicians. It also has been a source of much debate and critical entrepreneurship. Unhappily, Dante's characterization of Francesca, even until recently, has engendered a number of critical expositions that safeguard what can only be described as a fallacious dichotomy, whereby the figure of Francesca has been subjected to rigid stereotyping, resulting in extemporaneous fictions that are not borne out by the text.

The nineteenth century's Romantic portrayal of Francesca did much to promote a distorted view of her as "(un) essere fragile, appassionato" [a fragile, passionate creature] (De Sanctis 1955: 80; Rossi and Galpin 1957: 39),[2] one who "nella fiacchezza e miseria della lotta serba inviolate le qualità essenziali dell'essere femminile, la purità, la verecondia, la gentilezza, la squisita delicatezza de' sentimenti" [in the weakness and distress of her struggle, preserves inviolate the essential qualities of womanhood – purity, modesty, gentleness, exquisite delicacy of feeling] (De Sanctis 1955: 81; Rossi and Galpin 1957: 40–41). De Sanctis's view of the living Francesca as a delicate being "in cui niente è che resista e reagisca" [without the strength to resist or react] (De Sanctis 1955: 80; Rossi and Galpin 1957: 40) implies that Francesca yields to desire through no fault of her own. In other words, she cannot be held responsible for her actions and decisions because she is a weak and passive woman.

1. All quotations in Italian from Dante's *Divine Comedy* are taken from the 1966–67 edition (edited by Petrocchi). All English translations of the passages quoted are taken from the translation by D. Sayers and B. Reynolds.

2. All English translations of the passages by De Sanctis are taken from *De Sanctis on Dante.* Essays edited and translated by J. Rossi and A. Galpin (1957: 39).

13

However, such a view negates the practice of *libero arbitrio*, free will, the importance of which is stressed in the *Purgatorio*:

> Color che ragionando andaro al fondo,
> s'accorser d'esta innata libertate;
> però moralità lasciaro al mondo.
>
> Onde, poniam che di necessitate
> surga ogne amor che dentro a voi s'accende
> di ritenerlo è in voi la podestate.
>
> (*Purgatorio* 67–72)

> [They who by reasoning probed creation's plan
> Root-deep, perceived this inborn liberty
> And bequeathed ethics to the race of man.
>
> Grant, then, all loves that wake in you to be
> Born of necessity, you still possess
> Within yourselves the power of mastery.][3]

In the polarity of responses to Francesca, there is also the equally misleading view that she cannot be other than a morally abhorrent and evil character. To these critics she is narcissistic (Bergin 1969: 84; Grandgent 1933: 48–49; Musa 1971: 46–48), one of "le creature del male" (Montano 1956: 183) [an evil creature], a "lying temptress" and the "pathetic protagonist of an infernal encounter" (O'Grady 1987: 84).[4] The latter remark is in stark contrast to the poet's engaging portrayal of

3. The importance of free will is stressed also in the Epistle to Can Grande della Scala: "The subject is man according as by his merits or demerits in the exercise of his free will he is deserving of reward or punishment by justice" (Epistola X, 8, Toynbee 1966: 200), although the question of the letter's authorship is still the subject of critical debate. For example, Dronke's study of the *clausulae* in the Epistle throws doubt on Dante's authorship of the expository part of the letter (Dronke 1986: 103–11). In any case, the focus on the faculty of free will in the *Divine Comedy* is clearly a move away from the sentiments expressed in sonnet CXI, "Risposta di Dante a messer Cino," in which Dante denies that the will can be free under the rule of "Amore":

> Però nel cerchio della sua palestra
> liber arbitrio già mai non fu franco,
> sí che consiglio invan vi si balestra. (9–11)
> [Thus within his arena's bounds free will was never
> free, so that counsel looses its shafts in vain there.] (Foster and Boyde 1967: 201)

As the Francesca episode was written only a few years later, it is possible to identify an element of "palinodic self-analysis," as Barolini terms it (1984: 3). In Canto V, the mature poet Dante is reasserting his belief in the positive effects of literary achievement. The preoccupations of his early work, notably the theme of love, have been transformed and universalized to reflect his "convictions about the proper use of literary art" and the "social effect of his art, for good or for ill" (Taylor 1983: 5).

4. See also Shapiro (1975) and Kirkham (1989).

Francesca, in which outbursts of moral indignation are conspicuously absent. Dante's Francesca is not prevaricating. While there are no illusions as to the serious nature of the lovers' sin, Francesca is neither the passive, frail flower nor the wanton, licentious creature circumscribed by either of these two opposing groups of critics.

Historical evidence of the lovers is somewhat sketchy. It is known that, soon after 1275, Francesca, daughter of Guido da Polenta, lord of Ravenna, was given in marriage to Gianciotto Malatesta, lord of Rimini, in order to guarantee peace between the two feuding families. Francesca became enamored of her brother-in-law Paolo (who was already married), and the two lovers were murdered by Francesca's husband between 1283 and 1286. It is likely that Dante saw or perhaps met Paolo Malatesta when the latter was Capitano del Popolo in Florence, from February 1282 to February 1283.

In Canto V, then, powerful human emotions are cardinal points in a poetic structure born of reflection and order. In the Second Circle, where the souls of the lustful are carried aloft and buffeted by the angry currents of a howling black wind, the Wayfarer first encounters sinners in a circle of Upper Hell, and the violence and disorder of the storm are a reification of the irrational nature of blind sexual passion. Amid the strong visual and aural effects of the canto and its emotional impact on the Pilgrim, the author constructs an episode that is rich in literary associations and "associative relationships" (Scott 1979: 8).[5] A closer examination of the episode reveals that the figure of Francesca serves an important function in the poet's exploration of the reforming power of literature. Francesca is presented as a reader of books, and her articulate and intelligent discourse demonstrates a familiarity with a number of literary works, the most obvious being Guido Guinizelli's poetry and the Old French prose romance *Lancelot du Lac*. However, there are a number of other texts whose presence signals the possibility of a new poetic direction for Dante the pilgrim, who has emerged from the "selva oscura" [dark wood], and whose shifting, evolv-

5. Textuality in the Francesca episode is also discussed in Carli (1950); Poggioli (1957); Cambon (1961); Mattalia (1962); Pagliaro (1967 vol. I: 115–59); Caretti (1968 vol. I: 105–31); Hatcher and Musa (1968); Hollander (1969: 106–14); Perella (1969: 140–57); Dronke (1975); Cossutta (1977); Mazzotta (1979: 160–70); Paparelli (1979); Popolizio (1980); Della Terza (1981); Bàrberi-Squarotti (1982); Bonora (1982); Noakes (1983); Taylor (1983); Barolini (1984: 4–14).

ing nature is in contrast to the stasis of the infernal inhabitants. Moreover, if one appropriates the journey motif, one could say that Canto V contains important "signposts" or "markers," which not only indicate the edification of the Pilgrim, but which also further the reader's understanding of Dante-poet's intention to create a new poetic credo that will surpass both the efforts of the *stilnovisti* and his own youthful poetic works.

In Canto V, Dante underlines this intention through the use of the book image, where the reading motif is an essential factor in the poet's exploration of how literature can reveal truths. Ernst R. Curtius states: "The highest activities and experiences of the mind are for Dante connected with learning, with reading, with assimilating through books, a preexistent truth. Hence, for him, writing and the book can be the media of expression for the 'highest moments' of poetry and human life" (1953: 326).[6]

Francesca's gracious speech, with its marked referentiality of text, offers important lessons, whereby, without concealing or diminishing the lovers' guilt, Dante shows how their limited response to literature, that is, to the courtly-chivalric literature of the day, is characteristic of the narrowness of their perception of the human condition. Clearly, those critics who perceive Francesca as merely a diabolical personification of *lussuria* [lust] overlook the literary dimension of Dante's characterization of her. The view should be rejected, therefore, that in *Inferno* Canto V Dante is "unable to comprehend the potential danger of Francesca" (O'Grady 1987: 73); danger, not in a physical sense, but in what the critic sees as Francesca's attempt to conceal a deceitful nature to elicit sympathy for her plight. On the contrary, Dante is able to comprehend the lesson offered by Francesca as a result of her intellectual pursuits. Although the focus on one type of literature can be seen as a motivating factor in the lovers' abandonment to sexual passion, Francesca's monologue, a remarkable concentration of literary references, contains a positive message for the Wayfarer-poet, for whom the highly charged encounter elucidates his own attitude to literature and human relationships. Moreover, the Wayfarer's fall into a death-like swoon does not arise simply from a sense of

---

6. John Freccero believes that Dante's poetic career was "a continual *askesis* in preparation for his last work" because "Dante's poetic history derives its significance retrospectively from its ending" (1973: 73). See also Hollander (1975: 348–63).

overwhelming pity and grief for the lovers' suffering in Hell. Rather, it constitutes a moment of self-realization and cognizance. The Pilgrim-poet recognizes that he has the potential to advance from poetry "per diletto" [for enjoyment] to literary art that uplifts and transforms the human spirit. Thus Dante's fall is not a condemnation of the lovers, nor indeed of the authors of courtly literature. It is, however, an affirmation by the poet of the further possibilities that Francesca's reading could have offered had she and Paolo not chosen to remain "earthbound" (like doves bound "ferme al dolce nido" [to their sweet nest]), unwilling to develop further and discover the truths that might have saved them from eternal perdition. The Wayfarer's loss of consciousness signifies his recognition that he has avoided that same unhappy fate. It is a moment of self-awakening; an awareness of his own fallibility in the light of Francesca's experience.[7]

The motif of reading and literature, what we may term the image of the book, is a crucial theme in the Francesca episode. Although Dante-protagonist is overcome with emotion when he hears the lovers' tale, Dante-poet is seeking an alternative to the romantic literature that acted as a catalyst for Paolo's and Francesca's illicit liaison. There are, of course, other instances in the *Commedia* where Dante highlights the reading motif. The most beautiful occurs in *Paradiso* XXXIII where, at the moment when the Pilgrim contemplates the Divine Light of God, the universe is described as a volume whose scattered leaves are bound together by the love of the Creator:

Nel suo profondo vidi che s'interna,
legato con amore in un volume,
ciò che per l'universo si squaderna.   (*Paradiso*, 85–87)

[In that abyss I saw how love held bound
Into one volume all the leaves whose flight
Is scattered through the universe around.]

7. Antonio Enzo Quaglio defines Francesca as "questa donna libresca, questa creatura cartacea, che proietta sul pellegrino le ombre della propria ambivalenza morale" [this bookish woman, this papery creature who projects onto the pilgrim the shadows of her own moral ambivalence] (1973: 29). Fredi Chiappelli is equally dismissive of Francesca's literary pursuits in his description of "la trivialità delle sue parafrasi dottrinali," [the triviality of her doctrinal paraphrases] (1990: 16). However, Francesca's discourse fulfills an all-important function for the Wayfarer's development. As Vittorio Russo states: "Egli (Dante) ha riconosciuto nelle parole di Francesca gli echi della sua passata esperienza morale e intellettuale" [He (Dante) has recognized in Francesca's words the echoes of his past moral and intellectual experience] (1965: 102).

In Canto I of *Inferno,* the poet states that he applied himself to the study of Virgil's "volume":

> O de li altri poeti onore e lume,
> vagliami 'l lungo studio e 'l grande amore
> che m'ha fatto cercar lo tuo volume.   (*Inferno,* 82–84)

> [Oh honor and light of poets all and each,
> Now let my great love stead me – the bent brow
> And long hours pondering all thy book can teach.]

And we learn in *Inferno* XX that Dante knows the *Aeneid* by heart: "ben lo sai tu che la sai tutta quanta" [well thou knowest that hast by heart the whole long rhyme] (114). Of course, Dante's familiarity with the *Aeneid* is evident in Canto V. For example, Francesca's statement:

> Ma s'a conoscer la prima radice
> del nostro amor tu hai cotanto affetto,
> dirò come colui che piange e dice   (*Inferno,* 124–26)

> [Yet, if so dear desire thy heart possess
> To know that root of love which wrought our fall,
> I'll be as those who weep and who confess]

is a direct echo of Aeneas's words in Book II, where he gives an account of the fall of Troy:

> Sorrow too deep to tell, your majesty,
> You order me to feel and tell once more
> . . . .
> But if so great desire
> Moves you to hear the tale of our disasters
> . . . .
> However I may shudder at the memory
> And shrink again in grief, let me begin.[8]

Since Paolo does not utter a word for the entire duration of the canto, Dante pays homage to his "auctore" by means of a female character. However, why choose Francesca da Rimini? It is striking that Dido, who in *Aeneid,* Book VI, gives a long monologue, should be mentioned only briefly by Dante in Canto V: "cotali uscir de la schiera ov'è Dido" (85) [so these from Dido's flock came fluttering]. Instead, Dante chooses a pair of contemporary lovers who are of comparable social standing. This fact differentiates Francesca and Paolo from

---

8. Virgil, *The Aeneid,* translated by Robert Fitzgerald (1985: 33).

Guinevere and Lancelot, to whom Francesca alludes in the closing lines of her monologue. Guinevere is Lancelot's queen and therefore her bestowal of a kiss in the French prose romance is in keeping with this difference in social status. Dante's choice of a pair of contemporary lovers gives a sense of immediacy, since their experience would have seemed more pertinent to his readers.

Of no less importance than the book motif is the bird imagery that occurs in the canto. Prior to Francesca's monologue, Dante employs three sets of bird images: "stornei," "gru," and "colombe" [starlings, cranes, and doves]. Lawrence Ryan states "From ancient Christian times, the properties of these birds had been charged with moral and spiritual meaning, since all creatures were meant to be taken as signs written by the divine hand in the Book of Nature" (1976: 27).

Thus the starlings signify lust, the cranes order, and the doves "amore" [love]. Ryan goes on to mention an analogy between the aimless flight of the starlings and the movement of the eagle, whose flight heavenward was interpreted as the goal of philosophers who attempt to arrive at a clear vision of the truth through the exercise of their intellectual powers (1976: 30). The parallel with the starlings and the eagle has important implications for an understanding of the Francesca episode, where the starlings are seen flying in a wheeling, disordered way: "E come li stornei ne portan l'ali / nel freddo tempo, a schiera larga e piena" [Like as the starlings wheel in the wintry season / In wide and clustering flocks wing-borne, wind-borne] (40–41), the cranes flying in a direct line: "E come i gru van cantando lor lai, / faccendo in aere di sé lunga riga" [And as the cranes go chanting their harsh lay, / Across the sky in long procession trailing] (46–47), and the two doves flying down toward the earth. There are, therefore, three types of movement or flight: disordered, ordered, and earthbound. One could say that the cranes and starlings form an antithetical pair denoting human society in a state of order and chaos – that is, with the faculty of Reason guiding human affairs on the one hand, and with the free reign of emotions and desires threatening to destroy ordered social networks on the other. The downward flight of the two doves therefore would constitute an inversion of the eagle's upward flight. This idea is represented vividly in the first canto of *Paradiso*, where Dante describes Beatrice's heavenward gaze in terms of bird imagery,

19

specifically those virtues associated with the eagle's legendary ability to gaze into the sun and the remarkable power of its flight:

> Quando Beatrice in sul sinistro fianco
> vidi rivolta e riguardar nel sole:
> aguglia sì non li s'affisse unquanco
>   E sì come secondo raggio suole
> uscir del primo e risalire in suso,
> pur come pelegrin che tornar vuole,
> così de l'atto suo, per li occhi infuso
>   ne l'imagine mia, il mio si fece,
> e fissi li occhi al sole altre nostr'uso. (*Paradiso*, 46–54)

> [When Beatrice, intent upon the sun,
> Turned leftward, and so stood and gazed before;
> No eagle e'er so fixed his eyes thereon.
>   And, as the second ray doth evermore
> Strike from the first and dart back up again,
> Just as the peregrine will stoop and soar,
>   So through her eyes her gesture, pouring in
> On my mind's eye, shaped mine; I stared wide-eyed
> On the sun's face, beyond the wont of men.]

Later, in Canto XXV, Beatrice is said to be guiding Dante in his "alto volo" toward the contemplation of the Divine:

> E quella pïa che guidò le penne
> de le mie ali a così alto volo.[9] (*Paradiso*, 49–50)

> [And Beatrice, compassionate, the same
> Who led my pinions soaring thus on high.]

In harnessing her intellectual skills to contemplate "amor sensibilis," Francesca can be seen as choosing the earthbound flight of the doves, thereby neglecting the contemplation of higher goals, "amor intellectualis," that is, the heavenward flight of the eagle and the lessons of Lady Philosophy. Particularly when the presence of Boethius's *Consolation of Philosophy* is noted among Francesca's reading matter ("Nessun maggior dolore/ che ricordarsi del tempo felice/ ne la miseria" [The bitterest woe of woes / Is to remember in our wretchedness / Old happy times]), it becomes clear that Dante is pointing the reader in a particular direction. In her reading, however, Francesca does

---

9. See Shankland (1975 and 1977), Shoaf (1975), and Moleta (1980: 98–100).

not continue the process of cognition and illumination that leads to the ultimate goal of Paradise. Together with the other lustful sinners, the two lovers subvert reason to carnal appetite, "la ragion sommettono al talento"(39), and thereby ignore both the nurturing of the intellect and the soul's capacity for knowledge and virtue (the goal of sanctifying grace). In so doing, they forfeit all possibility of peace ("pace"), a word mentioned twice by Francesca. In the fulfillment of her nascent desire, Francesca, the exemplary reader, ultimately neglects the supreme text that would have promoted the possibility of peace among the Blessed in Heaven.

For Paolo and Francesca, the act of reading is the "prima radice" [first root] of their love; not only does it mark the realization of their mutual desire, "li occhi ci sospinse/ quella lettura" [as we read on, our eyes met now and then] (130–31), but it also signals the moment of their renunciation of the higher goals of learning and the development of a spiritual outlook; "quel giorno più non vi leggemmo avante" [we read no more that day] (138). Not surprisingly, therefore, when Francesca speaks of the reason for her love, she makes reference to her reading and to a variety of texts and authors that may be grouped into three broad categories: classical (the works of Virgil and Ovid), medieval/contemporary (*Lancelot* prose, the works of Boethius and Cappellanus, *stilnovisti*), and divinely inspired works (the Bible, St. Augustine's *Confessions*). As with the symbolism of the cranes and starlings (order and disorder in human affairs), the first two groups of authors and texts may be seen as works dealing with the vicissitudes of human existence (themes of love, betrayal, suffering, and death), whereas the third group is the one neglected by Paolo and Francesca (the earthbound doves), and this action leads to their spiritual perdition.

Taking a closer look at the densely packed literary references, it can be seen that in verses 100–107, where the anaphora of the word "Amore" occurs, echoes of the stilnovistic credo may be found:

Amor, ch'al cor gentil ratto s'apprende,
prese costui de la bella persona
che mi fu tolta [. . .]   (*Inferno*, 100–102)

[Love, that so soon takes hold in the gentle breast.]

The words recall the opening line of Guinizelli's "Al cor gentil rempaira sempre amore" [Love returns always to a noble

21

heart], but omit the simile "come l'ausello in selva a la verdura" [like a bird to the green in the forest]. The Guinizellian echo is one of a number of literary reverberations that serve to stimulate both Dante's faculty of memory and his self-awareness.[10] For example, the notion of the gentle heart harks back to Cappellanus's treatise on love, while the death of the lovers calls to mind the tragic account of Pyramus and Thisbe in Ovid's *Metamorphoses*, Book IV, in which the fruits of the mulberry tree (where the lovers had planned to meet secretly) are stained with blood and have changed to a dark purple color. Ovid says, "The fruits of the tree were sprinkled with his blood, and changed to a dark purple hue. The roots, soaked with his gore, tinged the hanging berries with the same rich colour" (1955: 97).

This may be compared to Francesca's words to Dante:

O animal grazïoso e benigno
che visitando vai per l'aere perso
noi che tignemmo il mondo di sanguigno.   (*Inferno*, 89–90)

[O living creature, gracious and so kind,
Coming through this black air to visit us,
Us, who in death the globe incarnadined]

The idea of staining the earth with blood and the inclusion of the adjective "perso," which, we are told in *Convivio*, denotes a color that combines purple with black where black predominates, certainly has links with Ovid's tale.[11] The stilnovistic overtones also continue with "Amor, ch'a nullo amato amar perdona" [Love, that to no loved heart remits love's score] (103), and the final "Amor condusse noi ad una morte" [Love to a single death brought him and me] (106) again recalls Thisbe's words: "our steadfast love and the hour of our death have united us" (Ovid 1955: 38). While the death of the two classical lovers is described by Ovid in vivid detail, Francesca and Paolo's murder is only alluded to, and links with the classical story thus serve to heighten the dramatic tension for Dante's readers, who knew only too well what grisly fate lay in store for the two contemporary lovers.

At first glance, Francesca's literary references appear to deal

10. With regard to "Al cor gentil rempaira sempre amore," Moleta states: "The discreet changes by which, in *Inf.* V, Dante 'delyricises' the text which he so admired, are part of the complex moral vision through which, in the *Commedia*, he reviews his cultural formation" (1980: 97–98).

11. "Lo perso è uno colore misto di purpureo e di nero, ma vince lo nero, e da lui si domina" (*Il Convivio*, IV, xx, 2).

exclusively with themes of love and the vagaries of the human heart; for example, the lover's anguish, the physical aspect of the beloved, Love's driving force, and the credences of Love. Francesca's account of the reading of the Lancelot story, and the resulting awareness of desire, seem to confirm this (130–31). Moreover, comparisons may be made with Dante's account of his youthful experience of love in the *Vita Nuova*, where the sight of the beloved causes him to tremble and to turn pale.[19]

Dante's early poetry explores and analyzes the physical and psychological changes wrought by "Amore" and, in her doctrine of love, Francesca also emphasizes the various ways in which Love manifests itself. This is particularly evident in the choice of verbs that signal a dynamic change in her relationship with Paolo, for example, "s'apprende," "prese," and convey its tragic outcome; "condusse noi ad una morte" (106) and "chi a vita ci spense"(107) [Love to a single death brought him and me / Cain's place lies waiting for our murderer now]. Like the youthful protagonist in the *Vita Nuova*, the Wayfarer in Canto V experiences a powerful emotional response. In the latter case, Dante is moved to tears by Francesca's revelation, "i tuoi martìri / a lagrimar mi fanno tristo e pio" [Thy dreadful fate, / Francesca, makes me weep, it so inspires / Pity] (116–17). At the same time, he desires to know more, and the concluding part of Francesca's monologue begins and ends with two literary "markers" that are crucial to the Wayfarer-poet's development. The first of these is contained in the observation that Francesca makes at the beginning:

Nessun maggior dolore
che ricordarsi del tempo felice
ne la miseria; e ciò sa 'l tuo dottore.   (*Inferno*, 121–23)

[The bitterest woe of woes
Is to remember in our wretchedness
Old happy times; and this thy Doctor knows.]

The phrase is a direct echo of Boethius's words:

12. "Mi parve sentire uno mirabile tremore incominciare nel mio petto da la sinistra parte e distendersi di subito per tutte le parti del mio corpo," (XIV, 4) and "quasi discolorito tutto per vedere questa donna" (XVI, 4) [I felt the beginning of an extraordinary throbbing on the left side of my breast which immediately spread to all the parts of my body] and [all pale as I was, to go and see my lady].

In the midst of adversity, the worst misfortune of all is to have once been happy.[13]

The reference to Boethius's sacred dialogue with Philosophy precedes the moment of Paolo and Francesca's mutual awakening to sexual desire, with the description of the latter set within the context of a famous courtly-chivalric episode, that is, Sir Lancelot and Queen Guinevere's first kiss:

> Quando leggemmo il disïato riso
> esser basciato da cotanto amante,
> questi, che mai da me non fia diviso,
> la bocca mi basciò tutto tremante.   (*Inferno*, 133–36)

> [We read of the smile, desired of lips long-thwarted,
> Such smile, by such a lover kissed away,
> He that may never more from me be parted
> Trembling all over, kissed my mouth.]

Unlike Boethius, who reflects on the nature of happiness and the human condition, Francesca and Paolo misdirect their energies and disregard their responsibilities. They lose sight of the multiform aspects of human nature and surrender to the demands of carnal appetite. It is at this point that the noble Francesca seals her fate. She reads no further – a metaphor that conveys the narrowing of her vision. Conversely, her words help the Pilgrim-poet gain new insight into the future direction of his poetic voice. The full import of the message becomes clear only when Francesca's concluding words are set against the context of their literary source. The reference, although not an obvious one, endows the episode with great dramatic force, and is, in fact, the moment of Saint Augustine's dramatic conversion as recorded in his *Confessions*. Saint Augustine opens the Bible at random and reads from Saint Paul's Epistle to the Romans:

> Let us pass our time honorably, as by the light of day, not in revelling and drunkenness, not in lust and wantonness, not in quarrels and rivalries. Rather, arm yourselves with the Lord Jesus Christ; spend no more thought on nature and nature's appetites.[14]

He then adds:

---

13. *The Consolation of Philosophy*, Book II, 4. The phrase also recalls *Aeneid*, Book II (see note 8).
14. Romans 13: 13–14. Saint Augustine does not quote the entire passage.

I had no wish to read more and no need to do so (nec ultra volui legere).[15]

Francesca's words are a direct parallel, but the comparison does not end there. Previous to the moment of revelation and conversion, Saint Augustine has been intent on soul-searching:

> I probed the hidden depths of my soul and wrung its pitiful secrets from it, and when I mustered them all before the eyes of my heart, a great storm broke within me, bringing with it a great deluge of tears.[16]

The experience of Paolo and Francesca has been in the reverse order to Augustine's. They have neglected the study of God's text and so, in Hell, Paolo is unable to stop his flow of tears.[17] In this way, Augustine's internal struggle, the "great storm" and the "deluge of tears" that precede his spiritual conversion are evoked by Paolo's fitful crying midst the stormy wind that is now his eternal punishment:

> Mentre che l'uno spirto questo disse,
> l'altro piangëa; sì che di pietade
> io venni men così com'io morisse.
> E caddi come corpo morto cade.   (*Inferno*, 139–142)

> [While the one spirit thus spoke, the other's crying
> Wailed on me with a sound so lamentable,
> I swooned for pity like as I were dying,
> And, as a dead man falling, down I fell.]

The Pilgrim is overcome at this point, not by feelings of grief or helplessness, but by the gravity of his insight. He recognizes that he must change course, so that he may undergo the redemptive experience of *Purgatorio* and ensure that his literary endeavors follow the upward flight of the eagle, and in so doing, promote social and political reforms. In the richness of its literary dimension, Francesca's characterization reveals the direction that the Wayfarer-poet must take. Her fate is that of a character who no longer can experience change or renewal, but her impressive speech, with its subtle hues and intelligent articulation, is nei-

15. *Confessions*, Book VIII, 12. See Swing (1962: 299), Hollander (1969: 112–14), and Scott (1979: 14).

16. Book VIII, 12. See also Dronke (1975: 113–14).

17. Douglas Radcliff-Umstead states: "Part of the task of writing the *Divine Comedy* was to direct humankind away from romantic literature with its message of earthly love's supremacy to experience the redeeming grace of celestial affection" (1978: 54).

ther the whimsical fancy of a simpering maid nor the fatal lure of a beguiling siren. It is a speech of multiform elements, and the message contained therein offers hope and the possibility of change for the Pilgrim-poet and for all pilgrims undertaking the "cammin di nostra vita" [journey of our life].

THREE

Men Framing Women: Sabadino degli Arienti's *Gynevera de le clare donne* Reexamined

STEPHEN D. KOLSKY

For men to write about women in the fifteenth and early six- teenth centuries involved a complex series of choices. At its most pragmatic level it meant evaluating the possibilities of advancement offered by a woman-oriented text. Writing for and about women presupposed that the female presence at court participated in and initiated patronage networks. Court women were perceived as alternative sources of patronage by writers, in particular by poets who performed their own work. Other intellectuals wrote theoretical "treatises" on women, usu- ally with the express aim of winning patronage from a high- ranking lady. As shall be seen in Sabadino degli Arienti's case, a text of this type easily could have a dual function: both to encourage the more powerful female figures at court to act sep- arately from their husbands and to pay indirect homage to the male partner for having so exemplary a wife. Most writers were not totally committed to the female patron; the treatise on women was often just one work among several on diverse sub- jects usually of more interest to the prince.

Another factor that needs to be taken into account is that the profemale treatise was relatively easy to write; preparation could be kept to a minimum.[1] This was because there already existed a model that fulfilled the requirements, providing an illustrious literary precedent: Boccaccio's *De mulieribus claris*.[2] It is perhaps

---

1. It is clear that many writers just borrowed numerous *exempla* from other writings without any clear intellectual structure. See Kolsky 1990 (especially 47–49).

2. *De mulieribus claris*, edited by Vittorio Zaccaria, is in vol. X of Boccaccio (1970). It has been translated into English by Guido A. Guarino (Boccaccio 1964). All the translations in this paper are my own. See also Torretta (1902–1903).

too tempting to consider the choice of this text rather cynically – as the manipulation of an archetype for purposes for which it was not originally intended. The composition of *De mulieribus claris* was partly an exercise in erudition, a learned compendium of famous women along humanist lines. It undoubtedly had an ideological aim, namely that of making possible a comparison between men (who already had their *De viris illustribus*) and women, to the disadvantage of the latter. It would seem that the idea of dedicating the work to a lady was an afterthought: "I realized that since the work spoke about women, it should not be dedicated to an important man but to a famous woman" [adverteremque satis non principi viro, sed potius, cum de mulieribus loqueretur, alicui insigni femine destinandum fore] (*De mulieribus*, 18). Accordingly, on completing *De mulieribus*, Boccaccio dedicated it to Andrea Acciaiuoli, after considering dedicating it to Giovanna I, Queen of Naples.[3] But the dedication is somewhat misleading, since the work does not lend itself very easily to the interpretation presented by Boccaccio in the pages to Andrea Acciaiuoli. Indeed, it has been argued that the treatise could be regarded as a virulent antifemale tract (Jordan 1987).

Later writers did not, in fact, follow Boccaccio's example mindlessly. *De mulieribus claris* offered, above all, a model for structuring a discourse on women that avoided extensive discursive writing. It left hardly any room for generalized comments or entry into the long-standing debate over women's position in society. It favored narrative discourse over more "committed" forms; often the entries under separate women are no more than novellas with an obvious moralistic point.[4]

3. Boccaccio states in the dedication that he originally intended offering the work to "Giovanna, most serene Queen of Jerusalem and Sicily" [Iohanna, serenissima Ierusalem et Sicilie regina] (18) but he changed his mind: "Fearing the lesser light might be completely eclipsed by the greater, I gradually changed my mind" [Timens ne a potiori lumine minor omnino fugaretur in tenebras, sensim retraxi consilium] (18).

4. Boccaccio is always more than ready to criticize the behavior of the women he describes, even if sometimes he is willing to acknowledge their more positive aspects. For example, his entry on Europa, Queen of Crete, contains the following comment after recounting how she was left alone tending her father's flock:

Vagari licentia nimia virginibus et aures facile cuiuscunque verbis prebere, minime laudandum reor, cum contigisse sepe legerim his agentibus honestati non nunquam notas turpes imprimi, quas etiam perpetue demum castitatis decus abstersisse non potuit. (*De mulieribus*, 60)

[I deplore the fact that young women are allowed to go as they please and listen to anyone's words because I have often read that precisely for these reasons their reputation is shamefully stained so that not even the honor of perpetual chastity can cancel the dishonor.]

Furthermore, the schema of individual biographies imposes a rigid formula on the enunciations. Women are not discussed as a group having specific social desires. They are instead represented as isolated social beings who have a personal story to tell; even if they have a historical dimension, women in *De mulieribus claris* seem to be fictitious.

The Boccaccian archetype expressly avoids, whenever possible, the problematic issue of women in Christianity. There are no saints or female martyrs and very few biblical figures of primary importance in *De mulieribus claris*. It might be argued that Boccaccio wished to avoid difficulties with the religious authorities. Even so, he is asserting clearly, albeit indirectly, the power of the secular, perhaps creating a lay version of sacred hagiography, which would also explain why court writers were attracted to the text.

The court writer also would have perceived the possibilities for *encomium* inherent in the structure of the text. In the first place, contemporary (or near-contemporary) women might substitute the heroines of myth and early history and, in the process, they would be enhanced by implicit reference to the great women of the (mythical) past. Second, the composition of a court version of *De mulieribus claris* would demonstrate the power of male writing to structure female lives; male writing encoded the values by which a woman's existence was to be framed. What is more, these values implied a series of judgements about female behavior that inevitably were mediated by the male voice. Reputation and fame were dispensed with the aim of increasing the prestige of both writer and lady.

It is all too easy to dismiss such writings as examples of courtly adulation resulting in mediocre texts, or "copies." It will be argued here that, apart from implications regarding the way women are viewed in court society, the treatise to be examined represents an interesting case study in the substantial variations that can occur within a specific literary genre.

The work to be considered is *Gynevera de le clare donne* by Sabadino degli Arienti, written in 1490 (Arienti [1969]).[5] It is dedicated to Ginevra Sforza, wife of Giovanni II Bentivoglio, ruler of Bologna.[6] There seems nothing untoward in all this, given the courtly ethos of Sabadino. Nor is there anything

---

5. For Arienti's biography see the entry by Ghino Ghinassi (1962) in *Dizionario biografico degli italiani*, which also has a useful bibliography.
6. The standard history of Bentivoglio Bologna is Ady (1937).

29

exceptional in his reference to Ginevra's husband on the second page of the manuscript: "Tu sei ad contento del Bolognese populo copulata al più felice Cavaliero del mondo, Joanne Bentivoglio secundo, strenuo in arme [. . .] et Senatore perpetuo, primo de tanta illustre città" [To the joy of the Bolognese people you are joined in marriage to the happiest knight in the world, Giovanni II Bentivoglio, skilled in arms [. . .] and Senator for life, first citizen of such an illustrious city] (*Gynevera*, 2–3).

So courtly and conventional is the passage that it appears to require no further comment except that two years earlier Sabadino had compiled an anthology of poetry that can be seen to support a minor branch of the Bentivoglio and even persons indirectly associated with the Malvezzi conspiracy against Giovanni II (1488).[7] It seems that Sabadino was beginning to rethink his political choices in the two years between the conspiracy and his writing the *Gynevera*. Although he had not yet completely abandoned the line represented by his longtime employer Andrea Bentivoglio, a member of the senatorial branch of the family, he was expressing a political openness or awareness that eventually led him into the service of the Estensi at Ferrara. The *Gynevera* represents an attempt to come to terms with mainstream Bentivoglio politics in the aftermath of the Malvezzi conspiracy and, at the same time, to challenge them by offering a subtle revision of the dominant power ideology.[8]

The composition of the *Gynevera* also might be viewed as the work of someone wishing to demonstrate his credentials in the aftermath of the Malvezzi conspiracy while confirming his continuing allegiance to the principal branch of the Bentivoglio family. It may have been with some regret that Arienti felt compelled to submit more completely than before to the dictates of signorial power politics.

The senatorial branch of the Bentivoglio clan could no longer offer him the guarantee of a livelihood. Arienti looks at the possibilities of exploiting the network of ruling families in

7. For the Malvezzi conspiracy see Ady (1937: 103–10). The anthology is discussed by Vecchi Galli (1984).

8. Arienti was associated for twenty years with the senatorial branch of the Bentivoglio as Andrea Bentivoglio's secretary (1471 to 1491, the year of Andrea's death). He also composed a biography of his employer, *Vita del conte e senatore Andrea Bentivoglio* (Arienti 1840; see also Ambrosini 1909). A passing reference to the cultural divergences between the two branches is found in De Benedictis (1984: 28–29). It is, thus, not altogether surprising that Arienti began making overtures to Ercole I, Duke of Ferrara in the period immediately following Andrea Bentivoglio's death.

northern and central Italy, and the theme of dynastic alliances is associated here with Ginevra herself in the role of childbearer: "You have also had from such a husband, glorious Madam, angelic bearer of sixteen children" [Hai anchora havuto de tanto marito, gloriosa Madonna, angelica sobole de sexdeci figliuoli] (*Gynevera*, 4). Her children are then enumerated and usually the only detail given is whom they married:

[C]um molta gloria et triumpho de tuta la cità nostra, matrimonialmente [ottavo figliuolo Hannibal secundo] se congiunse cum Lucretia, savia figliuola dell'alto Duca Hercule Estense, come difusamente habiamo scripto ne l'opera de lo *Hymeneo*. (*Gynevera*, 5)

[To the great glory and triumph of all our city [Annibale II, the eighth son] was married to Lucrezia, the high-minded daughter of the noble Duke Ercole d'Este, as we have written at length in our work the *Hymeneo*.]

The reference to the marriage alliance and to his own work that celebrates it is politically expedient: the wedding marked Giovanni II's coming of age as the "ruler" of a state worthy to enter into matrimonial alliances with its neighbors and capable of putting on magnificent displays equal to those of other northern Italian courts. Arienti's recalling the *Hymeneo* serves to underline his loyalty to the signorial regime. In all this description of political alliances, Ginevra appears almost irrelevant; even the fact of childbirth is passed over in favor of her husband's capacity to produce politically useful children:

La natività de quisti toi figlioli, certo non è manco presso noi iocunda per loro futura alteza, et augumento del felice nome Bentivoglio. (*Gynevera*, 6)

[The birth of your children is indeed no less joyful for us because of their future greatness and of the increased prestige of the happy Bentivoglio name.]

The marriages are clearly part of Giovanni II's policy of finding allies in northern and central Italy. Thus, language becomes rhetoric used expediently to represent the Bentivoglio as part of a dynastic system, hence increasing its prestige.

It will be immediately apparent that the *Gynevera* has aims other than the praise of women. Indeed, it would not be hard to think that women are a secondary concern, given that the *Gynevera* gives priority to other discourses, principally the political discourse.

Yet Arienti's innovations with regard to the Boccaccian archetype should not be underestimated. First of all, Arienti's women are relatively recent and do not include any mythical or classical figures. Nor are there to be found many women of humble birth. Perhaps sensitive to such a radical change and the consequences it may have had for the status of his women, Arienti introduces parallels between the modern *exempla* and Boccaccio's women. For example, he quite often employs a formula of this type:

> [N]on haverebbe [Arienti's wife] perdonata a faticha nè a spesa, secundo le sue force, de honorare el mio terreo corpo di exequio et de sepulcro, et non cum manco amore che facesse Artamixia regina, moglie de Mausolo re de Caria. (*Gynevera*, 362)

> [She (Arienti's wife) would not have spared energy nor expense, as much as her resources would have allowed her, in honoring my earthly body with exequies and burial, with no less love than that displayed by Queen Artemisia, wife of Mausolus, King of Caria.]

The comparison clearly defines Arienti's ideological position. He insists on traditional virtues and structures within which he inscribes his discourse on women. Not surprisingly, the reference to Artemisia has its source in Boccaccio's *De mulieribus claris*. Thus, even in the case of his own wife Arienti was intent on creating a mythic dimension to lend her and other modern women a certain prestige, a literary pedigree and, by so doing, he sought to render Bolognese history more "universal" and in a particular sense, "grander." In *De mulieribus claris*, "Maria Puteolana bellatrice [the warrior]" is compared to Penthesilea, Queen of the Amazons (XXXII), Francesca Venusta to Busa [Paolina] (LXIX), Joan of Arc to Camilla (XXXIX), Isabella of Aragon to Veturia, mother of Coriolanus (LV) and so on.

Arienti's treatment of the biography of "Maria Puteolana" has considerable interest in the context of the *Gynevera*. Its ideological perspective would seem to place it in conflict with the dominant view of women as peacemakers. It may be that Arienti felt obliged to insert such figures for the sake of balance or through a sense of loyalty to his Boccaccian model. A collection of female lives may have seemed incomplete without the Amazons. Arienti specifies the fundamental notions that constitute the warrior-woman, at odds with those activities traditionally associated with women in contemporary society:

Non era data al tessere, a la rocha, all'aco, al fuso, nè al spechio, ma a l'arco, a la faretra, al dardo et tuta a l'arme. (*Gynevera*, 53)

[She was not interested in weaving, not in the bobbin, spindle or wheel nor in looking at herself in the mirror but her passion was weapons, the bow, quiver, arrow.]

The writer ensures that he "normalizes" her central activity in order to make other activities appear more grotesque:

Costei non era nobilitata de lascivi baci et de abraciamenti de gli ho mini, ma illustrata de cicatrice aquisite ne le bataglie. (*Gynevera*, 53)

[She did not seek nobility in lascivious kisses and embraces with men but was famous for the scars acquired in battle.]

She is represented as an asexual being, secure in her virginity. She is also the object of the male gaze as a kind of circus freak; for example, Arienti notes that "Robert, that most contented king of Sicily, renowned for his glorious virtue, did not refuse to go and see this brave woman" [Roberto felicissimo de Sicilia, come re de gloriosa virtute, non sdegnò andare ad vedere questa valorosa donna] (*Gynevera*, 55).

By contrast, the woman he next deals with (Francesca Venusta) is outstanding for her beauty: "[S]he was subjected to the stare of young men and had to fight other lascivious battles" [Fu molto combatuta da gli occhij de'giovani et da altre lascive battaglie] (*Gynevera*, 59). She does not take part in battles but spurs captains on to greater deeds in defense of Bologna, signing a letter to the captain of the Bolognese army "tua devota feminella" [your devoted little woman] (*Gynevera*, 62). The central narrative only indirectly involves the female "protagonist" who, indeed, becomes a pretext for Arienti to indulge in nostalgia for the lost civic virtues of Bologna:

[M]e doglio che li nostri primarij citadini de la republica patri circunscripti, che non sono curiosi conservare lo exemplo de le glorie de loro passati per reputatione de la nostra cità, et per acendere li posteri ad simile, overo a magior glorie. (*Gynevera*, 63–64)

[I am saddened by our leading citizens of the republic, shortsighted fathers, who are not interested in conserving the example of their ancestors' glorious deeds for the fame of our city and in order to inspire their descendants to similar or even greater glories.]

It is this declaration and the confirmation of an idealized past by Arienti that form the nucleus of the chapter. Perhaps because of the neglect of his female subject the writer institutes the parallel between Francesca Venusta and the Boccaccian Busa. The latter is treated positively in the *De mulieribus claris*, principally because she is represented exclusively in the well-defined role of mother: "She had the wounded treated with maternal love" [Vulneratos materna affectione curari fecit] (*De mulieribus*, 274). The implications are multiple for Arienti's text. Firstly, there is the connection between Republican Rome and Republican Bologna, and second, these political ideals inscribe women in a subordinate role. They constrain her to work for the state, matching male virtues with female ones (motherliness, chastity, virginity, and so on). Undoubtedly, the woman is involved in politics and in public events, but in no way does she set the political agenda. In fact, she becomes an image of a particular social regime preferred by the writer. Caterina Visconti, for example, has the courage and intelligence to save the Duchy of Milan – for her male progeny.[9]

Another way in which Arienti seeks to circumscribe his female subjects is to make them the object of male discourse on sexuality. He deals only with specific categories of women: virgins, wives, and widows. The latter play a particularly prominent role in the *Gynevera*, maybe as a result of the civil strife that is a backdrop to many of the narratives in the work; the husbands are frequently killed in factional disputes or in large-scale wars (Herlihy 1985). There are also demographic factors to take into account, such as the age at which men got married. It also has been suggested that "getting married empowered women in the princely courts of northern Italy" and the influential presence of married women is hence reflected in a text such as the *Gynevera* (see Ward Swain 1986: 194). The implications of this hypothesis become apparent on careful reading of some of the biographies in the text.

Arienti's narrative account of "Diana Saliceta di Bentivoglii" provides a convenient starting point. Diana Bentivoglio is "a woman made resplendent by noble lineage and virtue" [una donna fulvida de famoso sangue et de virtute] (*Gynevera*, 327), with nobility and virtue being interchangeable terms. The following analysis is not intended to be a discussion of the histori-

9. It is perhaps ironic that her eldest son for whom she made so many sacrifices turned out to be a terrible tyrant over whom the mother had no control. She could only reproach him with her tears and words, obviously to no avail (*Gynevera*, 78).

cal reality of this woman but is rather an examination of how she is inscribed ideologically in the text.

What seems to interest Arienti is the relationship between power and women, when the latter, that is, have the opportunity to influence society. In order to be acceptable to the male-constructed institutions of power, such women must be chaste and accept absolutely the constraints of marriage on female sexuality:

> Fu sempre honestissima ne le sue parole, le quale mai lasive se poterono existimare. Fu pudicissima et castissima et de l'honore et gratia del caro marito fu sopra tutte le cose del mondo observatrice. (*Gynevera*, 329)

> [Her speech was always honorable and nothing indecent was ever uttered by her. She was most modest and chaste and, above anything else in the world, she maintained the honor and favor of her dear husband.]

The conventionality of Arienti's position is indisputable, but perhaps it would be pertinent to add that Moderata Fonte, writing on *Il merito delle donne* toward the end of the sixteenth century, maintains that chastity is essential to a woman's sense of self since, by necessity, it is unique to women (Moderata Fonte 1988: 14, 52–55). It is not a coincidence that Arienti is himself the author of a tract, known as the *Trattato di pudicizia*, written for his late wife's sister some years before the *Gynevera*.[10] It is interesting to note that in the *Trattato* Arienti includes chastity among those "virtues of moral and political life" [virtute del morale e politico vivere] (f.3v) that have a positive influence on "this inconstant world, full of deceits, avarice, and betrayals" [questo mondo instabile pieno de inganni, avaricia e tradimenti] (f.4r).[11] Thus, Arienti stresses the political value of chastity as cementing social institutions. Failure to adhere to its dictates leads to social chaos and disorder:

> Di che molte volte ne segue incendii, morte, rapine et ruine de le famiglie e de le republiche et damnatione eterna de l'anime. (*Trattato*, f.5v)

> [From which many times there result burnings, deaths, pillaging and ruin of families and republics and eternal damnation of souls.]

10. See Chandler (1954), 110–13. The manuscript I have used is Bodleian Library, Oxford, Broxbourne ms. 85.7 (undated).

11. In this method of manuscript citation, f means folio (manuscript page), v means verso (back side of page), and r means recto (front side of page).

It is, however, understood that most women do not possess the qualities of a heroine and are overwhelmed by their own sexuality. Thus, it is only a political and moral elite who manage to overcome the inherent "defects" in female nature. The implication is that women have to struggle against their own nature in order to ensure that their behavior conforms to the norms imposed by men. It would no doubt be easy to criticize Arienti's stance for the way his key concepts control female behavior and relegate the majority of women to obscurity, only bringing to light a few carefully selected examples that do not have a great impact on social institutions. These presuppositions are behind the more important biographies of the *Gynevera de le clare donne*, the biography of Diana Bentivoglio being no exception.

She was, in all respects, a model wife: loving to her husband, producer of male offspring, "careful at all times and in all circumstances" [misurata in ogni tempo et fortuna] (*Gynevera*, 329). She also knew how to manage family affairs properly; she is indirectly praised for her skill in looking after her husband's property, guarding against "senseless profligacy" [disordinato consumamento] (330).

It becomes apparent that Arienti is gendering political ideologies. "Discreta misura" (330) – a feminine quality in this case – implies a particular social system based on civic values originating in an oligarchic view of city government. Magnificence, that is, conspicuous consumption, an increasing part of mainstream Bentivoglio politics, is implicitly criticized through Diana Bentivoglio's thrift:

> [Q]uesta prudentissima Diana gubernò la grande sua famiglia cum splendore, prudentia et misura, priva de cupidità et avaricia; et non solamente de le substantie de la casa fu salvatrice et dispensatrice, ma quelle augumentò cum le proprie mane et ingegno, de egregii ornamenti. (*Gynevera*, 330–31)

> [This most prudent Diana governed her great family with splendor, care and discretion, free from cupidity and avarice; and not only did she protect and distribute the wealth of the family but she greatly increased it with her own hands and intelligence.]

Her achievement lies in her ability to unify the extended family of which she is an integral part:

> [I]nfra marito, cognati, fratelli, figliuoli, nepoti, consobrini, nore, famigli, serve, et il concorso de la visitatione de' parenti et de li

amici, che per virtù de tanta donna dire pur possiamo, una minima parola discrepante de la pace et unione se sentisse già mai. (*Gynevera*, 331)

[From her husband, brothers-in-law, brothers, sons, nephews, cousins, daughters-in-law, familiars, servants, and the great rush of visiting relatives and friends, we can even say that, through the offices of such a woman, never was there heard a single word that contradicted the peace and union of the family.]

It is the description of a patronage network, with a woman at its center, extending outward from the nuclear family to include finally all supporters of the clan. Arienti goes much further than this. Diana Bentivoglio is metamorphosed into a Circe-like figure, having power over the domestic animals – "the dogs do not howl" [né li molti cani ululavano] (331) and so on – all because they are "happy at such a union" [lieti de tanta unione] (331).

The Bentivoglio even have at this time the approval of Pope Pius II who called the family "most holy" [sanctissima] (331) Although there may be an unintentional comic effect, the discourse is central to Arienti's vision of a tranquil Bologna and perhaps to his perception of the function of women in society:

Non è questa beata virtù in costei dignissima de memoria, casone de tanta unione et pace, che siano state le memorande opere in le grande fortune de l'alte donne? Certo sì. (*Gynevera*, 331)

[Is not this blessed virtue of hers most worthy to be remembered, the reason for such harmony and peace in the same way as those memorable deeds performed by noble women in moments of importance? Certainly they are.]

"Questa beata virtù" does not receive a full definition; it remains rather vague. Yet, it can be said to be an amalgam of the wifely virtues and, in addition, there is the unstated *dictum* that women, as homemakers, are biologically peaceful and tranquil. Arienti is suggesting that certain women have a specific political role to perform.

However, it is legitimate to ask at this point whether women are merely being used by Arienti to fulfill his own desired political ends; in other words, are they merely instruments for a higher political goal? Do women benefit at all? The most obvious answer would be that Arienti's female constructions are just that – constructions to fill a political need. The writer makes a point, however, of showing some of these women actively helping their less fortunate sisters (though charity was a traditional part of some women's duties). Discussing Ippolita Sforza, Arienti writes:

> Havea compassione a quelle misere donne che non se conservavano in pudica fama; le amoniva cum sancto modo Li rancori et le discordie che infra li suoi sentiva, levava via, reducendoli ad benivolentia et a pace. (*Gynevera*, 340)

> [She felt compassion for those poor women who had not preserved a reputation for modesty; she would religiously reprove them. [. . .] She settled grudges and disputes that occurred among members of her family, bringing about good will and peace among them.]

Ippolita Sforza was extremely generous to men and women alike, "she gave generously to charity" [era elemosinatrice molto] (341). Both Diana Bentivoglio and Ippolita Sforza can be seen as alternative responses to the dominant power politics that held sway over Bologna and, indeed, over the rest of the peninsula. It is paradoxical that the confirmation of traditional female values and roles can lead to a revision of [male] power politics perceived in a negative light. Thus, it is extremely hazardous to label such a text either reactionary or progressive, though undoubtedly it has elements of both in unequal measure.

Arienti in the *Gynevera* was looking back to a golden age where the "tranquil life" [quiete vivere] (260) was attainable through adherence to norms that had become "old-fashioned." The women he discussed are all exceptional. They have managed to overcome the deficiencies of their sex in contrast to most women who, according to Arienti, are in no position to leave their mark on society:

> La quale virtute et magnificentia tanto la dobiamo più lampegiante iudicare, *quanto rara in donne se vede*, perché la tenacità et avaritia non solo gli è famigliare, *ma innata e de propria natura cum el picolo animo*. (*Gynevera*, 162; emphasis added)

> [We have to judge her virtue and magnificence the more startling as it is rarely seen in a woman, because stinginess and avarice are not only common in them, but innate and part of their nature together with a small soul.]

Arienti believes implicitly in the natural weakness and shortcomings of women.[12] Hence he is able to separate the exceptional women from the unexceptional, held in low esteem by

---

12. The ultimate source is Aristotle; see Cline Horowitz (1976).

him. These relatively few heroic women are able to cast aside their "femaleness" and come closer to the ideal of men active in public life. Arienti is especially interested in that moment of crisis when certain women are able to extend their sphere of action: "At least you did not consume your years by the fire with the bobbin, wheel, reel and frame, speaking ill of your neighbor" [Che almeno non consumasti li tuoi anni [Cleofe di Lapi] intorno al fuoco cum la rocha, fuso, naspa et arcolaio dicendo male del proximo] (*Gynevera*, 138). They go beyond their female selves ("oltra misura del sexo muliebre," 265), but only in certain conditions.

The women, in fact, are often lost from sight in the narratives, as Arienti seems more interested in writing about general political issues. To participate in the political processes women have to observe certain rules. Most important, they have to demonstrate their total support for the institutions of marriage, virginity, chastity, and widowhood. In other words, such values are considered the backbone of civic society, without which political regimes go to ruin. One might interpret Arienti's insistence on these values as an attempt to return to a more traditional way of life, an indirect attack on the politics of *magnificentia* as practiced by northern Italian rulers in the late fifteenth century. This conservative vision of the city-state emphasizes the "honest pomp" [honesta pompa] (154), the "great frugality" [molta parsimonia] (159), and, in general, the Christian faith of the women discussed in the *Gynevera*. A Queen of Scotland provides Arienti with the opportunity to perorate on contemporary mores:

> Non fece lei, come molte fano, che postergandose l'honestate et il timore divino, per obtemperare a le loro disordinate lasivie, inquinano il sacro matrimonio; quale in summa reverentia se debbe havere, essendo da l'omnipotente Dio ordinato. (*Gynevera*, 315–16)

> [She did not, as many women do, poison holy matrimony by neglecting her chastity and fear of God in order to give rein to their disordered lust. Holy matrimony must be held in the greatest respect since it was commanded by the omnipotent God.]

It is implied that obedience to one's husband further strengthens the possibility of political power for women, in that matrimonial harmony can become an extended metaphor for social harmony. The woman, then, is regarded as the repository for values long since abandoned by men who often lack the virtue of *temperantia*, that is, "moderation and balance." They are dispensers of justice and clemency. It is perhaps precisely in the contradictions of the text, with its conservatism becoming a motivating force to change society, that Arienti's ambiguous female figure emerges.

FOUR

Female Protagonists in Late Sixteenth-Century Italian Comedy: More Errant Than Erring

NICOLE PRUNSTER

It would make little sense to attempt any evaluation of the nature and function of the female protagonists in sixteenth-century Italian comedies following the Council of Trent (1545–1563) without first making some reference, no matter how cursory, to their forerunners in plays written in the first half of the century. Much of early erudite comedy in Italy is written according to a formula established by the Latin plays of Plautus and Terence. The plot variations are relatively few, the character variations even fewer. Miserly fathers or avaricious slave dealers cause servants to exercise their wits in devising deceptions intended to aid their enamored young masters in attaining the young women of their choice; gluttonous parasites, vainglorious captains, and fatuous pedants provide comic relief while also allowing a critical jibe at particular aspects of contemporary society.

Of no less importance in the portrayal of female characters is that all erudite comedy throughout the century was written exclusively by male dramatists for the entertainment of courtly audiences. There were very few contributions by female writers to any genre in Italy in the sixteenth century. As Carlo Dionisotti observes, "Soltanto nella letteratura del medio Cinquecento le donne fanno gruppo" [Only in the literature of the mid-sixteenth century do women (writers) form a group] (Dionisotti 1965: 327), and of this group of female writers at least two were renowned courtesans: Tullia d'Aragona, whose *Rime* and *Dialogo dell'infinità d'Amore* were published in 1547 and

1560, respectively; and Veronica Franco, responsible for perhaps the most noteworthy contribution to Italian literature
between 1560 and 1580.

Women thus had no active part in the comic process, since
the Church interdiction against women appearing on stage was
upheld until the late sixteenth century. Yet on the whole, the
Church resisted being drawn into the debate over theater, possibly because of the popularity of theatrical representations, not
least among representatives of its own ranks. Although it did
not ban the comic theater as a whole, it issued two interdictions
regarding drama: it prohibited the use of ecclesiastical costumes on stage, and prohibited the participation of women in
theatrical productions. The latter interdiction, however, was
observed only in sacred drama; by the end of the century,
women already were interpreting female roles (Dejob 1884).

The role of women therefore was limited to that of receptor.
Even as part of the audience, however, women hardly were likely to be instrumental in determining to any appreciable extent
the nature of female protagonists in erudite comedy, because
any identification between middle-class female characters, who
usually converse in colloquial language, and the noble women
of the audience, with their refined speech, was highly improbable. Hence the changes apparent in female characterization in
comedies postdating the Council of Trent occurred as a consequence of societal changes and of the (male) dramatists'
response to them. So it is that the female characters in most
comedies of the latter part of the Cinquecento assume a didactic function within a sometimes disturbing hierarchy of patriarchal values. Their apparent autonomy and relative independence are not absolute qualities indicative of any hard-won
emancipation. The female protagonists are endowed with a
new, unintended ambiguity stemming from the discrepancy
between their actions and the system of values they promote;
that is, between their seemingly liberated, autonomous behavior and the covert moral conservatism underlying this behavior.

The force motivating the action in learned comedies of the
early sixteenth century is invariably love: not the sublime love of
the *stilnovisti* for their *donna angelicata*; not the unrequited and
ambiguous love of Dante and Petrarch for their respective married muses; but instinctual, hedonistic passion in the best tradition of Boccaccio's *Decameron*. The young female characters,
whose mere appearance kindles this passion, exist only as

objects of carnal desire. They have no other function apart from this, thus at times (as in Niccolò Machiavelli's *Clizia* and Ludovico Ariosto's *La Lena*) they do not even appear on stage, all question of social decorum aside. When speaking of his love for this conceptualized female, the lover often has recourse to precious, Petrarchesque language in an attempt to elevate his feelings, but the servant delights in bringing his master down to earth, thereby defeating this attempt to present lust in a more refined, that is, hypocritical, form. Any residual doubt as to the true nature of this sensual passion is removed when lovers and gluttons converse at cross-purposes, each totally engrossed in an obsession that has a different focus but similar terms of reference.

Unlike their correlatives in the contemporary short story, these female characters are simply catalysts, as stereotyped as their male counterparts, as lacking as they are in autonomy and independence, the product and object of male fantasy. On those occasions when this comic formula is varied in any way, when, for example, a female character resists and is reluctant to be made a sexual plaything, the ensuing seduction takes on serious implications. Lucrezia in Machiavelli's 1518 comedy *La mandragola* is not a compliant object of desire but a character forced to play this part despite her deeply felt moral principles. Likewise Lena (in Ariosto's eponymous comedy of 1528) is compelled to resume an adulterous relationship with a man whom she despises. It is only when the female characters unsuccessfully try to avoid a sexual relationship, when their resistance is overcome by importunate male characters, that comic hedonism is replaced by a power struggle, by sexual politics, in which the female faction is dominated by the male. More than two hundred years were to pass before Carlo Goldoni's Mirandolina in *La locandiera* was to redress the balance by seducing and publicly humiliating the misogynistic Cavaliere. Yet it is a hollow victory with no less disquieting implications about male/female relationships.

The Counter-Reformation in Italy had particular repercussions for women at all levels of theatrical activity. In 1558, Sextus V decreed that women in Tuscany were not to attend theatrical performances and were never to appear in theatrical productions. More important for the purposes of this essay are the changes apparent in the female protagonists of erudite comedy postdating the Council of Trent (1563). No longer a passive, generic noncharacter, the heroine emerges from the shadows to occupy center stage. She now eclipses in importance her male counterpart (and other formerly prominent comic characters, such as the servant) precisely because she can be made to exemplify such characteristically female virtues as chastity and fidelity, which the new climate of moral restraint encouraged. She has become extraordinarily mobile and enterprising, prepared to adopt disguises – usually male attire – and travel great distances in order to be reunited with her lover. Whereas in earlier comedies the young lovers are either caught in *flagrante delicto* and then bustled off to church, or their marriage at the end is a formality to be observed before they can consummate their passion, later heroines already may be married, albeit clandestinely as a rule, as the comedy begins – and this despite the 1563 decree of the Council of Trent making such marriages unlawful. Drusilla in Girolamo Bargagli's 1589 comedy *La Pellegrina* is anomalous in that she has been married for ten years but is still resolutely virgin, while Lepida in the same drama is also secretly married and pregnant to boot. The drama, that is, deals with what happens after a woman has been wooed and wed. The relationship between this new breed of female characters and their lovers is of a correspondingly different kind, compared to that of their predecessors, one born of a relative maturity acquired, at times, at the expense of a separation that may have spanned many years.

With such lofty sentiments as constancy and chastity now governing their behavior, these heroines at times inspire correspondingly admirable sentiments in their male counterparts. In the light of this newfound capacity of theirs to engender noble feelings in the men they love, *a posteriori* reasoning leads to the conclusion that if the hero of early comedy is singularly lacking in laudable sentiments, then the heroine is to blame for not having instilled them in him.

It is evident from this composite picture of the post-Tridentine heroine that now she is intended to have a particular didactic function in the hybrid "serious" comedies of this period. A treatise on comedy, written in 1572 after its playwright author Bernardino Pino had read Sforza Oddi's comedy *L'erofilomachia*, published in the same year, implicitly confirms this.[1]

---

1. See Bernardino Pino da Cagli, "Discorso di messer Bernardino Pino intorno al componimento della comedia de' nostri tempi," in Oddi (1578). A number of treatises written by men in Italy during the fifteenth and sixteenth centuries argued that women were equal or even superior to men, a stance fre-

After proposing an Aristotelian definition of comedy and its dual Horatian aim ("dilettare giovando" / to entertain while edifying) – both commonplaces routinely appearing in comic prologues and treatises throughout the century – Pino implies the role of female characters in carrying out this aim by asking rhetorically of Sforza Oddi how a woman of questionable thoughts can learn to mend her ways if she sees a procuress (*ruffiana*) at work on stage. The implication is, of course, that female characters evincing positive moral qualities will aid comedy in carrying out its didactic purpose. Yet it is difficult to overlook the bias that sees women spectators as being particularly prone to corruption and certain female characters as particularly apt to corrupt. It is this same ambiguity that underlies the portrayal of women characters in several of the better-known serious comedies of the time, including Oddi's own *L'erofilomachia*, which Pino at the end of his treatise suggests can serve as a model of good comedy.

Benedetto Croce, who in 1946 reedited Oddi's comedy, clearly concurs with Pino's judgement of *L'erofilomachia,* and is unequivocal in his appreciation of Ardelia, the courtesan in the drama, identifying in her all that is aesthetic in the play. While acknowledging that, where plot and structure are concerned, Fabio must be considered the drama's principal character, where its poetry is concerned, Ardelia is the undisputed protagonist (Croce 1970: 240). Croce describes her effusively as "creazione individuata e nuova, dissimile da tutte le altre [cortegiane], semplice e armonica nel suo sentire, che non oltrepassa mai l'amore, che rimane sempre sotto il suo imperio assoluto, che, innalzata dall'amore e per l'amore, non perciò ricompone e purifica la vita a cui il destino l'ha condotta e, in mezzo a questa, attraverso di questa, è pietosa e gentile, retta nel suo comportarsi, ed è una creatura umana, che parla al cuore umano" [an individualized and original creation, unlike all other [courtesans], simple and consistent in her feelings, never going beyond the limits laid down by love but remaining ever under its absolute power, ennobled by it, yet not changing and purifying the life to which destiny has led her; despite her

---

quently undermined by the use of paradoxical arguments. Women entered the debate in the seventeenth century, offering a female point of view that negated the "perfect equality" mooted by earlier male treatise writers such as Ortensio Lando. For two early seventeenth-century treatises written by women, see Lucrezia Marinelli (1600) and Moderata Fonte (1988).

circumstances she is compassionate and kind, virtuous in her behavior, a humane creature who speaks to the human heart] (1970: 244). Ardelia is, however, a more problematic character than Croce would have the reader believe. As a courtesan she is sexually experienced, yet she has been faithful to Amico, a courtier and gambler, since he became her lover. She is that peculiarly male creation, a virtuous whore. All moral opprobrium is clearly directed at Amico, since he accepts expensive clothing and money from Ardelia, though she exacts no payment from him for her services. Social opprobrium, however, is directed at her alone because of her profession; she complies with the edict requiring her to wear a yellow veil in public and she declines an invitation to enter a private home as she considers herself unworthy. And Amico's servant Sandrino, although generally sympathetic toward Ardelia, implies that she is something less of a woman ("quella povera femina, che pur femina è" [that poor woman, who nevertheless is a woman]) for being a courtesan.

Submissive and totally subjugated to Amico, Ardelia is almost pathological in her willingness to be exploited both sexually and financially: "[M]i par d'essere beata quando [Amico] s'inchina a chiedermi qualche cosa," [I feel blessed when [Amico] lowers himself by asking something of me] she admits to the procuress, Giubilea (Oddi 1978: act I, scene 5). Deaf to all Giubilea's reasoning, Ardelia sees Amico's imminent abandonment of her as justified punishment for whatever fleeting opposition she raised in the past to his exploitation of her. She attempts to win back his favor with costly gifts and the avowal that he will be responsible for her suicide should he leave her. Her total dependence on Amico, her desire to renounce all autonomy, is already metaphorically suicidal, a denial of self, little short of total self-abnegation. Giubilea intuits that Ardelia is ill, but wrongly identifies her illness as tuberculosis.

Ardelia's faithfulness differs from that of Flamminia, the other prominent female character in *L'erofilomachia*, only in that it applies to an unworthy subject, Amico, whereas Flamminia's steadfast loyalty is to Fabio, who demonstrates that he is indeed worthy of it. Female constancy, then, may transcend social class and personal situation. Typically, in the case of Flamminia, a lengthy separation tests her faithfulness – she and Fabio have not seen one another for five years; if necessary, she will flaunt all decorum by returning alone to Genoa from Florence to find him in order to avoid the marriage arranged by her father. She is no less willing to die should all other attempts at remaining faithful fail.

It is a sort of Penelope syndrome, common to many heroines of post-Tridentine comedy. It is not surprising, therefore, that the prolific Neapolitan dramatist Giambattista Della Porta, in adapting the concluding episodes of the *Odyssey* in his tragicomedy *La Penelope* (1591), should have made the faithful Penelope the protagonist. Her didactic function is stated explicitly in the prologue: "Onde imparar potran tutte le donne, Quali esser denno verso i lor mariti" [Whence all women will be able to learn, How to behave toward their husbands] (Della Porta 1591: 4). No mention is made of whether men were likewise to see a moral example in Ulysses, whose dalliances with women largely were responsible for his delayed homecoming.

Oriana, the protagonist in *Il moro* (1607), the second of Della Porta's three serious comedies (the other two are *I due fratelli rivali*, 1601, and *La furiosa*, 1609), is influenced directly by Penelope. She is unique among Della Porta's comic heroines in that she has been married technically for ten years already when the representation begins. Her woes, no less than those of Penelope in the tragicomedy, stem from her determination to remain married to a man generally believed dead. She, too, is exemplary for her faithfulness: Oriana speaks of "la costanza della mia fede" [the constancy of my faithfulness] and calls herself "la tua fedel consorte" [your faithful consort], while Pirro, marvelling at his wife's constancy, derives from it a moral lesson that echoes the prologue of the tragicomedy:

Quando fu visto amor di donna così costante?
quando simile a questo? Resti in ogni tempo
viva la memoria del tuo amore. Imparino
tutte le donne, che sono, e che saranno, ad
esser così costanti negli amori, come tu sei
stata: a tanti mariti, ed innamorati aver
fatta così onorata resistenza, e col soffrir
solo aver vinte cotante miserie.   (Della Porta 1726: act V, scene 5)

[When has the love of such a faithful woman
as this ever been seen? Let the memory of your
love live always. Let all women, present and
future, learn to be as constant in their love
for their husbands and lovers as you have

47

been with your praiseworthy resistance and
suffering which only conferred grief upon you.]

The sexual license and hedonism that motivated the male
lovers in early erudite comedy has been replaced with the sexual restraint and fidelity now attributed to the female protagonists.

Given Croce's warm appreciation of Ardelia in Oddi's *L'erofilomachia*, his condemnation of Raffaello Borghini's 1578
drama *La donna costante*, which he describes as "cosa del tutto
frigida, senza alito alcuno di vita," [something completely cold,
without any breath of life] (Croce 1958, vol. 2: 156) holds some
promise that its female characters may be of a different stamp
than Ardelia. *La donna costante* is a reelaboration of the Romeo
and Juliet story, presenting star-crossed lovers from rival families and the subterfuge of a sleeping potion and subsequent
burial so that the heroine may remain faithful to her lover
exiled seven years earlier. There are once more two female
characters outstanding for their constancy and fidelity:
Elfenice, the "morta viva" [living dead woman] who, in male
attire, is prepared to depart for Lyon to search for Aristide; and
Theodolinda, Aristide's sister, in love with Milciade who, in
order to protect her honor, claimed to be a thief when he was
caught entering her window.

Constancy, the attribute that qualifies Elfenice as a true
Counter-Reformation heroine, is alluded to first in *La donna
costante* in an amusing soliloquy by the doctor, maestro Herosistrato, ostensibly a champion of women but one whose sophisti-
cal defense of female steadfastness gives rise again to a certain
ambiguity (Borghini 1578: act I, scene 3). With mock indignation, maestro Herosistrato observes that, to the timeworn accusation of fickleness, some detractors of women also would add
obstinacy, which they are wont to illustrate with a popular anec-
dote: a man, enraged by his wife's obstinate repetition of the
word "scissors," lowers her into a well to drown her but as the
water rises over her head, she raises her hand to imitate the cut-
ting action of a pair of scissors. Even accepting for the sake of
argument that such a tale were true, the doctor astutely points
out that, as fickleness and obstinacy derive from two opposite
causes and two opposites cannot coexist in the one subject,
then it follows that, at worst, women are either fickle or obstinate but not both. Yet the fundamental error made by these
slanderers of women is, maestro Herosistrato concludes, mis-

taking obstinacy for what is, in fact, the virtue of constancy. The soliloquy reads as an amusing, mildly chauvinistic joke directed not only against women but against Borghini himself as the creator of Elfenice, a paragon of the very virtue that he ridicules.

Lack of virtue is now to be found only in female characters of low social station. The servant and procuress Acradina in *La donna costante*, a true champion of female rights, chaffs at length in a soliloquy (act III, scene 7) over the restrictions placed on females at all stages of their life. She is particularly irked by their lack of freedom in courtship. After some initial hesitation, she resolves to dispense with decorum and approach a youth in the street whom she finds attractive: "E no, no, chi si proferisce è peggio il terzo, le donne deono esser pregate, e non esse pregar, gl'huomini. E perche non ha da esser lecito ancora à noi il pregare? Non siamo noi di carne, e di sensi composte come gl'huomini? O' quante venture scioccamente si perdono per non saper pigliare l'occasioni. Io son disposta per questa volta di rompere la regola" [Ah no, women who openly declare themselves are really reprehensible. Women ought to be pleaded to by men, and not themselves do the pleading. And why should not we, too, be allowed to plead? Aren't we made of flesh and feelings like men? Oh, how much good fortune is foolishly lost by those not seizing the opportunity! Just this once I'm inclined to break the rule] (Borghini 1578: act III, scene 8). Her advances, however, are rejected indignantly by the youth who is, in fact, Elfenice disguised as a male. Yet her failed bid for sexual emancipation highlights the actions of Theodolinda and Elfenice, who not only have defied convention but also have jeopardized their honor in order to love the man of their own choice.

The treatment of honor in these comedies may have disquieting implications where female characters are concerned. Honor for them is tantamount to virtuous conduct. Carizia in Della Porta's *I due fratelli rivali* (1601) is renowned in all Salerno for her "incorruttibil onestà" [incorruptible virtue] and Oriana in *Il moro* likewise has an invaluable asset, "la fama" [her reputation]. The heroines of Della Porta's serious trilogy have particular reason to safeguard their virtuous reputation, since the family to which they belong possesses a collective honor that can be stained by the conduct of one member. In the case of Vittoria in *La furiosa* (1607) and Carizia in *I due fratelli rivali*, responsibility for their honor rests with their fathers, as neither girl is married. As concerned as he is for Vittoria's safety, Agazio is no less concerned for the family honor, imperiled by his daughter's clandestine departure. Although Carizia herself does not actively expose the family honor to shame, the repercussions are considerably more grave when her unwanted suitor Flaminio does this by impugning falsely her virtue. The reaction of Eufranone, Carizia's father, on being informed of her supposed unchastity, exceeds all expectations and he attempts to kill the innocent victim of Flaminio's calumny. Yet the play, having raised serious questions about male dominance, about domestic and social violence directed at women, ultimately falls back on comic formula to conclude with the requisite happy ending.

At times, the female characters of serious comedy are prepared to jeopardize their reputations for love. Theodolinda (in *L'erofilomachia*) determines to save Milciade's life by confessing that robbery was not the motive for his entering her bedroom window; and Elfenice in the same drama is also prepared to renounce all honor by appealing to the Governor for clemency for Aristide. Where fathers are concerned, however, honor outweighs love for their daughters. Both Eufranone (*I due fratelli rivali*) and Clotario (*L'erofilomachia*) think only to kill Carizia and Theodolinda when they believe them guilty of having sullied the family's good name. When young male members of the family transgress, however, a show of repentance suffices to restore harmony and the family honor. The treatment of honor thus at times suggests that these Counter-Reformation heroines, as exemplary as they may be in their personal relationships, are only of relative worth in the patriarchal family context.

Girolamo Bargagli in his comedy *La Pellegrina*, first published in 1589, leaves no doubt that for a female to renounce her virtue is madness. Lepida, married clandestinely, must feign intermittent insanity to avoid the match proposed by her father, particularly in view of the fact that she is pregnant. Since one of the play's characters points out that clandestine marriages are no longer approved by the Council of Trent, the association between unchastity and madness is explicit. In contrast to Lepida, Drusilla is a model of sexual probity. Although she, too, was wed clandestinely years earlier, she refused to consummate the union until she and Lucrezio could be married publicly. Thus her outward appearance as a devout pilgrim is no less appropriate than Lepida's assumed madness. She arrives in Pisa from Valencia in search of Lucrezio and lodges with Violante, a procuress and bawd who, disappointed that the Pilgrim is not the kind to entertain clients, describes her as "una donna maschia e terribile [. . .] tanto fredda e [. . .] tanto insensata" [a woman both masculine and terrible [. . .] so cold and [. . .] so foolish] (Bargagli 1971: act II, scene 3). The attribution to her of a certain male quality endows her with ambiguity; it is as though Violante wished to imply that Drusilla's exceptional character is more typical of a male than a female.

Despite the particular character and centrality afforded to this new breed of heroine, Bargagli's comedy confirms that it is still very much a man's world wherein women remain subservient, if Drusilla can declare that she would rather have Lucrezio "ingrato ed infedele" [ungrateful and unfaithful] than another who was "leale" [loyal]. Her independence, then, is relative, her enterprise proof that she is a worthy match for Lucrezio. "Dilettare giovando" or "giovare dilettando" [To entertain while edifying or to edify while entertaining]? Either way, the didacticism of post-Tridentine Italian comedy owes a great deal to the character of its female protagonists who have acquired a set of moral standards that serve, in the first instance, as an example to other women. Those that will benefit in the last instance from the application of this moral lesson are, of course, men.

FIVE

The Women Characters of Carlo Emilio Gadda

MARGARET BAKER

Carlo Emilio Gadda (1893–1973), like his predecessors in Naturalism, has given us women characters of remarkable vitality. By the time of his first recorded writing, during World War I, the earlier (male) view of female beauty had shifted focus; the tradition that had found its poetic symbols in the figures embodying woman's virtues, desirability, vulnerability, and pathos had broadened its typology of women to allow for a representation that included, among other things, qualities verging on the irregular and the bizarre, to which the trio of Fosca, Giacinta Marulli, and Elena Dorello testifies.[1] This characteristic of the bizarre is also a feature of many of Gadda's women characters who display an astonishing range of physical defects, which, as the examples below will show, seem themselves almost to justify the character's appearance. By contrast, his male characters exhibit far less extravagance in their individual physical aspects[2] and, apart from those in whom traces of Gadda himself

---

1. Igino Ugo Tarchetti, *Fosca*, 1869; Luigi Capuana, *Giacinta*, 1979; Giovanni Verga, *Il marito di Elena*, 1882.

2. The title story in the volume *Accoppiamenti giudiziosi* offers an unusual and uncommon example of caricature in the following description of the powerful but decrepit Beniamino Venarvaghi, obsessed with his desire to maintain his substance intact in his heirs: "Codesto ricchissimo prozio Beniamino si ritrovò in vecchiaia, a settant'anni, vedovo senza figli né discendenti diretti, col mento, e dopo il mento l'epigastro, tutto guernito e pavesato d'una interminabile barba color tabacco-ambra a due punte, con il capo calvo e la barba irretiti in una sorta di va e vieni per cui seguitava a parer significare no no anche quando nessuno gli proponeva, o richiedeva, esborsi di sorta: e con una vescica e un intestino in dissesto per cui, usufruendo dell'aiuto della Teresa e di speciali recipienti osculanti, vasi, bacinelle, fistole e cucchiaini a serbatoio, doveva, e poteva, far pipì dal fianco sinistro e pupù dal fianco destro [. . .]" [This very rich great-uncle Beniamino Venarvaghi found himself in his old age, at seventy, a widower without children or direct heirs, with his chin, and after his chin his epigastrium, all covered and decked out with an interminable beard, amber-tobacco colored and forked, with his bald head and his beard caught up in a

are discernible,[3] are often not defined in recognizable form. The author directs attention rather to their idiocies of action or attitude, isolating the middle class of property owners (in Lombardy, especially) for his strongest barbs.[4] In caricaturing the two sexes, he tends to divide their human fallibility into male misuse of the rational faculty and female grotesqueness in physical appearance and psyche. The line between these characterizations is not drawn so clearly as to preclude the middle-class women from equal criticism of their class attitudes, but whatever their station or literary function in his work, women are given the dimension of a physical reality that usually contains elements of distortion. As will be discussed, this more extensive use of physical description with regard to women characters does not always have the effect of individualizing them; their presence, nevertheless, is stated more emphatically and with greater variation than is the case with males, and they have a precise function in Gadda's representation of the world.

The physical deformities that afflict Gadda's women have bizarre parallels in an even earlier literary tradition: in the catalog of their abnormalities, we can find some of the same grotesque images of the body that Mikhail Bakhtin (Bakhtin 1968) identifies among the characters of Rabelais: the gaping mouth, the enormous nose, swollen bellies, large sweating bodies, and hunched back are present in the work of both writers, and the mention of urination in some unusual context is also common to both. Gadda's descriptions of women further insist on the impairment of the faculties of sight and hearing that inhibits relations with others. These topoi of the grotesque in

---

kind of coming and going by which he continued to seem to mean no no even when no one was proposing or requesting disbursements of any kind: and with his bladder and his intestine in difficulties so that, using the help of Teresa and of special curved receptacles, jars, basins, pipes and spoons as reservoir he had to, could, urinate from the left side and defecate from the right side. . .] (Gadda 1963: 369–70). (All translations are mine unless otherwise stated.)

3. This is particularly true of the description of the engineer Baronfo in *La Madonna dei filosofi* (Gadda 1931: 132–33) and of Gonzalo Pirobutirro, the male protagonist in *La cognizione del dolore* (Gadda [1963] 1987: 136–37).

4. A fine example of male idiocy is in the person of the industrialist Eucarpio Vanzaghi, "uomo probo e serio" [an upright and respectable man], who has such a firm conviction about the value of modern prophylactic medicine that he offers an utterly unnecessary appendectomy to each of his three sisters as a Christmas present ("La cenere delle battaglie," Gadda 1963: 327). The action of the father of Gonzalo Pirobutirro in *La cognizione*, who ruins the family by pouring money into the country villa, is amply castigated in the largely autobiographical pages of the book.

female bodies appear repeatedly in the following examples of Gadda's work, which span twenty or more years of writing.

At least three women are described in terms of a gaping hole of a mouth where front teeth are missing. In the volume *Novella seconda* that appeared in 1971, the segment of an unfinished novel "Notte di luna" (written in 1930) refers to the case of Filomena, whose two front teeth "se ne erano andati l'un dopo l'altro" [had gone one after the other]. We read:

> L'uscio si dischiuse a metà. [. . .] Filomena si offerse contro la luce del moccolo, mentre un sorriso sfrontato lasciava intravedere quel rettangolo buio, al posto dei due denti. (Gadda 1971: 112–13)

> [The doorway opened halfway: [. . .] Filomena appeared against the light of the candle, with a brazen [literally frontless] smile that showed the dark rectangle in place of the two teeth.]

In the same volume the (unfinished) "Novella seconda" refers to the "mammifero" (mammal) Dirce whose "due zanne porcine, apparendo a destra e a manca di tra la sottile fessura dei labbri e tutta la faccia, le davano un aspetto di cinghialessa in cerca di qualche porcheria dove intrufolare il suo grifo" (70) [two porcine fangs, appearing to the right and left in the thin slit of the lips and all the face gave her the look of a female wild boar searching for some filth or other in which to sink its snout]. This segment, written in 1928, ends with a description of Dirce gossiping with a servant – together they make "due autentici aspidi" [two undeniable asps] – a passage that is repeated almost verbatim in relation to Filomena and Linda in "Notte di luna." In 1949 the same image of toothlessness occurring in "Notte di luna" was used for Marianna in "La sposa in campagna":

> L'assenza totale degli incisivi dischiudeva allo sguardo l'oscuro boccaforno dove stanno di casa le bugie: e la lingua per raccontarle. [. . .] La saliva le andava infiorando le labbra di tante bollicine, come d'un delicato soffritto: e lei la riprendeva dagli angoli delle labbra lungo le fiancate della lingua in un sibilo gentile, o per succhi brevi e redditizi, come sorbisse l'amarena dalla cannuccia, ma di traverso. (Gadda 1963: 292)

> [The total absence of the incisors opened to view the dark hole of a mouth, the home of lies and of the tongue to tell them. [. . .] Saliva kept forming so many little bubbles on her lips, like the foaming of frying butter, and she caught them up from the corners of her mouth along the sides of her tongue with a gentle hiss, or with

short, satisfying sips, as if she were drinking an amarena from a straw, but sideways.]

In a more dramatic way the image belongs to the better-known Zamira, from the hills outside Rome, who is interviewed by police in *Quer pasticciaccio brutto de via Merulana* (written between 1946 and its final publication in 1957):

> Della Zamira, sì: nota a tutti, tra Marino e Ariccia, per la mancanza degli otto denti davanti [. . .], quattro sopra e quattro sotto: di che la bocca, viscida e salivosa, d'un rosso acceso come da febbre, si apriva male e quasi a buco a parlare: peggio, si stirava agli angoli in un sorriso buio e lascivo, non bello, e, certo involontariamente, sguaiato. (Gadda [1957] 1970a: 179)

> [La Zamira, yes: known to all, between Marino and Ariccia, by the lack of her eight teeth in front [. . .], four above and four below: whereby the mouth, viscid and salivary, red as if burning with fever, opened badly, like a hole, to speak: worse, it stretched at the corners into a dark and lascivious smile, not handsome, and, no doubt involuntarily, coarse.] (Gadda 1984: 200)

This last description continues to speak of the woman's face as if it were dark wood, furrowed by deep parallel lines, "come maga antica in sacerdozio d'abominevoli sortilegi" (*Pasticciaccio*, 180) [like an ancient sorceress, priestess of abominable spells] (*That Awful Mess*, 201), in an image of rigidity that fixes the features into a kind of gargoyle.

We find equal insistence on other features, such as noses and eyes, that attract attention by their gracelessness, size, or abnormality. In many cases the descriptions follow the typical Gaddian technique of dilating a point of observation until it encompasses its surroundings and establishes links to quite different realities. In the story "Cinema," for example, the author insists on a particularized account of the consequences of an accident of nature when the tailoress, thinking she is longsighted,

> [P]ortava degli occhiali che le annebbiavano un po' quei precisi rapporti cui gli occhi nostri soglion inoltrarci de' corpi contundenti. In realtà non era presbite, ma strabica: sicché se un occhio era al gatto, cosí morbido e pigro, l'altro le volava di là dai vetri, al di là dai passeri, di là dai tegoli, di là dai comignoli e lo fermava soltanto, tra un garbuglio di fili telefonici, la vetta stellante del Filarete. (Gadda 1931: 62)

> [W]ore glasses that clouded those relationships by which our eyes usually separate us from blunt instruments. In fact she wasn't long-

sighted, but cross-eyed, so that if one eye was on the cat, so soft and lazy, the other was out the window, beyond the sparrows, the tiles and rooftops and only the starry spire of Filarete in its haze of telephone lines brought it to a halt.]

The accumulated detail of digression has the effect of lessening the original impact, and the reader's attention shifts from concern for the woman to amazement at the sheer versatility of this divided gaze.

In the same story, the narrator is discomfited by a woman who misunderstands his movements; description is concentrated on her very sharp nose:

Mi guardava anche lei, a sua volta, e piuttosto maluccio: dai dintorni d'un naso aquilesco e pallido, affilatissimo, mi lanciava occhiate sature d'una viperina perfidia. (Gadda 1931: 96–97)

[She looked at me in her turn, and rather nastily: from near her pale aquiline and very sharp nose, she threw me glances full of viperish perfidy.]

Two other stories in the volume *Accoppiamenti giudiziosi* give the same attention to gracelessness. In "Socer generque":

[Q]uesta Dupont.[. . .] Il naso, povera creatura, era tutt'altro che 'un nasino francese voltato all'insù', perché era un nasone, e non si capiva di che paese, voltato all'ingiù. (Gadda 1963: 250)

[T]his Dupont.[. . .] Her nose, poor thing, was not at all 'a little turned up French nose' because it was a large nose, it was hard to tell from what country, and turned down.]

And Signora Batraci, in "La domenica," is described with even greater incongruity by comparison with the animal world:

Sorrise mansuefatta, commossa, negli occhi molli e vetrosi, gelatinosi, nelle palpebre piuttosto grevi, rigonfie, stancamente sedute sulle gote, pareva una buona cagna rappacificata col mondo. (Gadda 1963: 242)

[She smiled, meekly, touched, in her pale, glassy and weak eyes, and her swollen rather heavy eyelids, tiredly drooping, she seemed a good dog at peace with the world.]

There are also enough cases of awkward or cumbersome bodies to arouse our interest and curiosity, as these examples show:

'Mi sento delle ruote di bicicletta tra i ginocchi,' [says the narrator], 'mi sento carezzare affettuosamente le reni e contro la schiena un gran caldo molle, come il thermogène, dedicato proprio alla mia pleura. E' una signora enorme, che lo scirocco e il vin di Marino hanno resa carezzevole e termogenica, tutta in un felice bagno di sudore.'[5]

[I feel the wheels of a bicycle between my knees, I feel my back affectionately caressed by a great soft warmth, like a heating pad devoted to my pleura. She is an enormous lady who, made thermogenic and caressable by the hot wind and the Marino wine, is completely bathed in sweat.]

The unforgettable Donna Giulia de' Marpioni, "nata Pertegati, e cugina dei Borella di Villapizzone" [a Pertegati by birth, a cousin of the Borellas of Villapizzone], uses "la spettacolosa circonferenza e l'enormità della massa" [the spectacular circumference and the enormity of the mass] of her body to get her own imperious way: "donna degna del massimo rispetto: svelta, nonostante la ciccia, risoluta, 'energica', ben piantata in terra. [. . .] Di proporzioni enormi, purtroppo"[6] [a woman worthy of the greatest respect, quick, despite the fat, resolute, 'energetic', sturdy. [. . .] Of enormous proportions, unfortunately].

In "Prima divisione nella notte" (1950) we find inserted as an accompanying comment to a mother's hysteria the following rather gratuitous reference to characters who make no further appearance in the tale as we have it:

Un cane, fuori, abbaiava. Le due domestiche dal ventre a balconcino (non erano incinte, erano fatte così) giungevano le mani su quel ventre, su quel balconcino, si ritiravano spaventate facendo il segno della croce, si riducevano a dire il rosario in cucina. (Gadda 1963: 357)

[A dog barked outside. The two domestic servants with stomachs like balconies (they weren't pregnant, they were made like that) joined their hands on those stomachs, on those balconies, withdrew frightened making the sign of the cross, and went to say the rosary in the kitchen.]

Some further examples regarding the disabilities and deformities of servants are found in *L'Adalgisa* and *La cognizione del dolore*. In the house of the nobleman Gian Maria Cavenaghi, the condition of the domestics Carolina "in prestito" [on loan] and Caterina "a mezzo servizio" [employed half-time] is treated with

5. "La festa dell'uva a Marino" (first published in 1932), in Gadda [1934] (1973: 147).
6. "Quattro figlie ebbe e ciascuna regina" (first published in 1942) in Gadda [1944] (1955: 84, 87).

a pungent conciseness that reflects not so much on the two women as on the beleaguered state of the household once the commercial cleaning service has gone into insolvency:

> [S]ebbene la Caterina, strabica del sinistro, avesse poi la cataratta sull'occhio buono: la Carolina, semigobba, era sorda [. . .].[7]

> [T]hough Caterina, squinting in the left eye, had a cataract on the good eye: Carolina, half hunch-backed, was deaf [. . .].]

In the various points of *La cognizione del dolore* where the village women are brought into the action, their presence is signaled by reference to their deformity or idiosyncrasy, despite the variants of their common name that would distinguish them sufficiently. Through their various services to Gonzalo's mother and the villa, the women incur his anger by their association with the ritual that the villa represents, and the similarity between the points of view of Gonzalo and his creator colors the narration at the point where these women are introduced. They are first seen as:

> [L]a lavandaia Peppa, [. . .] una donna-uomo più dura e salda che non sia stato mai un facchino [. . .]. (*La cognizione*, 29)

> [Peppa the washerwoman, [. . .] a man-woman harder and tougher than ever [a] stevedore was [. . .].] (*Acquainted with Grief*, 21)

> [L]a pescivendola a piè scalzi Beppina, notissima in tutto il territorio di Lukones e delle vicine ville, non tanto per il commercio dei lavarelli, quanto per il suo modo sbrigativo e piuttosto amazonico di far la piscia, (il tempo è denaro): che adibiva per lo più, la pipì, a uno scopo nobilmente agronomico [. . .]. (*La cognizione*, 31)

> [T]he barefoot fishwife Beppina, famous in all the territory of Lukones and in the neighbouring villas, not so much for her trade as for her brisk and rather Amazonic way of pissing (time is money): and she directed her pee to a nobly agronomical end [. . .].] (*Acquainted with Grief*, 21)

> [L]a Pina [. . .] ch'era la moglie nana dell'affossatore principale e vestita sempre di nero [. . .]. (*La cognizione*, 32)

> [Pina [. . .] who was the dwarf wife of the chief grave-digger and always dressed in black [. . .].] (*Acquainted with Grief*, 21)

Subsequent mention of them is in these terms: "la viriloide Peppa" (470), "la vecchia senza mutande" (416), and "la moglie

---

7. "Quando il Girolamo ha smesso" (first published in 1943) in Gadda [1944] (1955: 43).

nana e ingobbita dell'affossamorti, nera come una blatta" (411) [the viriloid Peppa (213), the old woman without drawers (185), the gravedigger's dwarfed and humpbacked wife black as a roach (183)].

Again in *La cognizione* there is a lengthy description of the servant Battistina that concentrates almost exclusively on the woman's goiter: the swelling is of such a size that it is impossible for her to look ahead, but she must keep her face constantly turned to the left – "la faccia si rivolgeva a sinistra, che parve si fossero sbagliati a inchiodargliela sul busto, quasi d'un pupazzo dignitoso verso occidente: in realtà per far luogo al gozzo, tre o quattro ettogrammi" (*La cognizione*, 116–17) [her face was addressed to the left, so it seemed that they had been mistaken when they fastened it to her bust, like a dignified puppet facing west – in reality, to make room for her goiter, three or four hectograms (*Acquainted with Grief*, 54–55)]. The description of the deformity consists of an accumulation of extended images that has the same effect of dissolving our empathy with the character as happened regarding the squint-eyed dressmaker of "Cinema." There is digression from the first extended simile to a secondary one:

> [E] il gozzo pareva un animale [. . .] che, dopo averla azzannata nella trachea, le bevesse fuori metà del respiro, nascondendosi però sotto la pelle di lei come il fotografo sotto la tela. (*La cognizione*, 11)

> [T]he goiter seemed an animal [. . .] which, after having clawed at her trachea, was now drinking forth half her breath, hiding however under her skin like the photographer under his cloth.] (*Acquainted with Grief*, 55)

This is followed by a further extended image:

> Dal gozzo della donna ribollí un 'buon giorno signor dottore', cosí sommesso e bagnato, che parve il cuocere d'una verza e carote in una terrina, a cui per un attimo si sia tolto il coperchio. (*La cognizione*, 117)

> [From the woman's goitre bubbled forth a 'Good day, doctor', so subdued and damp that it seemed the cooking of a cabbage with carrots in a pot from which for a moment the lid has been removed.] (*Acquainted with Grief*, 55)

Where the objective detail is given such prominence, as here, it has a reductive effect on the paragraph's hierarchy of meaning, bringing it all into parallel, undifferentiated components. It is a technique that elsewhere serves Gadda in breaking up conventional hierarchies of values.

The repetition of negative images of lower-class women, shown with blemish, ugliness, or deformity, is a trait that links Gadda to a certain kind of naturalism: the almost photographic reproduction of the consequences of not supplying appropriate care to women at this level may be coincidental with Gadda's intent, but his work nonetheless documents the presence of toothless, obese, physically decrepit women in service at the center of a country during the years of its proclaimed political and social emphasis on progress, fitness, and probity. Given the implosive, redundant effects of Gadda's language, the intent of social criticism through humor is quite clear. The avalanche of language overwhelms the servants as well as their employers, but the satire seems to discriminate more against the less numerous middle-class women characters, who are observed in greater detail at the level of their social performance. The criticism of them (most sharply felt in *L'Adalgisa* and *La cognizione del dolore* from the mid 1930s) is pointed at the class that had taken upon itself the role of the protector of social values.

These examples of negative female typology seem to contrast with the view of women in the short essay "Il seccatore," written in 1955 (Gadda 1981: 77–81), in which the author finds that, in an epoch that has confirmed the equality of the sexes, there is one positive characteristic still belonging solely to the female sex – they, unlike their male counterparts, are not bores (accepting this statement at face value, without the possibility that it implies criticism of women's loquacity). Far from possessing the male ability to bore others, women, he claims, represent for males a "senso sororale e crocerossistico" [a sisterly, "Red Cross" attitude], a view that, while not negative, is hardly individualistic. The date of the writing of such a stereotype is an indication of the time fix we find in Gadda's imagery, since, in line with his usual distribution of women's roles (within the affective sphere or the private domains of society), it concentrates on the conventional models that refer to the turn-of-the-century Lombard society of his youth. The essay continues with the ideal of "il sorriso e la bontà di una donna, la sua carezza di madre, di sorella, di sposa, di figlia e magari di zia o di cognata" (77) [the smile and goodness of a woman, her caress as mother, sister, spouse, daughter or even aunt or sister-in-law], in which the emphasis rests on the role rather than on the personal characteristics of the women, and typifies them (in an effective denial of the equality mentioned earlier), simply as alleviators of their male relatives' problems.

Though abundantly present in all areas of Gadda's writing except that concerning the war and the technical essays, women characters are limited in their spheres of operation: the middle class is anchored to the routines and rituals associated with family or social interchange, while those without this status, if seen apart from their work function, are shown in their typical group activity. Between these two levels are the young marriageable women from wealthy families, single daughters who display audacity by driving fast cars at dangerous speeds – a phenomenon that is offered as a cliché of modernity from the 1931 *Madonna dei filosofi*, to the *Cognizione* of the late 1930s, to the story "Prima divisione nella notte", dated 1950. One other recurring female figure – that of the strong mother, educator of a young son[8] – if considered in relation to the personal references throughout Gadda's writing, beginning with his war diary of 1915–1919 (Gadda 1955), leads us to the autobiographical threads in his work that, as often as not, produce lyrical treatment rather than the bizarre and the misogynistic, such as are recorded in this essay.[9] The early traumas that have been

8. See in particular the Countess Brocchi guiding the education of Gigi in "San Giorgio in casa Brocchi" in *Accoppiamenti giudiziosi*, and the determination of Donna Teresa Velaschi in relation to her son Paolo in *La meccanica*, written between 1924 and 1929 (Gadda 1970b). The theme is continued through allusions that can be read into passages of *La cognizione del dolore* and in the more open statements in "Dalle specchiere dei laghi" of 1941 (Gadda 1964): "Se altri avesse lasciato dondolar la gamba, bimbo irrequieto, o avesse tentato di stropicciarsi le mani diacce da poter sostenere la sua penna, di certo non sarebbe incorso nelle ammonizioni 'illuminate', poi nelle punizioni feroci [. . .]" [If another, a restless child, had let his leg swing, or had tried to rub his icy hands so as to be able to hold his pen, certainly he would not have incurred "enlightened" admonitions and then ferocious punishment [. . .]] (22). Gadda draws specific attention to his interest in the theme when, in reviewing a translation of Ramón Perez de Ayala's *Luna de miel, luna de hiel*, he mentions his own work and the theme of education: "La frase tematica è un accordo a carattere geneticosessuologico-pediatrico-pedagogistico di notevole (per me) interesse: e mi fa rivivere l'accordo di fondo d'una novella di autore italiano innominabile: *San Giorgio in casa Brocchi* (Solaria, giugno 1931)" (Gadda [1945] 1958: 218). [The theme is a concordance of a genetic-sexological-pediatric-pedagogic nature that is of notable interest (for me): and it brings me back to the basic concordance of a short story by an unmentionable author: *San Giorgio in casa Brocchi* (Solaria, June, 1931).]

9. Since writing this essay I have been able to read Lucilla Sergiacomo's more detailed work on the subject of Gadda's treatment of female characters, in which she identifies a typology of women observed largely with a misogynist's eye (Sergiacomo 1988).

hinted at and discussed by others (particularly Manzotti 1984) and Gadda's possible misogyny are contributing strands no doubt to his general representation of women with such limitations or distortions as we have seen. Any general view of his work, however, shows the writer's consistency in reflecting the deficiencies in all human manifestations, since the world appears to him as a jumble of often discordant phenomena that impinge on each other, with a limiting or distorting effect; as such it excites his criticism. The dialogue entitled "L'Editore chiede venia del recupero chiamando in causa l'Autore" that accompanies *La cognizione del dolore* contains the author's explanation for his representation of the world, and his disclaimer of any unmotivated violence in representing it:

La sceverazione degli accadimenti del mondo e della società in parvenze o simboli spettacolari, [. . .] e in moventi e sentimenti profondi, veridici, della realtà spirituale, questa cérnita è metodo caratterizzante la rappresentazione che l'autore ama dare della società: i simboli spettacolari muovono per lo più il referto a una programmata derisione, che in certe pagine raggiunge tonalità parossistica e aspetto deforme: lo muovono alla polemica, alla beffa, al grottesco, al "barocco": alla insofferenza, all'apparente crudeltà, a un indugio "misantropico" del pensiero. Ma il barocco e il grottesco albergano già nelle cose [. . .]: grottesco e barocco non ascrivibili a una premeditata volontà o tendenza espressiva dell'autore, ma legati alla natura e alla storia [. . .] talché il grido-parola d'ordine "barocco è il G.!" potrebbe commutarsi nel più ragionevole e più pacato asserto "barocco è il mondo, e il G. ne ha percepito e ritratto la baroccaggine." (*La cognizione*, 481–82)

[The division of the world's happenings and of society into exterior aspects and symbols [. . .] and the profound, truthful reasons and feelings of spiritual reality, this selection is the method characterizing the representation that the author likes to give of society: the exterior symbols cause the representation to become a programmed derision that in certain pages reaches a tonality that is paroxysmal and of ugly aspect: (these symbols) induce polemics, jeers, the grotesque, the "baroque": intolerance, apparent cruelty, a lingering in "misanthropic" thought. But the baroque and grotesque already inhabit things [. . .] grotesque and baroque not ascribable to the author's premeditated wish or expressive tendency, but tied to nature and history: [. . .] so that the catch-cry "G. is baroque"! could be changed into the more reasonable and placid assertion "the world is baroque, and G. has perceived and portrayed its baroqueness".]

The cross-referenced allusions within Gadda's work, as well as the illuminations offered by some of the posthumous publications, provide a gloss for most of the repeated minutiae of private experience embedded in this narrative, and reveal how frequently these experiences are projected through the figures of women characters.[10] The centrality of women in the expression of Gadda's themes may correspond to the personal history and condition of the author, but also it seems that the more dominant presence, and enthusiastic participation, of women in all areas of social exchange – more so at a time when their circumstances were otherwise restricted – gave him an ample canvas on which to trace, and then embroider, his design of the endless transmutations inherent in his riotous view of reality. In the most recent edition of *La cognizione,* we find among the author's notes for the preparation of the novel the following plan, in which we can see an intention that does not seem to have been confined to this work alone:

> Sviluppare il tema delle donne, delle fidanzate, delle supposte fidanzate. Claque non ingenua, ma interessata. Svilupparlo tra il mito, la caricatura e la verità. (*La cognizione,* 542)

> [Develop the theme of women, fiancées, supposed fiancées. Claque that is not ingenuous, but self-interested. Develop it somewhere between the ideal, the caricature and truth.]

The ideals and their inversions into caricature are equally truthful aspects of that constant flux that marks his "baroque" world, where known forms dissolve and deform into strange new combinations.[11]

10. The two extremes of this experience are manifest in the ideal represented by Donna Elsa in "Al parco in una sera di maggio" ("[P]oichè tutto, di lei, pareva significare senza nostra speranza, dopo bruni alberi: 'sono io, sì! Quella che avete veduta e sognata; ancora per un poco, oggi, sono con voi!' " (Gadda [1944] 1965: 220) [[S]ince everything about her seemed to signify without our hope, after dark trees: "Yes, I'm the one! The one that you have seen and dreamed about: for a little while longer, today, I am with you!"], and in the threat to the protagonist's inner peace that comes from Emma Renzi ("Le spaventose scenate con cui Emma Renzi l'aveva accolto poi a ogni nuovo dente che Gigetto mettesse [. . .] avevano avuto per lui ripercussioni un po' dure, ma era il minore de' mali" [Gadda 1931: 130–31]) [The frightening scenes with which Emma Renzi had met him every time that Gigetto had a new tooth [. . .] had had rather difficult repercussions for him, but that was the least of his troubles].

11. See the essay "Il faut d'abord être coupable" – "quel deflusso di deformazioni multiple che sogliamo chiamare 'la vita' " [that ebb and flow of multiple change that we are wont to call "life"] (Gadda [1950] 1958: 232–33).

Criticism moves from the level of personal vindication, then, to a sociocultural concern that castigates the combination of arrogance and complacency guiding the conduct of a certain society. The women that are targeted are from the author's own background, and in *L'Adalgisa*, where so many of these figures are concentrated, the narrator addresses the reader from the standpoint of a witness who sometimes is relating his own participation in the social rituals described. Such intradiegetic-homodiegetic narration (that is, narration by someone who participated in the action) is set aside on occasions when the narrator moves back to the heterodiegetic distance (that is, the distance of someone who has not participated in the action) of "Sembra, da quanto mi riferirono [. . .]" [It seems from what they told me [. . .]]. The presence of his narrator at both the primary and secondary levels of the text, sharing and at the same time acting as critical recorder of his society, signals something of the author's conflicting feelings about his *patria* Lombardy and the social phenomena he describes. The focus falls on such women as Donna Carla, who is traversed by "un lampo di cordialità che rischiara per un attimo i vecchi contrafforti della degnazione"[12] [a flash of cordiality that lights up for a moment the old buttresses of condescension]. Their ritual appearance and behavior at concerts is captured in the following:

> E sfanalarono su di lei occhialacci [. . .]. Puntarono su di lei, acuminate, lucide da dietro spesse lenti, le loro pupille inevitabili, i due zii ottimi massimi [. . .]. Riuscí perfino a poterla avvistare, se pure dentro un mare di nebbie, la cataratta eroica di alcune dame dalla pelle di geco, coeve di Gaetano Negri: [. . .] ed ella, Elsa Delmonte maritata Caviggioni, le supponeva integralmente defunte![13]

> [And they beamed onto her their eyeglasses [. . .]. They, the two most excellent uncles, directed at her, sharpened, bright from behind thick lenses, their unavoidable pupils [. . .]. The heroic cataract of certain grandames with gecko skin, coeval of Gaetano Negri, also managed to pick her out, even though through a sea of haziness: [. . .] and she, Elsa Delmonte, Mrs. Caviggioni, had imagined them entirely defunct!]

An aspect of the characterization of this class is the vacuous and narcissistic attitude that is attributed to them, from which

---

12. "Claudia disimpara a vivere" (Gadda [1944] 1955: 65).
13. "Un 'concerto' di centoventi professori" (Gadda [1944] 1955: 177).

derives their idolization of material possessions and power,[14] as is seen in the following reflection by the Commissario Ingravallo:

> Quel dare, quel regalare, quel dividere altrui! [. . .] [O]perazioni, a suo modo di vedere, tanto disgiunte dalla carnalità e in conseguenza dalla psiche della donna [. . .] che tende viceversa a introitare: a elicitare il dono [. . .]. La personalità femminile – brontolò mentalmente Ingravallo quasi predicando a se stesso – che vvulive dì? . . . ['A] personalità femminile, tipicamente centrogravitata sugli ovarii. (*Pasticciaccio*, 124–25)

> [That giving, that donating, that sharing out among others! [. . .] [O]perations, to his way of looking at things, so removed from carnality and, in consequence, from the psyche of women [. . .] which tends, on the contrary, to cash in: to elicit the gift [. . .]. The female personality – Ingravallo grumbled mentally, as if preaching to himself – what did it all mean? [. . .] The female personality, typically gravity-centered on the ovaries.] (*That Awful Mess*, 138–39)

Ingravallo is here highlighting another feature that we find throughout these texts: the generalization appearing above in "il sorriso e la bontà di una donna" is common to Gadda's writing and can be traced through a surprising array of examples. A further version in *Pasticciaccio* of this limitation to a function or to a single attribute is evident in the succession of young girls who are brought to live with Liliana Balducci and her husband, all beautiful and all helping to fulfill Liliana's lack of children of her own. In *La cognizione*, the confusion that Gonzalo registers over the numbers of similar female names in his vicinity is another regrouping of the individuals into the anonymity of repeated labels:

> Il figlio Pirobutirro ebbe l'aria di navigar nel vago: confondeva facilmente le Juane con le Pepite, e anche con le Teresite: ma più che tutto, a terrorizzarlo, era l'insalata delle Marie e Maria proclitiche, cioè le Mary, le May, le Marie Pie, le Anne Marie, le Marise, le Luise Marie e le Marie Terese, tanto più quando le riscopriva sorelle, a cinque a cinque, da doverle discriminare lì per lì [. . .]. (*La cognizione*, 149)

> [The Pirobutirro son seemed to be navigating in vagueness; he easily confused the Juanas with the Pepitas, and also with the Teresitas;

14. The disastrous consequences of this at a national as well as at a personal level are the subject of the tract *Eros e Priapo* (Gadda 1967), but the theme is there from *La Madonna dei filosofi*, in reference to "analfabetissime donne, sazie d'ogni cibo, sdraiate nelle fanfaronesche automobili de' spaccamonti falliti" (Gadda 1931: 133) [completely illiterate women, every appetite satiated, sprawled in the blustering automobiles of failed braggards].

but more than anything, to terrorize him, there was the mixed salad of Marias, and proclitic Marias, namely the Marys, the Mays, the Maria Pias, the Anne Maries, the Marisas, the Luisa Marias, and the Maria Teresas, especially when he discovered they were sisters, five in a bunch, and he had to distinguish them then and there [. . .].
(*Acquainted with Grief*, 72)

In his characterization of women of all levels Gadda makes reference to what is common in their experience: this serialization involves not only such as Signora Menegazzi who, "come tutte le donne sole in casa, trascorreva le ore in uno stato di angustia o per lo meno di dubitosa e tormentata aspettativa" (*Pasticciaccio*, 26) [like all women alone in the house, spent her hours in a state of anguish or, rather, of suspicious and tormented expectancy] (*That Awful Mess*, 27), but involves equally Maria Ripamonti, one of the ideal figures, who seems to share some of the author's own thoughts. Yet Maria is undifferentiated from others at the level of her deepest sentiments: "sentiva bene dal più profondo dell'animo, come tutte forse le nobili e gentilissime donne della sua vecchia famiglia, che qualcosa di men che cretino ci doveva essere" (Gadda 1931: 114) [she clearly felt from the depth of her soul, like perhaps all the noble and kind ladies of her old family line, that there had to be something less than cretinous].

Even the forcefulness of such a woman as Adalgisa, the former opera singer, is measured by the fact that she belongs to the class of "quelle meravigliose donne lombarde che il proprio vigor di cervello manifestano [. . .] col postulare dovunque, davanti a chiunque, la certezza nella propria infallibilità" (Gadda [1944] 1955: 220–21) [those marvelous Lombard women who make manifest the vigor of their thought [. . .] by postulating wherever they are, in front of anyone, the certainty of their infallibility].

In this respect, the narrative possibilities of beauty seem to offer Gadda less interesting and more stereotyped images than those of some degree of ugliness; a girl of exuberant beauty and spirit, for example, is described as "stupenda" or "meravigliosa," in what reads like a formula akin to that listing color of eyes and hair.[15]

15. See "La stupenda Zoraide" (Gadda 1970b: 8): "Dalla lunga Aprilia color granato uscì, pallida, una ragazza stupenda" [From the long garnet-colored Aprilia, there emerged, shaken, a stupendous girl]; "Prima divisione nella notte," in Gadda 1963: 347–48; and "Una meravigliosa fanciulla, unica viaggiatrice [. . .] la deliziosa viaggiatrice [. . .] la stupenda Ellen" [a marvelous young girl, the sole traveller [. . .] the delightful traveller [. . .] the stupendous Ellen] in Rodondi 1982: 279.

The description of ugliness, however, as we have seen, is only apparently particularized, and, especially in its most startling manifestations, is accompanied by the same deflection of the author's gaze from the specificity of the person to an emphasis on the incidentals or on the margins that lead to other figurations of reality.

Young people, likewise, are represented anonymously, as the following early example from the *Racconto italiano di ignoto del novecento* shows (written 26 July 1924):

> [I] giovanetti si diportano in bicicletta. [. . .] Alcuni vestono larghi pantaloni di fustagno [. . .]. I tintori, per l'effetto del cloro e gli allievi salumicri per effetto del sale hanno mani gonfie. (Gadda 1983: 43–45)

> [T]he young people pass their time cycling. [. . .] Some wear wide trousers of fustian [. . .]. The dyers, because of the effect of chlorine, and the apprentice sausage-makers because of the salt have their hands swollen.]

This frequent diminution of individual expression in the characterization of women is consistent with a more general aspect of style in Gadda: it reflects the particular quality of abstraction that accompanies his use of imagery. Throughout his work nature is represented in reiterated generic images, in particular the stars and the night wind, and the personification of trees as a race of ancient people – the latter in positive contrast with human activity; and as accompaniment to lyrical reflection, beside and within nature, there is the passage of trains, or their smoke, over the distant landscape. All function as group images in which the specific is blurred in response to a predilection for lyricized expression. In such a context, the tendency we have seen to generalize female characters into various typologies lessens their individuality and independence so that, despite the frequently vivid and realistic details attached to them, their function approximates that of carriers of associations.

Given the direction toward which he leaned in his characterization, it is not surprising to find that Gadda deliberately chose to represent others from an external viewpoint. The *Racconto italiano di ignoto del novecento* documents an interesting discussion in which, as early as September 1924, the author considered the question of whether male writers are capable of representing females "ab interiore." His conclusion was that we are all able to intuit the sentiments of the opposite sex, since we are a polarization of maleness and femaleness. His reason for rejecting multiple points of view was that the constant movement between the characters' points of view is aesthetically tiring and difficult for the reader to follow. The novel then in gestation was meant to be "un romanzo della pluralità" [a novel about plurality], and his own inclination was for the variety to be achieved through the narrator's perceptions, without the use of interiorized characterization; it is also more realistic, he found, to acknowledge that we continually interpret others from our own point of view. In choosing this path of representing the world from the narrator's point of view, he established a distance from other-than-narrator's-self, so that women characters in particular became a lens through which he took the measure of reality – the frustrations and negations of a personal and a social nature then could be mirrored with a certain detachment. We thus have the contradiction of vibrant women characters that are more often than not passive, rarely initiators of action and still less in command of their situation; they are not allowed to be self-identifying individuals.[16] Women are, instead, the vehicle through which Gadda offers criticism of the distortion of the social and private rights and values that he observed within his own experience: natural deterioration, as seen in the neglected health of the poor, is matched by another kind of impoverishment, which is seen in the obtuse attitudes of the middle-class and the wealthy that contribute, in extreme cases, to social degeneration. In this further example of the process of change and deformation that Gadda identifies as synonymous with life, his women characters provide both a specific historical set of examples of Italian society, seen from a particular early twentieth-century male orientation, and a metaphor through which he represents the world.

---

16. I am grateful to my colleague Raffaele Lampugnani for his reminder that the figure of Jole in "San Giorgio in casa Brocchi" is a bringer of light. She is certainly, like other "stupende ragazze," the object of the author's delighted gaze, not only for her beauty but for the inadvertent role she plays in the mechanism that others set in motion and seek to control. Jole's most opportune visit as casual messenger to the house of Gigi Brocchi was the source of "nuovi dispiaceri che [. . .] doveva finir per dare ai Brocchi" [further displeasure [. . .] that she was to end up giving to the Brocchis], and in the context of the Contessa Brocchi's earlier anxiety about her, we can imagine that the risk of her unemployment was increased greatly by her adventure with Gigi.

SIX

The Failure of the Female Experiment: A Study of Women in Cesare Pavese's *La luna e i falò*

WALTER MUSOLINO

A Pavesian maxim might be a Pavesian line of verse:

Verrà la morte e avrà i tuoi occhi[1]

[Death will come and it will have your eyes],[2]

a line at once incorporating a chilling pronouncement about our mortality but also reversing the often traditionally redemptive function of eyes in poetry, which is to provoke passion, call it forth, rather than to deny or deflect it.[3] The poets of the *dolce stil novo*, ensnared in the bittersweet agonies of love's labors,

1. "Verrà la morte e avrà i tuoi occhi" (the opening line of an untitled poem written 22 March 1950) in the homonymous collection (Pavese [1951] 1981: 29).

2. All translations are my own, except where otherwise indicated.

3. Petrarch, the fourteenth-century Italian love lyricist par excellence who inherited and developed the "courtly love" tradition of the troubadors of Provence, provides numerous examples of how the eyes of his beloved Laura are the constant signifiers of the exalted power of love: "Benedetto sia 'l giorno e 'l mese et l'anno / et la stagione e 'l tempo et l'ora e 'l punto / e 'l bel paese e 'l loco ov'io fui giunto / da' duo begli occhi che legato m'ànno" – from sonnet LXI in Contini and Ponchiroli (eds.) 1964: 83, lines 1–4 [Oh blessed be the day, the month, the year, / the season and the time, the hour, the instant, / gracious countryside, the place where I / was struck by those two lovely eyes that bound me]. The English translation is taken from Musa (trans.) 1985: 35. "Chiare, fresche et dolci acque, / ove le belle membra / pose colei che sola a me par donna, / [. . .] / aere sacro, sereno, / ove Amor co' begli occhi il cor m'aperse" – from poem CXXVI, Contini and Ponchiroli (eds.) 1964: 167, lines 1–3, 10–11 [Clear, cool, sweet, running waters / where she, for me the only / woman, would rest her lovely body, / [. . .] / sacred air serene / where Love with those fair eyes opened my heart] (Musa 1985: 41); "Per la divina bellezza indarno mira / chi gli occhi de costei già mai non vide, / come soavemente ella gli gira" – from sonnet CLIX, Contini and Ponchiroli (eds.), 1964: 215, lines 9–11 [Who seeks for divine beauty seeks in vain, / if he has not yet looked upon those eyes / and seen how tenderly she [Nature] makes them move] (Musa 1985: 55).

were frequently apt to demonstrate as much:

> Ne li occhi porta la mia donna Amore,
> per che si fa gentil ciò ch'ella mira;
> ov'ella passa, ogn'om ver lei si gira,
> e cui saluta fa tremar lo core. (Dante)[4]

[In her eyes my lady carries Love,
so that what she gazes on becomes gentle;
wherever she passes everyone toward her turns,
and makes the hearts of those she meets tremble.],

> Viso di neve colorato in grana,
> Occhi lucenti, gai e pien d'amore:
> Non credo che nel mondo sia cristiana
> Sí piena di beltate e di valore. (Guinizelli)[5]

[Face of snow colored red,
shining eyes, gay and full of love:
I do not think the world has a Christian woman
so full of beauty and so worthy.]

> In un boschetto trova' pasturella
> Piú che la stella — bella al mi' parere.
> Cavelli avea biondetti e ricciutelli
> E gli occhi pien d'amor, cera rosata [. . .]. (Cavalcanti)[6]

[In a small wood I found a shepherdess
More than a star — beautiful in my opinion;
Blonde and curly was her hair
And her eyes full of love, her skin rosy [. . .].]

A chivalrous tendency toward aggrandizement and a tone of pleasant effusiveness establish the terms of a particular kind of correspondence between the poet and his beloved in the thirteenth century, but a correspondence that, in that line of Pavese's, clearly is altered now, darkened, hung with almost gothic overtones. And yet, although the *stilnovisti* and Pavese seem to be emotional and psychological opposites – they amorous, benevolently fawning, full of the sense of light and virtue; he grim, forbidding and blunt – both sets of poets reveal just how dominant the male sensibility can be. For if the male author is a metaphoric and microcosmic God-the-Creator, shaping a textual reality in the self-image of his own thought,

---

4. From sonnet XXI in *Vita Nuova*, edited by L. Pietrobono (1968: 69).
5. From "Le virtù di Madonna e i voti del Poeta," in Carli and Sainati (eds.) 1934, I: 88.
6. From "La ballata della pastorella," in Carli and Sainati (eds.) 1934, I: 95.

he allows (unlike the biblical God) remarkably little freedom to his creations.[7] The *stilnovisti* laud their ladies, but they also lord it over them, making their own devotional responses, their pleasure and tormented enchantment, the central concern of a poem. In their poetry the woman's already generic qualities – beauty, purity, love – amount to blissful, authorial bias; genial, authorial opinionatedness. The woman, ostensibly a presence (and the one to whom the poet is subservient), becomes really an objectification of the man's feeling. We discern the effects of the disease but glean little of its cause: who the woman is.

Now Pavese in that untitled poem from 1950, the first line of which is "Verrà la morte e avrà i tuoi occhi" [Death will come and it will have your eyes], in his own way subverts female independence as well, ensures that the function of literary woman conforms to his male need or visualization but does it, not like the *stilnovisti* by promoting her to a generously higher and more venerable order of existence among the angels and other godly mediators, but rather by drawing her down into the underworld of his own deathly perceptions. His nihilism, for example, is mirrored in her eyes as he sees them (". . . la morte avrà i tuoi occhi") [. . . death will have your eyes], but she, too, is condemned daily to face it claustrophobically in her own mirror (here are eyes evoking not optimism and life but the hypnotic negativities of futility and dying):

> I tuoi occhi
> saranno una vana parola,
> un grido taciuto, un silenzio.
> Così li vedi ogni mattina
> quando su te sola ti pieghi
> nello specchio.[8]

> [Your eyes
> will be a futile word,
> a mute scream, a silence.
> This is how you see them every morning
> when you bend down alone toward yourself
> in the mirror.]

The poem ends in a coolly gruesome image, too – Dantesque

---

7. In the book of Genesis, God, at the moment of making Man, confers on him the gifts of freedom and unconditional power to create and procreate. Even in imposing the limitation of not eating the forbidden fruit of knowledge, the biblical God allows free will, and thus allows Man to choose to disobey.

8. "Verrà la morte e avrà i tuoi occhi," Pavese [1951] 1981: 29, lines 5–10.

73

in origin though closer in spirit to a still from a horror movie – with poet and companion united in a sort of fatalistic pact:

Scenderemo nel gorgo uniti.[9]
[We shall descend into the vortex united.]

Pavese's pessimism can be as binding as that.

Still, such macabre instances of envisaged, climactic union in the poetry – moments of bleak victory at best – encapsulate Pavese's essential message, further elaborated in the more complex structures of the novels, that women never can be the saviors of men, never can provide enduring consolation for the loneliness or dissatisfactions of males, even though their attractiveness may be full of salutary potential as evidenced, for example, in one of Pavese's earliest novels, *Paesi tuoi*, where the protagonist's guarded cynicism about women actually softens when he suddenly discovers, in making love to Gisella – a voluptuous farm girl – a woman who is vulnerably honest and tenderly dignified. But ultimately, even at such a moment, it is impossible not to register his coarse, (stereotypically) masculine phraseology after the act and the latently chauvinistic sentiment that validates female virtue only insofar as it imitates male models and becomes recognizably manly:

Una volta cessato il rumore di lei che se ne andava, resto là fiacco sotto il sole e pensavo che a qualcuno l'avevo fatta. E' un momento quello, che uno non ne ha piú voglia di donne; ma di andarmene come avevo fatto con Michela non mi veniva neanche in mente. Sarà perché Gisella era piú naturale, e appena in piedi guardava e si muoveva come un uomo, e cosí doveva aver fatto a suo tempo quando perdeva quel sangue. Chi sa che lagna, se fosse toccato a Michela! – Se fai forte, mi fai male – , lei aveva detto, e basta. (Pavese [1941] 1968: 54)

[Once I could hear her no longer as she walked off, I stayed there under the sun, tired, and thought of how I had cheated someone out of some pleasure. It's a moment when one no longer desires women; but it didn't even cross my mind to leave the way I had left Michela. It's probably because Gisella was more natural, and as soon as she stood up she looked and moved like a man, and that is how she must have behaved that time when she was losing blood. Imagine the whining, if it had happened to Michela! – If you do it too hard, you'll hurt me – , she had said, and that's all.]

---

9. "Verrà la morte e avrà i tuoi occhi," line 19. Of course, the "gorgo" as "vortex" is to be found in the violent winds that spin about and buffet the carnal sinners in Canto V. It may be added that the whole of Dante's descent into Hell resembles, paradoxically, what could be termed a slow or "static" vortex.

Worse ideologically – if we intend ideology in the narrow sense of sexual politics – are Pavese's consistently reductive, hope-denying, and reactionary conceptions of women as individuals in their own right and of their fate in life. They are obvious even when his characterizations are urgent with sensuality, as in that admirably combative but still incestuously violated figure of Gisella, or even when those characterizations may seem at first studiously romantic, as at times they do in his last novel, *La luna e i falò* (Pavese [1950] 1969). In one passage there are all the elements of the radiant, exquisitely trembling impressionism of a Claude Monet painting:

> Ma un giorno che Irene era venuta a far giocar Santina nella sabbia e non c'era nessuno, le vidi correre e fermarsi all'acqua. Stavo nascosto dietro un sambuco. La Santina gridava mostrando qualcosa sull'altra riva. E allora Irene aveva posato il libro, s'era chinata, tolte le scarpe e le calze, e cosí bionda, con le gambe bianche, sollevandosi la gonna al ginocchio, era entrata nell'acqua. Traversò adagio, toccando prima col piede. Poi gridando a Santina di non muoversi, aveva raccolto dei fiori gialli. Me li ricordo come fosse ieri. (*La luna e i falò*, 111)

> [But one day when Irene had brought Santina along to play in the sand and no one was there, I saw them run and stop at the water's edge. I was hiding behind an elder tree. Santina was calling out while pointing to something on the other bank. And so Irene had put her book down, had bent down, removed her shoes and stockings, and so blonde, with her white legs, raising her skirt to her knees, she had gone into the water. She crossed slowly, dipping her foot in first. Then calling out to Santina not to move, she had picked some yellow flowers. I remember them as if they were yesterday.]

Of course it is a stylized representation of human contentment, as implied by Pavese, who reproduces it, appropriately enough, through the impressionable eyes of the narrator as an immature boy. But still we would ask in any case, as the novel, too, implicitly asks: how do such women – apparently delicate, precious, self-involved – survive in life? How do the visions of them, captured like that, resist time? The answer is carried in that final, lingering sentence of the passage itself, alive with the recollected tenderness of the vision's loss.[10] In other words, I would argue that the heavenly heroines of the "sweet" poets of

---

10. The flowers are what is explicitly, and grammatically, referred to as lost ("fiori gialli": "Me li ricordo"), but the young girls are certainly the implied subject as well.

the late Middle Ages become antiheroines in the mid-twentieth-century Italian society of Pavese's novels. If they were partly divinities then, enticingly remote from their soulful admirers, Pavese's literary ladies have long since become corrupted by the world; and they perpetuate that corruption in their ambitions and their actions, thus becoming at once victims of that world and its agents.

This is how it appears in *La luna e i falò*, published only a few months after Pavese's suicide, after a liaison with the American actress, Constance Dawling, had ended with her return to America. In *La luna e i falò* Pavese would seem to have probed for the possibilities of love, to have measured, as always, the ultimate meaningfulness, or otherwise, of human involvements. His narrator is the male model for whom he chooses several compatible female models, only to discard them, for varying reasons. However, from the outset, Pavese operates love's experiments under the psychologically controlled conditions of a predetermined state of mind in the narrator; one of taciturn disillusionment, or alternately, of happy, glib condescension toward life, all of it caused by a succession of frustrated relationships on which he looks back. Thus, the novel's retrospectivity ensures that what we witness finally is not love explored but its failure proved, time and again. In *La luna e i falò*, in fact, the two most attractive and, in a way, most distressing portrayals of women are the sisters Irene and Silvia, the inveiglingly lovely young daughters of "sor Matteo," the head of a family of wealthy landowners who live at "La Mora," a sort of Brontian Thrushcross Grange, to which the narrator – as an inhibited, backward orphan – is apprenticed (a little like Heathcliff when he is placed for the first time among the intimidating newness of Wuthering Heights). In Pavese's novel the narrator's years of silent observation of these girls older than him breed the requisite infatuation, with Irene blonde, pale-skinned and aloof, the paradigm of cultured, untouchable beauty; and Silvia dark as the earth, recklessly sexual and disturbed, the paradigm of nonconformist passion (and in considering their natural appeal for him, we remember also that scene of subdued, boyishly furtive enjoyment at the sight – a somewhat overripe depiction – of Irene with her youngest sister, Santina, bending over at the riverbank picking yellow flowers).

Yet the "affair" with Irene and Silvia remains for the narrator purely platonic, a melancholy fantasy, attributable in part to

their differences in age and social position (and to his perception of the girls' forbidding sophistication), but attributable as
well to his timid nature and to what would seem his youthful
uncertainty about such things as arousal and sex. However,
beyond him, seen legitimately in isolation, the lives of these two
young women, set in the context of what goes on in the world
between men and women, carefully suggest to us that there never
can be an auspicious future for them. Despite their material
advantages – money and good looks – Pavese methodically
exposes their flaws, magnifies them, revealing how wretchedly
fatal those flaws must be. Irene's inability to realize her social
aspirations of marrying into the lower ranks of the local aristocracy – the family of a countess – blinds her to the unctuous false-
ness of the man she eventually marries to escape the scene of her
great failure. Silvia hemorrhages to death after an illicit abortion,
an act both horribly symbolic of the perpetual threat of abuse by
men of women and a metaphor for the consequences of a life
lived without the twin restraints of dignity and shame. In other
words, it would seem that in his last novel, Pavese was proving his
own philosophy correct. The struggle to make a success of life is
the revelation of need, but need for Pavese is like a corruption
(again that term we used in relation to the world), a corruption
that invades the very core of human beings, compromising the
integrity of the self. Pavese would have agreed with the nineteenth-century Italian poet Giacomo Leopardi's sense of how all
life, even the most beautiful women, is chronically susceptible to
the forces of relentless decay (whether those forces be death
itself or simply our own despair), which beauty may disguise for a
while but never oppose or elude:

> Ahi come,
> come passata sei,
> cara compagna dell'età mia nova,
> mia lacrimata speme!
> Questo è quel mondo? questi
> i diletti, l'amor, l'opre, gli eventi
> onde cotanto ragionammo insieme?
> questa la sorte dell'umane genti?
> All'apparir del vero
> tu, misera, cadesti: e con la mano
> la fredda morte ed una tomba ignuda
> mostravi di lontano.[11]

11. "A Silvia" [To Silvia] in Leopardi 1975: 190, lines 52–63.

[Ah how,
how you are gone,
dear companion of my youth,
my lamented hope!
Is this that world? These
those pleasures, the love, the deeds, the events
of which we spoke so much together?
This the fate of human kind?
At the appearance of the truth
you, wretched, collapsed: and with your hand
you pointed to cold death and
a naked tomb far off.]

Life oppresses us, then, robs us of our natural impulse to hope, the unstated paradox being for Pavese, as it is for Leopardi, that it becomes demonstrably unnatural to maintain hope when our defeats in life show how hopeless human effort is.[12] To insist on hope, as Pavese and Leopardi would seem to understand it in their writings, is merely to increase our human suffering, though not commensurately our ability to tolerate it, as the cases of Irene and Silvia tragically illustrate. As Pavese plainly declared in "Verrà la morte e avrà i tuoi occhi": "Per tutti la morte ha uno sguardo." [For everybody death wears a look.]

At its most somber, in *La luna e i falò*, the truth of Pavesian existential law – what Pavlovian theory might have identified as "conditioned reflex philosophy"[13] – is ultimately, and curiously, to be verified in Pavese's most "successful" and most important character: the male narrator whose life has defied the forces of negation, whose good fortune in America and Genoa give him an air of alluring, capitalistic authority, at least where the excited locals back in his old home town are concerned (often motivated, some of them, by cloying self-interest).

> Volevano sapere che affari facevo, se compravo l'Angelo, se compravo la corriera. In piazza mi presentarono al parroco, che parlò di una cappelletta in rovina, al segretario comunale, che mi prese in disparte e mi disse [. . .] (*La luna e i falò*, 53)

[They wanted to know what business I was in, if I was going to buy the Angelo bar, if I was going to buy the coach. In the square they

---

12. "Amaro e noia / la vita, altro mai nulla; e fango è il mondo. / [. . .] / [. . .] Al gener nostro il fato / non donò che il morire." [Bitterness and boredom / life, never anything more; and mud is the world. / [. . .] / [. . .] To our kind fate / decreed but death.] "A se stesso" [To himself], Leopardi 1975: 252–53, lines 9–10, 12–13.

13. Ivan Petrovich Pavlov, Russian physiologist (1849–1936).

introduced me to the priest who spoke of a small chapel in ruins, to the town clerk who took me aside and said to me [. . .]]

Yet he is the one who, more than all others, confirms that essentially the Pavesian universe is negatively predeterministic, not necessarily in a material sense (success is possible: emigration, wealth), but in a human sense. Pavese simply cannot, for the most part, envisage triumph through close, human partnership, though when he does in *La luna e i falò* , it concerns, significantly, two men: Anguilla, the novel's protagonist, and Nuto, his best friend, who together pledge themselves to care for the orphaned peasant boy, Cinto (his father, finally driven to an act of cathartic madness by his impoverishment and exploitation, murders the other members of the family and then commits suicide). But if Pavese can be said to experiment at all with the notion of cooperation between men and women, his conclusions, as expressed through the unflattering judgments of men, are fundamentally condemnatory, generally dubious of the role and the value of women. As one female critic has asserted, referring also to another "questionable" Italian novelist in these matters: "Moravia's *Gli Indifferenti* or Pavese's *La luna e i falò* [are] both of them extremely oppressive texts for women, both of them extremely problematic to teach" (Caesar 1986: 2). And such a statement stands, of course, indirectly, as an accusation of misogyny against both narrator and author, one which close scrutiny of the text of *La luna e i falò* does not dispel:

Non voleva saperne. Strillava come fanno le donne [. . .] Per lasciarsi toccare [. . .] voleva essere sbronza. (*La luna e i falò*, 15)

[She did not want to know about it. She screamed the way women do [. . .] To let herself be touched [. . .] she wanted to be blind drunk.]

Il mio amico strinse le spalle, si chinò sul banco facendo cenno all'indietro con la mano: 'A te queste donne ti piacciono?' (*La luna e i falò*, 16)

[My friend hunched his shoulders, bent forward over the counter gesturing behind him: 'Do you like these women?']

Nei mesi che Rosanne fu la mia ragazza, capii ch'era proprio bastarda, che le gambe che stendeva sul letto erano tutta la sua forza [. . .] ma per lei una sola cosa contava – decidermi a tornare con lei sulla costa e aprire un locale italiano con le pergole d'uva – *a fancy place you know* – e lí cogliere l'occasione che qualcuno la vedesse e le facesse una foto, da stampare poi su un giornale a colori – only *gimme a break baby.* (*La luna e i falò*, 115)

[During the months that Rosanne was my girl, I realized that she was really a bastard, that the legs she spread out on the bed were all her strength [. . .] but only one thing mattered to her – for me to make up my mind to go back to the coast with her and open up an Italian place with vine-covered pergolas – *a fancy place you know* – and there wait for the chance that someone might see her and take a picture of her which would then be published in a color magazine – *only gimme a break baby.*]

Eppure mi piaceva quella donna, mi piaceva come il sapore dell'aria certe mattine, come toccare la frutta fresca sui banchi degli italiani nelle strade. (*La luna e i falò*, 116)

[And yet I liked that woman, I liked her like the taste of the air certain mornings, like touching the fresh fruit on the Italians' stalls along the roads.]

Born out of clearly visceral experiences with American women now – none of that adolescent voyeurism, that wistfully recalled spying on partly disrobed girls from behind trees – the narrator's comments (and that of his "amico") have a weary dismissiveness about them, a strange, dispassionate arrogance, or are casually bemused, though in a way that still can make allowance for women as an equivocal source of pleasure. (Here the implied ethical, behavioral, and aesthetic deficiencies of these women help identify them as part of the class of the inferior and the "victimized." This is true, too, of the one lover in the whole novel for whom the narrator comes closest to feeling genuine affection: Rosanne, the young ex-teacher from the Midwest in search of fame as a model or starlet on the East Coast. For, even in her case, his affection is mostly the expression of a fraternal kinship felt between misfits, of a compassion for this woman as a forlorn individual like him: "Venivamo tutti e due da chi sa dove [. . .]" (*La luna e i falò*, 116) [We both came from who knows where [. . .]]. In the end, though, he loses her as well because of his lackadaisical skepticism about the usefulness of having a permanent relationship with her.)

Such views prevail in the novel because repeatedly the accounts of individuals and incidents are described through the private looking glass of the narrator's rambling yet deceptively balanced memories. What we are told by him is subjective and relative (though Pavese is careful to portray a spectrum of political opinions, social classes, and human conditions throughout; and careful, as well, to undermine, when necessary, the authority of his narrator's own views, so that the impression we receive in reading the novel is a convincing attempt at ideological documentation as well as fiction). But, effectively unchallenged within the novel by other equally authoritative voices regarding the question of women, the narrator's way of seeing and his feelings about those women exercise a powerful influence over the narrative. And Pavese's narrator has a sensibility and outlook that are unmistakably masculine. But are they necessarily misogynist? If they are – and they seem to be – it also must be said that misogyny is only a partial explanation of this man's character, one that becomes more comprehensible when set against an appreciation of his broader state of mind. Because it isn't a single, problematical attitude that distinguishes the narrator, but a certain persistent – if intermittent, not absolute, and not always disagreeable – sense of dissociation from time and place in general, not just from one category of people. It is founded, partly, in his experiences as a waif, but also is confirmed gradually over twenty years of travelling the world; it is derived, that is, in great measure from a life of exile and dispossession spent yearning in America for the Italy of his past (before the Fascists and the war), or back in Italy, realizing the differences that divide him from it (which include his ignorance of what took place during the war, as well as simply his recognition that people he cherished had vanished, died, or had changed). The following passages poignantly point to the dissociation he feels back in the Langhe of his childhood:

> Ero tornato, ero sbucato, avevo fatto fortuna [. . .] ma le facce, le voci e le mani che dovevano toccarmi e riconoscermi non c'erano piú. Da un pezzo non c'erano piú. Quel che restava era come una piazza l'indomani della fiera, una vigna dopo la vendemmia, il tornar solo in trattoria quando qualcuno ti ha piantato. (*La luna e i falò*, 75)

> [I had returned, I had turned up, I had been successful [. . .] but the faces, the voices, and the hands that should have touched me and recognized me were no longer there. They had not been there for a long time. What remained was like a square the day after a fair, a vineyard after the harvest, a going back all alone to a restaurant after someone has just given you the flick.]

Such an implied state of almost cosmically profound emptiness is the culmination of a restless disillusionment that has resisted all his relationships with women and has brought him, variously, to conclude, as he disengaged himself from different female companions, that

> [D]i Genova ero già stufo, volevo andare più lontano – ma se le avessi detto questo, lei [Teresa] si sarebbe arrabbiata, mi avrebbe prese le mani e cominciato a maledire, ch'ero anch'io come gli altri. (*La luna e i falò*, 113)

> [I was already sick of Genoa, I wanted to get further away – but if I told her this, she [Teresa] would have got angry, she would have grabbed my hands and started swearing at me, saying I was like all the others.]

Then, in Fresno, he sensed that

> Rosanne me l'avrebbe anche fatto un figlio [. . .] [ma] Già allora sapevo che sarei ritornato. (*La luna e i falò*, 116)

> [Rosanne would have given me a child [. . .] [but] I already knew then that I would have gone back.]

And in Oakland, with Nora, he secretly determined that:

> Un bel mattino non mi avrebbe più visto, ecco tutto. Ma dove andare? Ero arrivato in capo al mondo, sull'ultima costa, e ne avevo abbastanza. Allora cominciai a pensare che potevo passare le montagne. (*La luna e i falò*, 18)

> [One fine morning she would not have seen me anymore, simple as that. But where to go? I had reached the top of the world, on the last coast, and I had enough of it. Then I began to think I could have crossed the mountains.]

Finally, what he is left with, this narrator, as a forty-year-old man and after myriad amorous encounters, is a laconic, resolved disaffection with all women,[14] a sense of their irrelevance in his life now:

14. His women were mainly from the working class, or from the lower middle class, which reflected, of course, his own modest socioeconomic background as a young man: "A Fresno dove vivevo, portai a letto molte donne, con una fui quasi sposato, e mai che capissi dove avessero padre e madre e la loro terra. Vivevano sole, chi nelle fabbriche delle conserve, chi in un ufficio – Rosanne era una maestra ch'era venuta da chi sa dove, da uno stato del grano, con una lettera per un giornale del cinema, e non volle mai raccontarmi che vita avesse fatto sulla costa." (*La luna e i falò*, 114). [In Fresno, where I lived, I slept with many women, I almost married one, and yet I never could figure out where their fathers and mothers were and where they came from. They lived alone,

82

Di donne ne ho conosciute andando per il mondo, di bionde e di brune – le ho cercate, ci ho speso dietro molti soldi; adesso che non sono più giovane mi cercano loro, ma non importa [. . .]¹⁵ (*La luna e i falò*, 118)

[Travelling around the world I met a lot of women, blondes and brunettes – I looked for them, I spent a lot of money on them; now that I am not young anymore they come looking for me, but it doesn't matter [. . .]]

That there should be moments of distraction and relief from states of disenchantment with love or of distress for the loss of the past: "Adesso a pensarci rimpiangevo quei tempi, avrei voluto ritrovarmici" (*La luna e i falò*, 184) [Now, thinking about them, I longed for those times, I would have wanted to be back there] is significant, however, because it is precisely in these moments that Pavese's narrator substitutes – with all sorts of provocative psychological implications – the doubts about human relationships, and life, with a belief in the possibilities of pantheistic adoration, the curative therapy of loving the earth. In fact, in having the narrator describe the land of his peasant childhood, Pavese seems to invoke the Freudian-linked metaphors of mother and lover, with the earth comforting as nurturer personified because it is constant, but also exciting the senses and the imagination by appealing to the power complex in the male observer (and with the male, in this instance, being the implied domesticator, the narrator's voice, for all its lyricism and benignity, reaches smugly patriarchal tones too):

[. . .] e mentre andavo rimuginavo che non c'era niente di più bello di una vigna ben zappata, ben legata, con le foglie giuste e

---

some in jam factories, others in offices – Rosanne was a school teacher who had come from who knows where, from one of the wheatbelt states, with a letter for a cinema magazine, and she never wanted to tell me about her life on the coast.]

15. Clearly, as a well-to-do bachelor in a small town, the narrator is the focus for scheming parental attentions concerning eligible daughters. His responses, though, reinforce the impression of an at times wry, mostly demure, but still steadfastly solitary individual: " 'Te l'ho già detto' dissi a Nuto, 'che il Cola vuol vendere?' 'Soltanto la terra?' disse lui. 'Stai attento che ti vende anche il letto.' 'Di sacco o di piuma?' dissi tra i denti. 'Sono vecchio.' "; "Non so se comprerò un pezzo di terra, se mi metterò a parlare con la figlia del Cola – non credo, la mia giornata sono adesso i telefoni, le spedizioni, i selciati della città [. . .]" (*La luna e i falò*, 13, 81). [" 'Did I tell you already' I said to Nuto, 'That Cola wants to sell?' 'Only his land?' he said. 'Be careful that he doesn't sell you somewhere to bed down as well.' 'With sackcloth or feathers?' I said, my teeth clenched. 'I am old.' "; "I do not know if I shall buy a piece of land, if I shall go to talk to Cola's daughter – I do not think so, my day is made up now of telephones, dispatches, the streets of the city [. . .]"]

quell'odore della terra cotta dal sole d'agosto. Una vigna ben lavo-
rata è come un fisico sano, un corpo che vive, che ha il suo respiro e
il suo sudore [. . .] e fa piacere posarci l'occhio [. . .] Le donne,
pensai, hanno addosso qualcosa di simile. (*La luna e i falò*, 51)

[[. . .] and as I walked along I thought about how there was nothing
more beautiful than a well-hoed vineyard, well-tied, with the leaves
just right and that smell of the earth being baked under the August
sun. A well-cultivated vineyard is like a healthy body, a body that is
alive, breathing and sweating [. . .] and you enjoy just looking at it
[. . .] Women, I thought, are somehow like that.]

Then we find:

[. . .] nelle piante, nella terra c'è qualcosa di tuo [. . .] anche quando non ci sei resta ad aspettarti. (*La luna e i falò*, 7)

[[. . .] in the plants, in the earth, there is something of yours [. . .]
even when you are not there it waits for you.]

Briefly, we also may note the significant coincidence of how the
female portrait that elicits a response of sober respect from the
narrator belongs to Virgilia, his peasant foster mother: an individual – a practical, dutiful, dour woman – again related to the
land.[16] It would seem, then, that in *La luna e i falò*, mother
earth, or Mother Nature, becomes the embodiment of the ideal
woman, the one woman who does satisfy; not just servile but
responsive to the male touch, even improved by it. This exem-
plification of "woman" is not purely sensuous but sublime, and
with moral connotations at that (of fidelity, for example). And
we seem here to be closer than at any other point in *La luna e i*

16. "Se sono cresciuto in questo paese, devo dire grazie alla Virgilia, a Padrino [her husband] [. . .] anche se loro mi hanno preso e allevato soltanto perché l'ospedale di Alessandria gli passava la mesata. [. . .] C'era chi prendeva una
bambina per poi averci la servetta e comandarla meglio; la Virgilia volle me perché di figlie ne aveva già due, e quando fossi un po' cresciuto speravano di
aggiustarsi in una grossa cascina e lavorare tutti quanti e star bene." (*La luna e i
falò*, 3–4.) [If I grew up in this town, I have Virgilia, Padrino to thank [. . .] even
if they took me in and raised me for the monthly subsidy the hospital at Alessandria paid them. [. . .] There were those who would take a girl in order to have a
little servant and boss her around easily; Virgilia wanted me because she already
had two girls, and when I was a bit older they were hoping to set themselves up
on a big farm and for all of us to work and be well off.]; "Mi ricordai come la
mamma Virgilia strappava la pelle ai conigli dopo averli sventrati." (*La luna e i
falò*, 27.) [I remembered how our mother Virgilia would skin the rabbits after
having gutted them]; "[. . .] da ragazzo [. . .] la Virgilia ci portava a messa [. . .]"
(*La luna e i falò*, 168.) [[. . .] as a boy [. . .] Virgilia would take us to mass [. . .]].
Virgilia's place in the novel, however, is not preeminent. She is recalled only
sporadically, undoubtedly due in part to the fact that she dies when the narrator is just ten years old.

falò to the idealizations of the *stilnovisti*. To put it another way, for all its physicality, for all its phenomenal realness, as an image of the best woman imaginable, the earth or nature is effectively more imaginary than real, a vision substantially in the imagination: a private exaltation. And for Pavese's narrator, the connection – let us stress and summarize it again – is explicit and intimate, and seductively, intoxicatingly so: "[. . .] non c'era niente di più bello di una vigna [. . .] con [. . .] quell'odore della terra cotta dal sole d'agosto [. . .] che ha il suo respiro e il suo sudore [. . .] Le donne [. . .] hanno addosso qualcosa di simile" [[. . .] there was nothing more beautiful than a vineyard [. . .] with [. . .] that smell of the earth being baked under the August sun [. . .] breathing and sweating [. . .] Women [. . .] are somehow like that]. So, for this narrator, the only acceptable woman is, finally, not a woman at all.[17]

Given this, it is not surprising to find that in *La luna e i falò*, Pavese's narrator sees nature's benefits as essentially escapist, too – that same nature in which the one redeeming vision of womanhood seems to be located for him; a vision too facile, too ecstatically offhand, though, to be credible or to be allowed to endure intact.[18] To contemplate nature's femaleness, imagining and feeling love regained through it (an emotion notori-

17. Even the self-satisfied dreaminess of that closing similitude – "Le donne [. . .] hanno addosso qualcosa di simile" [Women [. . .] are somehow like that] – points to a mind already quite comfortable with a sense of uncomplicated distance from life and others.

18. Yet the narrator's illusion about the innocence and integrity of the land around Gaminella where he grew up, his sense of privilege at "rediscovering" it, is challenged continually and is overturned by the facts, as in this example of how the countryside is no longer just farmland but has become a grotesque storehouse containing reminders of the evil men practiced during the war: "[. . .] Ma io [. . .] sapevo che tutto sommato solo le stagioni contano [. . .] e sulle colline il tempo non passa. [. . .] C'era uno, scassando un incolto, aveva trovato altri due morti sui pianori di Gaminella, due spie repubblichine, testa schiacciata e senza scarpe." (*La luna e i falò*, 56.) [[. . .] But I [. . .] knew that, all things considered, only the seasons count [. . .] and in the hills time stands still. [. . .] What happened was that a fellow who was digging up a piece of abandoned land had discovered another two dead bodies up in Gaminella's tablelands, two Republic of Salò spies, heads crushed and barefoot.]

Indeed, absorbed in fond, self-indulgent ruminating about the land, ascribing idealized feminine character traits to it, the narrator can fail to notice certain other weighty truths that concern him even more personally, such as the irony of his extolling the land's perceived quality of constancy – "[. . .] anche quando non ci sei resta ad aspettarti" (*La luna e i falò*, 7) [[. . .] even when you are not there it waits for you] – a quality his own life has so evidently lacked and one that he has failed to appreciate previously in those women, such as Teresa or Rosanne, who might have come close to displaying it with him.

ously independent of the world), is to stand outside time and have an experience of that Leopardian infinite in which the self discovers the healing order of its own contented stillness.[19] It is this restorative magic of nature that Pavese's narrator – in an image of primordial self-assertion – would have used to tranquilize his women, to transform them:

> Io avrei voluto portarmela in quella campagna, tra i meli, boschetti o anche soltanto l'erba corta dei ciglioni, rovesciarla su quella terra, dare un senso a tutto quel baccano sotto le stelle. Non voleva saperne. Strillava come fanno le donne. (*La luna e i falò*, 15)

> [I would have liked to have taken her into that countryside, among the apple trees, the groves, or even just the short grass of the embankments, to have thrown her down onto that earth, given some meaning to all that noise under the stars. She did not want to know about it. She screamed the way women do.]

In theory, it may be possible to act from such omnipotent determination, but the narrator eventually lacked the conviction and the strength (and we note the desperate tone of those words, the jerky, stumbling rhythms of the thought, and the frustrated and simplistic quality of the action envisaged, that already carry within them the sense of the scene's unconvincing absurdity). Unhappy in America, his impossible ambition would have been to impose a recognizable order on the chaotic elements of an alien universe, and thereby retrieve quiet for his heart. Instead, his very senses were disaffectedly alert to America's strangeness, were aggrieved and repelled by it. The vast night lights of California seemed either starkly imperial (manmade), like the great illuminated cities (*La luna e i falò*, 17) – also full of robotic menace was the startling incandescence of a train exploding past in the desert (*La luna e i falò*, 62) – or overwhelmingly indifferent (natural) like a cold sea of stars (*La luna e i falò*, 17). In their turn, the gross, invasive sounds he registered accentuated his dissatisfied, inner imbalance as he harped on the noise

19. In his poem "L'Infinito" [The Infinite] (1819), Leopardi's joy at the feeling of the profound absence of time and dissolving physical reality is not gender-significant, nor metaphorical or allusive, but it is quite sensorial, naturalistic, and immediate:
"[. . .] E come il vento / odo stormir tra queste piante, io quello / infinito silenzio a questa voce / vo comparando: e mi sovvien l'eterno, / e le morte stagioni, e la presente / e viva, e il suon di lei." (Leopardi 1975: 119–20, lines 8–13.) [[. . .] And like the wind / I hear in these plants rustling, I, that / infinite silence to this voice / compare: and I remember the eternal, / and the past seasons, and the present one / and alive, and its sound.]

("baccano") (15) of the crickets and toads, or on their voices ("le voci") (17), or on the so-called shouting or screaming ("urlare") (17) of those toads. Even a dog that sneezed, engendering fear in the narrator stranded in the lonely night time desert in a broken-down utility, is symbolic of his irremediable estrangement from America, as not even nature was a refuge from his disenchantment with life there. In this kind of situation, the simple act of love, as he realized himself, could not have resolved his dilemmas, which stretched beyond the significance of any relationship or woman:

> Quella notte, anche se Nora si fosse lasciata rovesciare sull'erba, non mi sarebbe bastato. I rospi non avrebbero smesso di urlare, né le automobili di buttarsi per la discesa accelerando, né l'America di finire con quella strada, con quelle città illuminate sotto la costa. Capii nel buio, in quell'odore di giardino e di pini, che quelle stelle non erano le mie, che come Nora e gli avventori mi facevano paura. (*La luna e i falò*, 17)

> [That night, even if Nora had let herself be thrown onto the grass, it would not have been enough. The toads would not have stopped croaking, nor the cars hurtling faster and faster down the slope, nor America being that road, with those illuminated cities below the coast. I realized in the darkness, in that garden and pine-tree fragrance, that those were not my stars, that they frightened me like Nora and the customers.]

The women of *La luna e i falò* may not have been incidental to the narrator's life, but as his life has progressed, the harmony it requires has become more self-centered, self-sufficient, either defying the needs of others or no longer able to embrace them. Pavese, in his own understated way, must have concluded as much by bringing that heavily introverted consciousness of the novel's guiding voice to an understanding that its own life would depend not on sharing it with others, but on a cautious detachment from unfamiliar conflicts, even on a gritty acceptance of a certain loneliness. It is an understanding that matures in the narrator over time; he has grown – unenviably we might think – toward it. In this context, the notion of love and closeness with a woman with whom Pavese was prepared to experiment through his central character alludes to the importance that just the possibility of merely imagining a successful human relationship must have held for him. The failure of the female experiment to open a window in the isolated room of

Pavese's philosophical darkness, providing the relief of some alternative vision of hope, is not a reflection of inherent creative inadequacies in the figures of the women as such, but a sign of the narrator's inability to sustain commitment, a symbol of the author's own crisis of faith.

SEVEN

The Double Gaze: Visibility of Sexual Difference in Photographic Representation (1908–1918)[1]

PAOLA DI CORI

Men look at women. Women watch themselves
being looked at. This determines not only
most relations between men and women but
also the relation of women to themselves.
  The surveyor of woman in herself is
male: the surveyed female. Thus she turns
herself into an object – and most particularly
an object of vision: a sight. (Berger [1973] 1985: 47)

Woman takes pleasure more from touching
than from looking, and her entry into a
dominant scopic economy signifies, again,
her consignment to passivity: she is to
be the beautiful object of contemplation.
While her body finds itself thus eroticized,
and called to a double movement of exhibition
and of chaste retreat in order to stimulate
the drives of the "subject," her sexual
organ represents *the horror of nothing to see*.
(Irigaray 1985: 26; emphasis in original)

In the last decade, historical and other types of research on
World War I has deeply changed what was known of the sub-
jective experience of men and women during the war years.
Also, a certain image has crystallized of the role played in this
period by European women – and, to a lesser degree, by their
American counterparts. This literature is characterized by a

1. This is a modified version of an essay published in 1986 in the proceedings
of the 1985 conference "La grande guerra. Esperienza, memoria, immagine"
(Leoni and Zandra, 1986). It has been translated here by David Watson.

noticeable sexual separatism. On the one hand, there have been studies of soldiers' experiences at the front in all their various forms – refusal to obey orders, day-to-day life in the trenches, psychoses, emotional and sexual disturbances, and the perception of landscapes and sounds.[2] On the other hand, there have been analyses of the situation of women on the home front – relief work, the massive presence of women in industry, their replacement of men in the work force, the strengthening of women's public image in Europe – which, after the war, was to pave the way for female suffrage (but only in England) – the change in political attitudes from radical feminism to interventionism and nationalism, and the emergence of the first mass women's movements of a politically conservative nature in Italy, England, and Germany from 1918 onward.[3]

What this literature offers, inter alia, is a picture of the reality of the enforced separation experienced for several years by the sexes. What still remains to be analyzed is an area to which this essay aims to contribute – that is, the translation of this experience at the level of the categories of masculine and feminine, and of the sexual identities of the two genders.[4]

Before World War I, the categories of male and female had relatively well-defined cultural connotations: the concerns of the male category were those of public life, extradomestic work and production, the outside world, and external space in general; the female category, on the other hand, had as its domain the private sphere, the sphere of reproduction, and internal space. Everything in real life that contradicted these oppositions was considered unnatural. Examples of such contradictions were women's involvement in intellectual, public, or military activities, or men's in the domestic field.

2. To confine ourselves to only a few recent contributions to the research in these areas, see especially Fussell (1975) and Leed (1979). Both studies were published in Italy by Il Mulino press in 1985. See also Forcella and Monticone [1968] (1972); Isnenghi (1970, 1977, 1978, and 1982); and Bianchi (1983). Recent essays dealing with socioeconomic factors are those collected by Procacci (1983). Melograni [1969] (1972) is still valid as a political study of the period.

3. The two studies by Pieroni Bortolotti (1974 and 1978) are indispensable. See also Bravo (1980) and Leoni and Zandra (1982). For legislative changes in this period, see Galoppini (1980); Scott (1988) is of great interest for its methodological fine-tuning.

4. See Rubin (1975). In recent years, the following important collections of essays have been published: S. Ardener (ed.) (1975 and 1978); Ortner and Whitehead (eds.) (1981). See also Harding (1983). Literature on the theme of gender in psychology is comprehensively discussed in Henley (1985). For a discussion of the problem of gender in history, see Scott (1983) and Pomata (1983).

These oppositions are represented in Table 1, in which one can see clearly the profound change undergone by certain central elements in the cultural definition of the two sexes in the first twenty years of this century.

An extensive analysis of the complex processes of these transformations in all their many and varied aspects falls outside the more limited scope of these pages, which are intended to be simply the seeds of initial research in an area that has been neglected almost totally. Table 1 is offered as a guide or framework, and its usefulness may be said to lie in the efficiently synoptic nature that it shares with all diagrammatic representations. A brief look at the items in the table discloses a few important aspects that give the present study its direction: the respective experiences of men and women are not balanced or symmetrical; there does not exist a one-to-one correspondence between masculinity and femininity, nor between the characteristics attributed to each.

Some of these elements are central in certain periods and economic circumstances, and marginal in other preceding and successive ones. This is true, for example, in the public and private spheres during the years under consideration. The characteristics of men and women are culturally different from those of masculinity and femininity. Even though the terms themselves are allied, they do not coincide (man is not always identified with masculine); nor is one term derived directly from the other (masculine attributes are not all derived from men, any more than their feminine counterparts are all derived from women).[5]

The points where these two poles differ, conflict, and overlap (highlighted in Table 1) are of primary interest if one is to go beyond the purely symmetrical approach. The case of World War I provides a clear example. Given the exceptional nature of the situation – a long period in which men and women were far away from each other – it is possible to study the experience of each sex in the absence of, and in the enforced separation from, the other. Moreover, it is possible to conduct this study in terms specifically related to the elements that contribute to the formation of gender identity (that is, those elements that constitute femininity and masculinity). This fact is of some import,

5. One of the few historical studies to address itself to these problems, applied to the specific case of a community of Cistercian monks, is Bynum (1982). See also Bynum (1984 and 1985).

91

TABLE 1

	1900–1908		1916–1917		1918–1920	
FEMALE		**MALE**	**FEMALE**	**MALE**	**FEMALE**	**MALE**
woman	:	man	woman : man		woman/man	
					mothers/widows	returned soldiers
private	:	public	private/public		private/public/political	
domesticity	:	politics	peace : war			
indoors	:	*outdoors*	*outdoors* : national border		*outdoors*	
home	:	work	home front : war front			
family	:	*country*	motherland : trenches		*country*	
domestic work	:	factory	factory : battlefield		demobilization	demilitarization
reproduction	:	production	reproduction/ production : death		reproduction/production	

for it is fundamental to the construction of sexual stereotypes, and to the determination of the norms that condition the roles and behavior of men and women in society.

World War I, which, in recent years, has been studied by Eric Leed as a cause of the profound splitting of the male identity, carried to the extreme the consequences of the crisis of those traditional elements that, culturally speaking, formerly had characterized the female identity – a crisis that had been fermenting for several decades. Of the various elements characterizing these transformations (which, in some cases, display clear signs of role-reversal and open transvestism), this essay will focus on an aspect that has not yet been analyzed in connection with this period: the visual representation of these transformations. Photography is taken as the main source of reference.

This choice is justified by a series of important factors relating to the private and public uses of the photographic medium. In its private use, photography became an essential instrument of communication between the two sexes during the war. For several years, men and women saw themselves and each other, and perceived their respective physical changes, above all through the photographs that they exchanged with each other, and through those published and circulated on both war and home fronts.[6]

In addition, photography played a leading role during this period in the construction of stereotypes related to gender identity, a function that, in the years following the war, was to be taken over by the cinema, and later by television and advertising. It is therefore those photographs distributed among a wide public that are of most direct interest here.[7]

There is, however, one aspect – perhaps the most important – that must be highlighted: it was in the war years that the female presence for the first time achieved mass visibility in a nondomestic context. This fact profoundly and irreversibly

6. For example, see Spitzer (1976) and Urettini and Guarnieri (1985). On photography during World War I, see the pictures and accompanying commentary in Bertelli and Bollati (1979), and the special issue of *La Rivista di storia e critica della fotografia*, 1981, no. 1, dedicated to the photographic representation of this war. A. Schwarz's contribution to this issue of *La Rivista* is of particular significance. For interesting considerations on the stereotypical aspects of war photographs, see Trichtenberg (1985).

7. The photographs taken into consideration here are principally those published in *L'Illustrazione italiana*, *La Domenica del Corriere*, and *Assistenza civile*, the fortnightly publication of the Federazione nazionale comitati assistenza civile, printed in Milan in 1917 and 1918.

cracked the edifice of the cultural stereotype based on the incompatibility of women and the public sphere – an idea derived, as far as Western societies are concerned, from the Enlightenment. This is in fact the root of the notion that women are extraneous to public life because of their role in physical reproduction, and their consequent close affinity with the world of nature.[8]

A photograph, once printed and circulated, not only documents this public dimension and exalts it to the highest level, but in the process also modifies the hierarchical ordering of, and the difference that exists between, the characteristics of the male and female genders. It is worthwhile underlining the importance of the female gender's march, as it were, toward the conquest of public visibility in the Italian cultural context. On the one hand, the latter was dominated by the Mediterranean code of honor (for which Italy, unlike Anglo-Saxon countries, provided a legislative counterpart), which conceives of the nondomestic arena as an area of constant threat to female purity, and consequently to the integrity of the entire kinship network. On the other hand, it was fortified by the age-old influence on upbringing and morality of the Catholic church. In both these traditions, the decree that consigned women to invisibility in any field beyond the purely domestic was near unassailable.[9] It is also important to remember the influence in this period of the Lombrosian school of thought, which advanced physiological and neurological arguments geared to reinforcing the ideology of the inadequacy of women in the public sphere, on the basis that female intellectual effort harmed reproduction, and was therefore a threat to the continuity of the species.[10]

In this cultural context, it is possible to divide photographs of women at the beginning of the century into four main categories: those relating to subjects considered criminal or abnormal (prostitutes, madwomen, sexual perverts); artists (circus performers, actresses, singers, models, painters, writers);

8. See the essay by Bloch and Bloch in MacCormack and Strathern (eds.) (1981) and MacCormack's introductory essay in the same volume. See also Mathieu (1973) and Brown and Jordanova (1981).

9. For the Mediterranean concept of honor, see the problems discussed by Davis (1980: 101–14); Peristiany (1966); Reiter in Reiter (ed.) (1975: 252–82); Chapter 13 of Lison Tolosana ([1966] 1983); Pitt-Rivers (1977); and Douglass (1984). For Italy specifically, see Schneider (1971); Blok (1981); and Alinei's comments regarding Blok's essay (1982).

10. See Law Trecker (1974); Porter and Venning (1976); Ongaro Basaglia's introduction to Moebius (1978); Pomata (1979); and Chaucey, Jr. (1982–83).

women working in factories, on the land, and in business; and finally, those concerning the domestic duties and family, and the context of everyday life.[11] As far as newspapers were concerned, the only photographs to be printed occasionally were those of female artists and, of course, of members of the royal family. In fact, in the Mediterranean context, the only group to escape the dictates and prescriptive rules of the honor code was that of the aristocracy, as Pitt-Rivers has noted with regard to Spain (1977: 37–46). Apart from those photographs of everyday life in the family context, all the photographs take as their subject women who are shown, or who show themselves, in the public sphere, and for this reason they occupy a somewhat anomalous position.

A review of this dominant iconography is useful in establishing a greater understanding of the way in which the relationship is articulated, for each of the sexes, between visual portrayal and political representation – that is, between the public, the private, and the political.[12]

The photographs of publicly visible women (such as actresses, workers, prostitutes, writers) always capture something individual and specific about the subject depicted.[13] Their public appearance does not confer on these women the right to represent also those women who generally do not appear in public; the photographed women remain closed in their uniqueness. A man, on the other hand, can be not only portrayed in a photograph, but is even capable (in parliament) of representing the entire human race, male and female alike.[14] Men can speak for

11. In addition to the major periodicals in the field, I also have consulted recent collections based on photographic exhibitions, such as *Esistere come donna* (1983); *Oltre la posa* (1984); and *Memoria fotografica (1908–1923)* (1985). See also Miraglia (1981). For various aspects of photography in general, see Sontag (1978); Arnheim (1981); Barthes (1981); and Gombrich (1982). For problems regarding visual anthropology, see the two special issues of *Ricerca folklorica*, 1980, no. 2 (dedicated to photography) and no. 3 (dedicated to cinema); Ruesch and Kees (1961); and Hockings (1975). On actresses, see the important essay by Blair (1981).

12. For the relationship between public and private, see the classic expositions by Arendt (1989); Habermas [1962] (1989); Firth (1973); and Bobbio (1980). For women and the public dimension, see Collier (1974) and Sanday (1974); Harris (1981); and Siltanen and Stantworth (1984a and 1984b). Of great interest from the philosophical and moral points of view are the essays edited by Hampshire (1978).

13. For a philosophical consideration of the problem of visibility, see Mulvey (1975); Fox-Keller and Grontkowski (1983); Gordon (1984); and Betterton (1985).

14. See Ardener's introduction to Ardener (1978).

both sexes; women cannot. This is one of the essential elements that distinguish photographs of men from those of women in this period. Hence the cardinal importance of captions.

Leaving aside considerations of its contents, any photograph of a woman that does not carry a caption creates an effect of almost ontological disorientation. The dependent and reified nature of the female subject portrayed makes it impossible for her to represent an entity other than herself – hence the need for an accompanying description that might justify her presence in the photo. A captionless photograph of a man, on the other hand, indicates simply that his identity is unknown.[15]

In the light of this difference, those photographs taken during the first National Conference of Italian Women (held in Rome from 24 to 30 April 1908), depicting participants and organizers at various moments of the conference, are to be considered genuinely revolutionary. For the first time, women are photographed as representatives of the female gender in all its difference and separateness from its male counterpart, but also as women who, in and of themselves, have the right to represent all other women as a species. In other words, it is no longer a question of a subgroup whose membership of the species can be represented by men alone (see Photo 1). This important historic event marks the point at which the principle of incompatibility of women and the public sphere begins to crumble.

The conference, organized by the liberal Council of Women, with the participation of socialist, radical, and Catholic feminist groups, enjoyed the support of the government and of Mayor Nathan, and was convened officially in the presence of Queen Margherita, government ministers, and members of the aristocracy.[16] There is little doubt that the solid participation of noblewomen and the queen was instrumental in giving the event a special aura. Their social position allowed the women the privilege of being excluded from the principles that regulated the relationship between public and private worlds. They availed themselves of this privilege to display their gender kinship to the outside world, just as the other participants at the conference were doing.

The organizers behaved in the full knowledge that they were

15. For the importance of captions, see Benjamin (1966: 77) and Gombrich (1977).

16. See especially *Avanti, Il Tempo,* and *Corriere della sera* for reports of the opening ceremony of the conference (22 April to 1 May 1908).

1. Delegates at the First National Conference of Italian Women.

displaying themselves openly, as if on a stage. In fact, they took advantage of the ambiguity of this forum to move back and forth between open theatricality – some of them turned up at the opening of the conference in the Campidoglio, dressed in the latest fashions and driving their own cars and carriages – and professional rigor in managing the conference sessions (in which some men also participated). The sessions of the final day – which closed with a rift between Catholics and socialists over religious education in schools – were followed by a farewell dinner for women only, which the newspapers reported with sarcasm.

For a whole week the national press reported the proceedings of the conference, which, in spite of its undeniable attraction for the beau monde, was in fact run along traditional lines, organized according to working groups, and including roughly two hundred papers.[17] It becomes clear from the newspaper reports that one of the principal aims of the participants was to make an impact at the level of social visibility, and, considering the high level of public interest, the conference was clearly suc-

17. The papers subsequently were published in the *Atti del I Congresso nazionale delle donne italiane*, Roma 24–30 aprile 1908, Rome, 1912, edited by members of the Consiglio nazionale delle donne italiane.

cessful. Journalists crowded the conference sessions, and the larger newspapers gave day-by-day accounts in front-page articles of their progress. Weeklies and cultural journals published long and detailed accounts. Reactions varied a great deal. One of the most interesting was the feeling, among men, of being demasculinized.

The *Corriere della sera* reporter gave free expression to the fears and the sense of suffocation that the sight of all those women together had provoked in him. The idea emerges clearly from his reports that a distinction between the genders had now been identified publicly:

> We are in a monosexual microcosm in which the sense of the male gender no longer exists. Even those few men present, even those who have been courteously granted the privilege of participating in the Conference debates, swathe themselves, it seems, in this feminine atmosphere, and they appear transformed, as if something had been softened and blunted inside them, in their physical appearance, in their voices, their gestures, in the very way they argue. [. . .]
>
> Every object around us seems to belong to the feminine gender. And so we are overcome by a wild desire to run away, to rush headlong down the stairs, so as to feel far removed from that all-too-soft atmosphere of womanish smells, sounds and colors, to find ourselves at last among men again, to rediscover at last our manliness, to smell once again the aroma of a cigar, and to see moustaches and beards that do not seem false [. . .] and that do not belong to women. (*Corriere della sera*, 28 April 1908: 3)

Other commentators take an opposing position, but one which, for the purposes of this essay, is equally important. They reveal the difficulty they have in perceiving gender difference, and therefore display a tendency to liken female to male. In *La Rassegna nazionale*, Giulio Vitali writes:

> It was indeed with great hesitation that I went to that unprecedented conference. I had the impression that I was taking part in a plot against the order of things, against the natural order. [. . .] Even today, after eight days of the Conference, I cannot eradicate that long-standing male claim that the interests of our women are best looked after by us men. [. . .] To tell the truth, I, too, and without difficulty, will have to stifle the deep-seated chivalrous urges of my heart, and resign myself to considering those assembled ladies a little as if they were men. (Vitale 1908)

The conference officially came to a close on 1 May 1908, and, in its closing moments, while the conference participants slowly were leaving, they "began, in every corner of the building, to pose before dozens of cameras" (*Il Tempo*, 30 April 1908: 3)

The captions beneath the photos of the participants say that every aspect of the world of Italian women was represented at the conference. Looking at them, one has a strange sensation; the images operate at several levels, combining public visibility with political representation. In them, it can be seen that the abstraction of belonging to the female gender (the gender that has here undertaken to represent itself), is harnessed to the palpable materiality of the physical bodies portrayed. This means that the women photographed cannot be seen as objects constructed by an eye that captures them for its own pleasure; but rather as representatives of an otherness that, in its turn, does the observing.

In all those countries involved in World War I, the presence of women in areas traditionally considered to belong to men became a quantitatively important and visibly widespread phenomenon. It was at this time that a progressive modification came about in those attributes that formerly had characterized membership of the female gender.

Both sexes spoke openly of the swift movement of women in the direction of the male gender – "women are about to become men," wrote Rosa Rosà in 1917 (Rosà 1981: 126) – while some pointed to the fact that men, in a way, had undergone a process of demasculinization, or even, in some cases, of open feminization. "They have become more sentimental, melancholic [. . .] they dream of the good wife or elderly mother getting the dinner ready," observes Palazzeschi in *Due imperi . . . mancati* (Palazzeschi 1920: 167).

This type of polarization is central to Sandra Gilbert's important study on the literary production of women in British society during the war. The study highlights the sense of liberation, erotic rapture, and enthusiasm present in the female imagination, as opposed to the anguished universe of the fragmented male identity that emerges from the research of Leed and Fussell (Gilbert 1983). However, the body of evidence – historical, medical, anthropological, and photographic – suggests another hypothesis regarding gender identity. In fact, few studies have paid attention to the effects, at the level of cultural gender characterization, produced by the separation of the two sexes.

The scant research into this problem, though it considers

very different periods and contexts,[18] has highlighted how the experience of separation and absence breaks down the order of those elements that identify gender, and how the categories of masculinity and femininity present themselves with much less well-defined characteristics than in situations of normal coexistence. In periods of separation, each sex tends to take on characteristics of its opposite. As a result of these modifications, the identities of both sexes, and therefore their respective behaviors and any concomitant stereotypes, are profoundly changed.

The 1908 conference had legitimized the visible presence of women in the public and political spheres, but not in the spheres of labor and production. It was to be the war that extended this presence in the entire social and industrial structure. In England, Belgium, and France, the massive participation of women in industry and in jobs traditionally carried out by men has been documented as far back as 1914. In Italy, this change occurred more slowly, and in two different phases.[19]

In the first half of 1915, the primary subject of photographs featuring women is the departure of their men for the front (that is, the moment of separation), and the new behavior that both sexes were beginning to adopt. This can be seen in the photo entitled "At the Front," taken in July 1915, which shows General Porro and his daughter (see Photo 2).[20] It was the first time since the beginning of the war that a woman had had the honor of appearing on the cover of *L'Illustrazione italiana*. The photo has didactic value; it is an exemplum, and represents the new model of behavior for men and women, each on a different front, and in a different uniform.

During the entire first year of the war, women were engaged in relief work in hospitals or sewing clothes for soldiers at the front. To judge from the photos, knitting seems to have been the female activity par excellence. At the same time, female patriotism was beginning to come into its own. Miss Maria Abri-

18. See Bynum's studies, cited in note 5 above. For the psychoanalytical point of view, see Salomè (1985), in particular the passage on masculine and feminine (79–83).

19. See Baronchelli Grosson (1917) and Ministero per le Armi e Munizioni (1918). For details of women's employment over a seventy-year period, see Bandettini (1959–60). For the role of women in the war industries, see Camarda and Peli (1980) and Peli (1983). For a comparison with other countries, see Williams (1972); for Britain and France, the most recent studies are Braybon (1981) and Hause and Kenney (1984).

20. *L'Illustrazione italiana*, 11 July 1915.

2. "At the Front: General Porro and his daughter."

ani, photographed in 1915 wearing the feathered hat of the Bersaglieri, was hailed as the first heroine of the war, having led the Italian army safely to the city of Ala. The comment of the reporter of *L'Illustrazione italiana* was: "When women set about doing something unusual, they acquit themselves every bit as well as men, if not better."[21]

In this period, a notable attempt was made to encourage women to act patriotically, and, at least initially, frequent references were made to the women of other countries, held up as models to be emulated. In the journal *L'Unità d'Italia*, women who enthusiastically supported Italy's entry into the war expressed their envy of English and French women, because they were allowed to work anywhere – Italian women were restricted to auxiliary tasks because of "men's excessive attachment to their jobs," as the writers said, sarcastically.[22] But the discourse articulated through photographs slowly changed. As

21. *L'Illustrazione italiana*, 12 September 1915.
22. *L'Unità d'Italia*, organ of the Comitato nazionale femminile per l'intervento italiano, II, 1 August 1916, no. 7.

early as the end of 1915, newspaper reports began to appear with the first batches of photographs depicting women carrying out tasks traditionally associated with men: driving and conducting streetcars, and sweeping the streets.

A significant feature of these photographs is what may be called the assemblage effect. Whenever it comes to illustrating the unusual female presence in public work areas, there is hardly ever one photograph alone, but many together on the same page (see Photo 3).[23] The representation of the female gender is no longer fragmented into the stereotyped categories (artists, prostitutes, workers, etc.) that had characterized it prior to 1908, and all prohibitions regarding extradomestic work have disappeared. Yet collective representation remains a peculiarity of the female gender, which is depicted as the sum of different parts, the unity of which needs to be reconstructed through the operation of a particular visual reading. Anyone looking at a page in which such a group of photos appears cannot concentrate on any one photograph, but is forced instead to cast her or his eye over the page as a whole, subjectively recomposing, in one single image, the multiplicity suggested by the printed page. The assemblage is extremely efficient. The photos show different parts of a space in which men have always been seen, and which is now occupied by women. The effect is that the observer begins to modify the image, to substitute and to superimpose on the traditional image of an exclusively male external space the reality of a female presence, which also has a highly positive function. Furthermore, in the photographs taken during the first year of the war, the female subcategories are no longer seen, and with them have vanished social differences between women, who are now grouped together without distinction, since national salvation requires a common effort. In fact, all women, including the queens and princesses from whom the others take their lead, dress in a similar fashion: they all wear auxiliary uniforms, and, in many cases, perform identical tasks. They all sew, for example – noblewomen and peasants alike.[24]

23. See *L'Illustrazione italiana* of 17 October 1915, and especially the issue dedicated to civil mobilization in Italy (21 November 1915). See also years 1917 and 1918 of *Assistenza civile*, the fortnightly publication of the Federazione nazionale comitati assistenza civile; and issues of *Attività femminile sociale* (the monthly publication of the Consiglio nazionale delle donne italiane) covering the war years.

24. See *L'Illustrazione italiana*, 12 November 1916 and 26 November 1916.

3. Streetcar drivers and street sweepers.

This new visibility of the female gender goes hand in hand
with the new way in which the women, for their part, look at the
photographer, and at the space that surrounds them. In the
most widely distributed photographs, women – often there is
only one woman in each photo – are smiling and are looking
straight at the camera; they are clearly proud and happy to be
photographed.

This is not the case for men. At the war front they are hardly ever photographed individually, but in groups, crouching in the trenches or on the march, or while skiing, climbing, resting, scanning the landscape, or shooting; and often they are looking away from the camera.[25] Their gaze, distracted or directed elsewhere, conveys great isolation and distance from the rest of the world, which the proximity of the photographer is powerless to mitigate. As Giulio Bollati wrote, "the photographs of the Great War are often solitary, as if they were not meant for anyone's eyes, not even those of the man pressing the button of his portable Kodak" (Bollati 1983: 174). The soldier does not care whether or not he is photographed. His very optic nerve seems atrophied, the lostness in his gaze symbolizing a genuine loss of the visual organ.

The immensely sad photographs of blind soldiers are powerful signifiers in this context. The blind soldier has lost not only his sight, but also his virility and his adult status. He is often compared to a child who needs to be reeducated, and in a photo taken in March 1915, a blind soldier is photographed while knitting (see Photo 4).[26] In another, taken in September 1917, blind soldiers are seen basket weaving, wearing long aprons that come down to their feet.[27] Yet, while women are compared to men, the opposite never occurs, not even in those cases when soldiers are dressed as women, or are photographed carrying out traditionally female tasks. The most significant caption in this regard appears in the British newspaper *The Illustrated War News*, and accompanies a picture of Belgian soldiers dressed in tutus (as in the film *La Grande Illusion*). The photograph is entitled "From Bullets to Ballets: Belgian Soldiers 'Resting,'" by way of explanation that what the viewer is looking at are courageous Belgian soldiers in a moment of relaxation (see Photo 5).[28]

It would be interesting at this point to look more closely at cultural differences. The British seem more ironical about some aspects of life at the front. The cover of *The Illustrated War News* carries a photo of wash day at the front, showing a soldier washing his clothes next to a pair of long johns that have been

25. See Touring Club Italiano (1965); Posani (1968); Stato Maggiore dell'Esercito (1978); and Manenti (1979).
26. *L'Illustrazione italiana*, 12 March 1916.
27. *L'Illustrazione italiana*, 16 September 1917.
28. *The Illustrated War News*, 20 September 1916.

4. Blind soldier doing macramé.

5. "From Bullets to Ballets: Belgian Soldiers 'Resting.'"

hung up to dry.[29] The Italians, on the other hand, tend to portray soldiers caught up in traditionally male jobs such as those of cobbler, barber, and butcher.[30]

One of the salient features of the British photos of the period and, to a large extent, of their French counterparts, is the intention to describe a world turned upside down. British women, in fact, were photographed while performing traditionally masculine jobs: driving ambulances and watering carts; baking; digging and working the land; engaged in industrial work and in scientific enterprises as doctors and researchers in laboratories; participating in the building industries; as gas workers and window cleaners, aviators, and airplane mechanics; and lumberjacking and carrying heavy weights. The whole spectrum of working activities was performed by women. Yet, the technique of representation was ambivalent; it had as its main genre reference the traditional representation of women as objects of the male gaze and of male pleasure. Female workers were then portrayed as if they were models in an artistic atelier or girls in a chorus line. Above all, British photography emphasizes the aspect of unreal reality of this widespread female presence in the public and working space. A woman's world was considered unbelievable, it was untrue, it could only belong to the realm of fantasy and imagination. A British commentator, Hall Caine, wrote: "There is at first something so incongruous in the spectacle of women operating masses of powerful machinery (as indeed any machinery more formidable than a sewing-machine), that for a moment, as you stand at the entrance, the sight is scarcely believable" (quoted in Braybon 1981: 161). British photographs reproduced the unreal experience of a female world through the many and different kinds of work performed by women.[31] Moreover, there was a strong emphasis on the individual characterization of these women.

The Italians, for their part, adopted the device of assembling several photographs on the same page. With the goal of making it believable that those photographed were real women, Italian assemblage of pictures has a clear purpose: the viewer is

29. *The Illustrated War News*, 9 August 1916.
30. Stato Maggiore dell'Esercito (1978), photographs 31, 72, 80.
31. In this area, two contributions that are fundamental from the methodological point of view are those of Zemon Davis (1975) and Davidoff ([1979] 1983). For certain characteristics of masculinity in the Mediterranean context, see Brandes (1981).

engaged in the optical exercise of turning the eyes around the page in a circular movement encompassing the different pictures. It is as if this female reality can be accepted only in stages, as a result of the accumulation of multiple images.

One of the most interesting things about the photographs of Italian soldiers is that as soon as they are photographed in uniform (that is, in their public capacity) but carrying out domestic chores, there is a shift to the privatization of the male role. The role of women during the war, on the other hand, is of necessity entirely public, and this publicness coincides with the elimination of a private female dimension unimaginable in a time of national emergency.

However, alongside this different articulation of the relationship between private and public, sensory perception comes to the fore as a new element of sexual characterization. Without doubt, one of the most ground-breaking aspects of Leed's study is his focus on the system of perception. This is an essential ingredient in his discussion of individual identity and its disaggregation in war. The accuracy of such a view has been amply confirmed by recent studies in the field of cognitive psychology. The studies emphasize the centrality of the functioning of the senses, both individually and together, in the apprehension and structuring of knowledge, memory, and self-perception.[32] The experience of the war, as can be seen clearly on examining the appropriate photographs, highlights yet again the emergence of a sexual difference: the senses acquire a strong gender connotation.[33] Female sight and touch find their correspondents in the male senses of hearing and smell.[34] Women's gazes range over objects and people, while men's gazes are desolate, narrowed, unidirectional, and voyeuristic. From the trenches, the only things visible are the barbed wire and rocks of no-man's-land. Otherwise, the landscape is viewed through telescopes and binoculars, the enemy camp is observed through slits, cracks, and rifle sights. This latter field of vision is oblong, filtered through lenses and glass, and forces one to strain the eyes or to shade them with the hand in order to get one's bear-

32. See Neisser and Kerr (1973); Neisser (1981); Lowe (1982).

33. Gregory Bateson and Margaret Mead have illustrated this aspect in a masterly fashion in their extraordinary study of photographs (Bateson and Mead 1942). For an analysis of the relationship between sight and touch from a cognitive point of view, see Gibson (1962).

34. Luce Irigaray in particular has insisted on the female nature of touch: see Irigaray (1982 and 1985).

ings. It is a vertically restricted and tubular field of vision, in which reality is either observed from afar or above, or miniaturized and delimited by a circle (see Photo 6).

Female vision, on the other hand, is circular and encompasses objects and human figures. It also is reinforced by the sense of touch. Other women's hands are seen in the foreground, gripping, clenching, and handling work tools and products. They also touch and care for the bodies of the dead and wounded (the relevant photos have not been reproduced here). The importance attributed to women's touch and sight finds its correlative in the exceptional sensitivity of men's hearing and

Osservatorii per la difesa aerea.

6. Observers and lookouts.

smell, amply documented in war journals. In Gadda's diary there is hardly a page that does not display this obsessive attention to sounds; whole days seem to be governed by the rhythm of broken silence and by the lesser or greater intensity of the smells of mud or the dead.[35]

This sensory polarization would appear to signal a deeper fragmentation of men's emotional universe and sexual identity. The photographs that bear witness to the massive influx of female labor into industry from the end of 1916 onward illustrate that, in addition to the higher public profile women had taken on, there had been a physical transformation. The lines on their faces have hardened, they are wearing overalls (this was apparently the year in which the use of overalls by female factory workers became widespread), and they have their heads covered (see Photo 7). On the factory floor they do not seem to be very different from their male companions, either physically or in their duties. Outside the factory, on the other hand, they put their skirts back on and their appearance reverts to something more traditionally feminine. In the public mind, women manage to represent both genders, occupying the male space and dressing in men's clothes.[36]

7. *Women in overalls.*

35. See Lussu (1945); Gadda (1955); Frescura (1981).
36. On transvestism, see Newton (1979 and 1984). See also Blackwood (1984).

In reality, this female duality, and the patent masculinization of women in the war years, were precursors of the desexualization of both sexes. The photographs of the period document the alarming process of dehumanization that the war had triggered on both fronts and for both sexes. For certain jobs, overalls were worn that cover the whole head, obscuring any sexual affiliation, the observer's attention being entirely focused on the industrial might of the machines. Like some huge steel Gulliver, the gun – and not the hundred or more men sitting or standing on it – is the true subject of the photo, which bears the chillingly terse caption "Fifteen-inch Guns," while in the top right-hand corner of the same photo can be seen an almost unrecognizable human being. The foreground of many photographs of the last two years of the war is reserved for the cogwheels of lathes and hydraulic forging presses, and it matters little that the operators are women, since, in reality, it is the machines that delimit the physical space and determine the way in which men and women move around them (see Photos 8 and 9).

Even so, it was not to be the factory machines that dominated the imagery of the latter period of the war, but rather, and inexorably, the materials of war. The spatial dimension on both the home and the war fronts is invaded by howitzers, projectiles, mortars, heavy artillery. These death-mongering objects were to become the custodians of a message that, in a way, has much to do with sexuality.

The area inside and outside factories now fills up with these elongated weapons and becomes a repository of artificial genitalia, while the figures dominating the landscape of the war zones are elements in the interplay between the show of strength of the heavy artillery on the ground and the airy lightness with which the penis-shaped balloons, standing out clearly against the sky, rise and fall back to earth (see Photos 10 and 11). But the shapes do not always relate to male sexuality; English air balloons even draw on the act of breast feeding for their name: nurse balloons (see Photo 12).

This hyperallusive visual language spreads its influence even to the world of advertising. But the important point is that the parade of images hides a reality in which male and female categories have lost the connotations that formerly characterized them, and therefore have lost the ability to be expressed by means of the symbols that traditionally represented them.

110

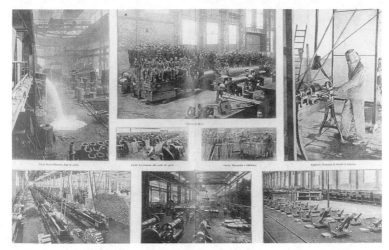

8. *Lathes and presses.*

9. *At the hydraulic press.*

10. Air balloon.

11. Air balloons.

The display of artificial genitalia, in the air and on the ground, is photographed and captioned, and becomes significant if it is considered alongside the process of desexualization referred to earlier. Its function is the opposite of the one it might have had in the period of peace before the war – a period that also coincides with the publication of Freud's *The Interpretation of Dreams*. In fact, it is not simply a matter of sexual symbols, as one might be tempted all too readily to observe. Rather, it is a question of the paralysis, brought about in the course of this technological and dehumanizing war, of the symbolic apparatus. To draw on Dan Sperber's intelligent analysis, this occurs because symbolism is not a property of objects, "but of the con-

12. 'Nurse' balloons.

ceptual representations which describe and interpret them."[37]
The shattering and transformation of the perceptual and cognitive system, and of its metaphorical and literal articulations,
are relevant not only to soldiers in the trenches but also to
those who, in the rest of the country, are related directly or
indirectly to the world of the trenches and to its reality of
remoteness, death, and destruction – images of which are transmitted, in turn, from the trenches to the home front. The great

37. Sperber (1981: 109). See also Sperber (1985) and Todorov (1972) for the
problem of sexual symbolism and the relationship between anthropology and
psychoanalysis; and the famous essay by Leach ([1958] 1980).

atrocity of war, and its ultimate message of desolation, are revealed in the disappearance of a universe of symbols and in the destruction of the human ability to symbolize.

The extreme devastating effects of this process at the level of male sexual identity already have been the subject of numerous psychiatric studies during the war.[38] Little or nothing is known, however, about female sexuality, which overly optimistic analyses reductively identify with the warlike activism of postwar politics.

A month before the end of the war, on 9 October 1918, a special pamphlet was published called *La Sirena*, with the subtitle, "Newspaper for the Workforce of Brescia," dedicated to women and their activities during the war. As is common in this kind of propaganda-oriented pamphleteering, the articles are written poorly and are brimming with chauvinistic rhetoric. But the center pages are very interesting from the point of view of the present study. They carry six photographs that illustrate the variety of jobs performed by women in these years: baking, digging, building, working flax. (The relevant photos have not been reproduced here.) In a key position, placed high and centrally on the page, there is a photo entitled "Women among Shells" (see Photo 13). It is an exceptionally unusual item in the spectrum of the numerous photographs of the war industry taken in this period. In it are seen hundreds of female workers putting the finishing touches on huge howitzer shells as tall as the women themselves. A little removed, at the sides of the photograph, there are some men – the ones on the left being most visible – standing by idly and watching the scene with their eyes facing the camera. The physical attitudes, headgear, and positioning of the persons in the space around the shells – and the shape and size of the shells – make the photo a disturbing composition, to say the least. It is an image that could serve as a figurative epigraph for the argument of this essay. It seems to be the radical and extreme conclusion of the profound fracture that occurred during the war years in the sexual identities of both genders. All the elements that have been instrumental in the forging of women's public profile are expressed here with a meaningfulness rarely observable in other war photographs.

38. See Abraham ([1918] 1975), originally a paper given at the fifth Psychoanalytic Conference (Budapest, 1918), which was dedicated to the theme of war neuroses. See also Freud ([1920] 1977), and the introduction to 'Psicanalisi delle nevrosi di guerra' in the same volume. For a historical perspective, see Gibelli (1980) and Bianchi (1983).

13. Women among shells.

Three aspects are immediately obvious: the similar heights of the women and the shells; the women's gestures and attitudes in relation to the shells; the total absence from the scene of traditional sexual meaning, in spite of the clearly phallic shape of the shells themselves. The most striking thing is the personalization of the relationship between the women and the howitzer shells, which do not seem to be objects, but human beings. We are struck by the delicate and almost affectionate gestures of the women, some of whom seem to be fondling the shells. In the space beyond the foreground, some of the women are seen with smaller shells, which are of a height comparable to that of children.

It is clear from the photograph that the women are not expressing a desire for absent men, because there are men in the photo (even if they are distant and passive). What the photograph conveys is something that may be defined as the paradoxical relationship that now goes well beyond that between two human genders. A new union between female human beings and deadly objects (as substitutes for the male gender) seems to have supplanted the age-old relationship between men and women.

The very peculiar positioning of the figures in the photographic space – they are arranged in couples, a woman to each shell – gives the entire scene the air of some sort of danse macabre on the eve of the end of the war: a heartrending ritual

115

or role-reversal, in which men seem lifeless, shells seem to be human beings, and women appear to be the ones directing this terrifying spectacle of sex and death. Of this transhuman group, only the men at the sides of the photo seem to be aware that they are being photographed, and they look straight to the right. The gaze of the women in the foreground is elsewhere; only those in the background reveal any curiosity for the photographer's activity.

Translated by David Watson

Tradition and Transformation

Women in Society and the Movement Toward Liberation

EIGHT

The Role of Women in the Lullabies of Emilia-Romagna and Tuscany

PIERA CARROLI

This essay[1] will explore the themes of poverty, family relationships, and the domestic world that are prevalent in the lullabies of Emilia-Romagna and Tuscany. In contrast to the picture of rural life presented by the idyllic poems and portraits of the Romantic era, many lullabies paint an image of the lives of peasants in general, and of peasant women in particular, that is often full of hardship. Women lament their loneliness and the difficulties they encounter in providing for their children. Poverty and oppressive traditional structures created a family environment offering women few outlets for their despair. In this environment the process of acculturation for females started with the lullabies mothers sang to their daughters. These lullabies state explicitly what lies in store for the adult female, and thus they are unique testimonies[2] of the peasant woman's perception of her own condition.

Lullabies[3] belong to the category of folk tradition called *ciclo della vita* [life cycle] and to the genre of "lyrical monostrophic" songs, the most popular of Italian folk songs. As opposed to the "calendar ritual" songs accompanying festivities such as Christmas, Carnival and Easter, the "life cycle" songs are connected with specific moments and stages of life, such as birth, childhood, conscription, marriage, and death. Unlike "narrative"

1. I acknowledge the assistance of Professor Antonio Comin, who was kind enough to offer helpful comments at the draft stage. All translations of the lullabies, except "Il bambino è della mamma," are mine.
2. Revelli (1985) and other similar documents of oral history were collected after the new awareness of the importance of oral history during the 1960s.
3. Definitions of lullabies can be found in Leydi and Mantovani (1970: 194–97); Leydi (1972); Saffioti (1978: 166–67); Saffioti (1981: 7–10); Straniero (1981: 89–99); Sanga (1978: 41); Currà, De Lucia, Lelli, and Riga (eds.) (1981: 10–11); Pianta (1982: 61–66 and 102–106).

songs, also known as ballads, "lyrical monostrophic" songs do not tell a story about a specific character, but express the feelings of the singer through discursive description in the first person. Because of their brevity and nonnarrative character, "lyrical monostrophic" songs allow the singer greater expressive freedom. Since each strophe is a self-sufficient unit, the singer can add, subtract, or create a strophe, according to her mood. There are some lullabies in which the mother starts off with a strophe expressing her love and affection for the baby, but then continues with menacing and angry strophes, presumably to vent her anger at her sleepless baby. In yet another kind of lullaby, the mother uses archaic magic formulae containing combinations of numbers, herbs, and flowers in an attempt to induce the child to sleep.[4]

The musical structure of lullabies, often irregular, is simple and functional, its rhythm following the movement of the cradle. According to Leydi and Mantovani (1970: 25) this indicates that they belong to "stage 1" of the "diachronic European folk music scale," that of "tribal society" (my translations). While the most archaic songs have a circular tune and contain nonsensical words, more recent lullabies are subdivided into strophes. The degree of archaism of individual songs is indicated also by the presence of lexical items[5] pertaining to a rural society or a rudimentary agro-industry such as that of the *canapini* [hemp workers], both of which gradually disappeared in Emilia-Romagna and Tuscany[6] in the first half of this century.

4. Since this type of lullaby is purely functional, it will not be discussed here. For examples, see Bacci ([1891] 1978: 24) and Raccolta Barbi (see note 10), G00015; G00020; G00052.

5. For example, the incipit "Nanén Kunkàta" (Stefanati 1986: 53); *kunkàta*, a diminuitive of *koka*, belongs to the archaic peasant word lexicon; a *koka* was a container made of wood, iron, or terracotta, and was used, according to its shape, to transport water, to feed chickens, ducks, and geese, or to do the laundry. For a comprehensive socioeconomic and linguistic analysis of the world of the *canapini* at Pieve di Cento, see Stefanati (1986).

6. It is impossible to establish exactly when these lullabies were created. Since there was considerable elaboration of the lullabies by the collectors, these textual versions must be placed into the historical context and sociocultural reality of mid-nineteenth-century Italy. However, political borders and governments had a relatively small impact on the lives of most Emilian, Romagnan, and Tuscan peasants. Culturally and economically, their lives were quite similar. Tuscany was already a united region under the rule of the Asburgo-Lorena. As a result of a plebiscite it was annexed to the House of Savoy with Emilia-Romagna in 1860. Emilia and Romagna did not exist as one region until unification; Romagna (in its modern form), Bologna, and Ferrara were under the authoritarian and regressive rule of the Church of Rome. The rest of Emilia was subdivided into two independent *ducati*. The deep anticlerical sentiment still alive in

The process of industrialization started at the end of the last century in Lombardy and Piedmont and parts of Emilia, and boomed after World War II in the whole of Italy, and the country very quickly was transformed from a prevalently rural into an overall industrial urbanized society. Although Emilia-Romagna still has a strong base in agriculture today, the socioeconomic situation has changed profoundly; many who worked on the land have gone from being peasants to being farmers; rather than working someone else's land, they often own their *poderi* [farms], and are reasonably well off. These big economic changes also have modified significantly the family structure

Romagna and in parts of Emilia today may be explained by the papal domination that lasted from 1757 until national unification in 1860, with minor interruptions (the longest of these interruptions being the Napoleonic period: 1796–1815).

and power relationship within it. The rural patriarchal family as it existed up to World War II has given way to the nuclear family unit.

Patriarchal families were, of course, male-dominated environments in which women were often reduced to a state of aphasia (Straniero 1981: 90). Legally and culturally they had no power, no say in decision making or in the handling of money and generally were considered little more than procreating machines and beasts of burden. They were supposed to be constantly active and had hardly any privacy; perhaps lulling the baby to sleep represented one of those rare occasions when the peasant mother, alone with her child who could not argue with her complaints, could vent her anguish and frustrations about her condition. The two major functions attributed to lullabies are, in fact, the conscious practical attempt to send the baby to sleep by using a lulling tune in conjunction with propitiatory and magic formulae (thus transmitting to her/him the cultural patrimony of the community); and the second, perhaps subconscious, function of relieving the mother of her anger. In contrast with the romantic image promoted by many scholars of folk culture, children for many peasant mothers were a burden rather than a joy. The most desperate lullabies, in fact, stemmed from the peasant world (Leydi and Mantovani 1970: 196), where sexual disparity was exacerbated by economic hardship. These lullabies and their major themes will be the major focus of this essay in order to deliver a realistic portrayal of the peasant women of Emilia-Romagna and Tuscany, within their social context.

The patriarchal family structure assigned to women most domestic tasks, including the raising of children. Since lullabies initially were created to send the baby to sleep, and since it was almost exclusively women who looked after babies, it is reasonable to assume that the lullabies were created by women rather than by men. The process of creation and transmission in folk culture is radically different from that of art culture. Whereas the latter is written and labelled with individual authorship, the former is oral[7] and typically is a community possession. Folk culture belongs to whatever community creates it or sanctions it by using it. It does not necessarily have to originate within the community, but it has to be validated by the community before

7. On the concept of orality, see Leydi and Mantovani (1970: 198–202) and Pianta (1982: 33–35).

being integrated into the cultural heritage of the community (Pianta 1982: 65). This, however, does not mean that folk songs were composed collectively by the whole community, as some early scholars believed, thus reinforcing their romantic view of peasant life. It is almost certain that folk songs were individually created, albeit as an expression of the whole community and not with the intention of the folk song remaining the private property of the creator. Instead, folk songs (and folk culture generally), not being fixed by writing and authorship, can be adopted and altered to suit the needs and situation of the performer who, by singing them, momentarily becomes their repository and transmitter.

It is hard to establish precisely when particular folk songs, and in this case lullabies, were "created." It was only toward the middle of the last century that scholars began collecting folk culture and committing it to print. Bonaccorsi (1956: 104) attributes the origins of the lullaby "Il babbo lontano" [The faraway father], to the first migration wave from Tuscany to America in the last century; he also states (1956: 105) that another lullaby, "Il bambino è della mamma" [Mother's baby], has more remote origins. Corazzini published a version of "La Malcontenta" [The unhappy woman] in 1877 in a chapter dedicated to lullabies (Corazzini [1877] 1968). Even though "La Malcontenta" belongs to a category of folk songs called "I canti della malmaritata" [Songs of the ill-married woman], it was often used as a lullaby, which probably means that it had been circulating within the community for quite a while. Unlike art culture, it is impossible in most cases to attribute exact dates to folk creations.

It is recognized, however, that lullabies generally are among the oldest and best preserved forms of folk song. This is probably due to their specific and practical function of lulling the baby to sleep, and also to particular characteristics that prevented both their diffusion outside regional and sometimes provincial boundaries and the alterations of them caused by outside influences. If the themes of hardship and family relationships seem to be common to lullabies not only from other regions of Italy and Spain,[8] the lexicon is usually peculiar to the region or province of origin. For example, the pet names used by mothers in the opening lines differ greatly, the most popular Tuscan

8. See Sanga (1978: 45) and Saffioti (1981: 19–32). For lullabies in Spain, see García Lorca (1980: 12, 16, 20).

123

one being *coscine di pollo* [little chicken legs] and the Romagnan, *giglio dell'orto* [white lily of the vegetable garden]. Lullabies and other songs pertaining to the female domestic environment are almost invariably in the local dialect or vernacular.[9]

The information contained in this essay is the result of a study conducted in 1987 on a corpus of lullabies from Emilia-Romagna and Tuscany. They were collated from a number of sources available at Flinders University (South Australia), the major one being a series of unpublished texts photocopied from a section of the Raccolta Barbi. 589 lullabies were collated: 520 from Tuscany, 42 from Romagna, and 27 from Emilia; 310 were drawn from the Raccolta Barbi, and 279 from other sources. These included 24 collections and 8 record booklets of popular songs, the earliest source being Francesco Corazzini's *I componimenti minori della letteratura popolare italiana* [Minor Works of Italian Folk Literature], first published in 1877, and the most recent, Gianni Stefanati's *Fòra la pórta d'Asìa: repertori di tradizione orale a Pieve di Cento* [Beyond the Asia Gate: Collections of Oral Tradition at Pieve di Cento], published in 1986.

The disparity in numbers does not necessarily reflect an imbalance in the richness of cultural background of one region as compared with another, but rather the limited sources available in Adelaide, and the unequal degree of collection and research carried out in each Italian region. According to the regional chart of ethnophonic recordings published by the Centro Nazionale Studi di Musica Popolare e dell'Archivio Etnico Linguistico Musicale, Emilia-Romagna is, in fact, one of the least-researched regions, while Tuscany is amongst the most intensely researched parts of Italy (see Natali 1977: 1).

The Raccolta Barbi, because of its size and quality, is among the most important collections of folk songs in Europe. Michele Barbi and his collaborators collected materials not just in Tuscany, but also in Emilia-Romagna, Umbria, Lazio, and Veneto, from around 1887 to 1930, with a long interruption during World War I. Most of the original Raccolta Barbi remains unpublished at the Scuola Normale Superiore di Pisa.[10]

9. For a comprehensive and succinct treatment of the language and content of Romagna folk songs, see Bellosi, Magrini, and Sistri (1980: 4–11); on the language of folk songs generally, see Sanga (1978: 32–33).

10. For more information on the Raccolta Barbi, see Barwick (1986) and Giusti (1986).

The research for this essay is limited by the criteria chosen by individual collectors and by historical trends, and the conclusions drawn are of necessity based on the material available and the texts the collectors chose to publish in their collections. Particular trends and personal attitudes to popular culture, in general, and to certain areas in particular, may have determined how many and what type of lullabies were collected and preserved. Corazzini and most early scholars, such as Barbi, classified lullabies as *componimenti minori* [minor works]. These songs were held in low esteem because they were sung almost exclusively in dialect and contained women's interpretations of the domestic environment.

As with most female literature concerned with domestic themes, lullabies suffered prejudice from scholars of popular culture, who underrated materials concerned with the domestic world of peasant women. Giovanni Giannini in his introduction to *I canti toscani* [The Folk Songs of Tuscany], first published in 1902, explains why many collectors excluded lullabies from their collections.

> [L]a maggior parte degli editori di canti popolari toscani [. . .] non ammisero nelle loro raccolte le Ninne-nanne e i Canti fanciulleschi, reputandoli indegni, per la povertà del concetto, di esser presentati al pubblico dei lettori. (Giannini [1901] 1981: 8)

> [T]he majority of editors of Tuscan folk songs [. . .] excluded lullabies and nursery rhymes from their collections, judging them unworthy of being presented to the readers due to their poor conceptual content.]

He then justifies having himself included such songs in his collection:

> E' vero, il contenuto di questi canti è ben povera cosa: ma che importa al bambino, se in essi il pensiero scarseggia? Vi è in cambio tutta una folla d'immagini graziose e attraenti [. . .]. (Giannini [1901] 1981: 9)[11]

> [It is true that the content of these songs is rather poor: but does the absence of thought matter to the child? In compensation, they abound in attractive, graceful images [. . .]].

Perhaps such images abounded after the polishing process he admits to having conducted on the whole collection to make it palatable to his genteel audience (Giannini [1901] 1981: 11).

11. See also Cioni ([1955] 1973: 213).

125

This superior paternalistic attitude toward popular culture has prevailed until recent times. Manipulative researchers molded the materials collected according to their own cultural values and aesthetic tastes, often perpetuating an idealized vision of peasant life to suit the bourgeois palate and consciousness. Descriptions of peasant life such as those in the introductions to Nino Massaroli's *Ninne-nanne romagnole* [Lullabies from Romagna] (Massaroli 1925) and Orazio Bacci's introduction to *Ninne-nanne, cantilene, canzoni di giuochi e filastrocche che si dicono in Valdelsa* [Lullabies, Singsongs, Songs for Games, and Nursery Rhymes found in Valdelsa], first published in 1891 (Bacci [1891] 1978: 11–13), blatantly romanticized life in the fields and the relationship between mothers and their babies. In their eyes, peasant mothers lived in heavenly harmony with nature while singing pretty songs to their children.

More recent collections, however, such as Saffioti (1981), contain a greater number of lullabies conveying messages of hardship and protest in conflict with the romantic view of peasant life. It also must be pointed out that lullabies disclosing family relationships and the theme of hardship are fewer in number than those fulfilling only their primary function of sending the baby to sleep. Of a total of 589 songs, roughly 100 expressed hardship and 110 included statements about the narrowness of peasant women's lives, the two themes often being associated within the same lullaby. This could be due to the fact that, as many collectors[12] report, many women informants were reluctant to sing lullabies, particularly those revealing intimate thoughts about their condition, in the presence of strangers.

The category of songs entitled "I canti della malmaritata," [Songs of the ill-married woman], however, disclosed married women's dissatisfaction with their condition, as seen in these two versions, the first from Tuscany and the second from Emilia:

Giovanettina che pigli marito
se tu lo pigli te ne pentirai,
ti converrà mangiare i' pan pentito
e tutti i sonni non li dormirai.
E quando crederai d'andar da mamma
ti converrà cantar la ninna nanna.
(Moscati 1975, section of "Stornelli senesi," record cover.)

12. See Lomax (1956: 129); Leydi (1972: 179); and Currà, De Lucia, Lelli, and Riga (1981: 10).

[Young woman taking a husband
if you take him you will regret it,
you will have to eat the bread of repentance
and you will not sleep all your sleeps.
And when you want to go to your mother's
you will have to sing lullabies instead.]

Tutt'im dis, tutt'im dis
Che a maridars as trova al paradis;
L'è tant temp ch'a son maridà,
Al paradis an l'ho ancora truvà,
Ma cred che, dop la luna d'miel,
Invez dal paradis as trova la fiel. (Ferraro 1967: 33)

[Everyone tells me, everyone tells me
that when you get married you find paradise;
I have been married for many years, but
I have yet to find paradise;
I believe that, after the honeymoon,
Instead of paradise you find bile [bitterness].]

The first song is addressed directly to a young woman about to
marry while the second one is a reflection on married life by a
woman who has been married for many years. It is interesting
to note the different tone of the two versions, the Tuscan one
being more dramatic and the Emilian one more sarcastic. Pier
Paolo Pasolini in *La poesia popolare* stated that Emilia's relative
prosperity influenced the quality of its folk tradition. According
to Pasolini, Emilian songs reflected this improved economic
condition in their openness and lack of inhibition (Pasolini
1960: 57). Perhaps this would explain why, contrary to
Romagna and Tuscany, the theme of hardship does not appear
in available Emilian lullabies. However, both versions of "La
malmaritata" actively discourage girls from getting married. In
another "malmaritata" song a wife laments being betrayed by
her husband and her mother-in-law, both of whom were scheming to find him a younger woman (Currà, Vettori and Vinci
1977: 68). Within the extended peasant family, daughters-in-
law were often powerless.

Female adultery is alluded to in some lullabies where the
mother uses the song to warn her lover at the door that her husband is at home. It is difficult to know to what extent such lullabies reflect real situations; perhaps, as Federico García Lorca
said about the same type of lullaby found in Spain, it is more
escapist fantasy than reality (García Lorca [1975] 1980: 21–22).

These teasing lullabies are predominantly from Romagna: of a total of 42 songs, in fact, 9 were found to contain this motif. Only 3 versions were found among the 520 Tuscan songs and 3 among the Emilian ones. Such allusions to adultery are hardly surprising, considering how often the motif of the *babbo lontano* [the faraway father] appears. The lullabies containing this motif, 78 in all, often include as well the theme of hardship. The father either had just come back, was expected soon, or might never return. The mother could not escape from a precarious existence until her husband came back. Often she tried to soothe her baby with the promise of a present her/his father would bring. The most commonly imagined gifts were shoes for the baby and clogs for the mother (25 out of 78 versions mention this type of gift). The practical nature of these presents shows the poverty of the world portrayed in these lullabies.

Mothers were often left at home to fend for themselves and their children whom, at times, they could barely feed. The following five examples testify to the hardship experienced by mothers and babies:

> Dormi, dormi, totolone;
> *e di pan non c'è un boccone;* *
> (Raccolta Barbi, G00258–G00264).[13]
> [Go to sleep, go to sleep, **totolone**;[14]
> of bread there isn't a mouthful.]

> Dirindina s'ha a fà le fritelle;
> *se ci manca la padella,* *
> *ci manca l'olio e la farina,*
> e si chiede alla vicina.
> (Currà, De Lucia, Lelli, and Riga 1981: 20.)

> [**Dirindina** I must prepare the fritters;
> if there is no frying pan,
> no oil and no flour,
> we'll ask the woman next door.]

> Fai la nanna corpo sodo:
> *Erano in sette a bere un ovo,* *
> *Al bambino ch'era nell'uscio*
> *Gli toccò soltanto il guscio.*
> (Rossi 1896: 80.)

* All asterisked underlining is the author's in this chapter

13. More examples can be found in Bacci ([1891] 1978: 18) and Saffioti (1981: 45).

14. Pet names (such as *totolone*), nonsense words, and other untranslatable terms, are **highlighted**.

128

[Rock-a-by **corpo sodo**:
there were seven drinking an egg,
For the baby on the door step
only the eggshell was left.]

Quattro stanghe son quattro pinecchie:
manca 'l sale, l'olio e 'gni cosa. *
Bambini piangano, ci hanno fame,
e ci ho fame anch'io:
fai la nanna, piscioccolo mio!
(Currà, De Lucia, Lelli, e Riga 1981: 22.)

[Four poles are four **pinecchie**:
there's no salt, no oil, and nothing else.
Babies cry 'cause they're hungry,
and I'm hungry too:
go to sleep, my **piscioccolo**.]

Ninàn, ninàn, ninàn, babé, la papa
a nun l'ho fata *c'an aveva e' pan* *
e nun ti posso dé ca nun l'ho fata;
sta bon e' mi baben *cl'é ch'ér e' gran*
a nun l'ho fata *ca'n aveva legna,*
a nun l'ho fata *c'an aveva e' sel,*
sta bon e'mi babén, speta c'a vegna:
sta bon e'mi babén *che la va mél.* (Massaroli 1925: 210)

[Rock-a-by, rock-a-by, baby,
I haven't prepared you pap 'cause I had no bread
and I cannot give it to you 'cause I haven't prepared it;
be quiet my baby, wheat is expensive
I haven't prepared it 'cause I had no firewood,
I haven't prepared it 'cause I had no salt,
be quiet my baby, wait till I get there:
be quiet my baby, things are going badly.]

In some cases, both parents were forced into seasonal migration and the children were left at home with the grandparents, an aunt, or whoever would look after them (Currà, De Lucia, Lelli, and Riga 1981: 23). These lullabies were the only means the mother had to vent her anguish and anger. Some lullabies culminate in bizarre threats toward the baby; in one particular song from Arezzo the mother, vexed and tired, threatens to throw the baby girl in a ditch so that neither her skin nor her bones will ever be found.

Fate la ninna, fate la nanna,
coccolino della mamma,
della mamma e del papà
e va a fatti buggerà.

Fa la ninna, fa la nanna,
coccolina della mamma,
della mamma e della zia,
se l'è cattiva si butterà via,
si butterà giù per un fosso
che 'un si trovi né pelle né osso. (Currà, De Lucia, Lelli, and Riga
1981: 19)

[Go to sleep, go to sleep,
mommy's little ducky,
and daddy's too,
go and get diddled.

Go to sleep, go to sleep,
mommy's little ducky,
mommy's and auntie's,
if she is naughty she will be thrown away,
she will be thrown down into a ditch
so that neither her skin nor her bones will ever be found.]

In the 32 versions of the lullaby "Il bambino a chi lo dò?"[15] the
mother creates imaginary figures with whom she can leave the
baby for a while. In the following lullaby, fantasy is juxtaposed
with harsh realism:

Nanna-ò nanna-ò
i' bambino a chi lo dò?
E lo dò all'omo nero
che lo tenga un anno intero,
e lo dò alla Befana
che lo tenga una settimana,
e lo dò all'omino di bronzo
che la sera lo porti a zonzo,
e lo dò all'omino d'ottone
che ci paghi la pigione. (Currà, De Lucia, Lelli, and Riga 1981: 10)

[**Nanna-o nanna-o**
who can I give the baby to?
And I give him to the bogey man
who may keep him for a whole year,
and I give him to the Befana

15. Some examples can be found in Raccolta Barbi, G00239–257.

who may keep him for a week,
and I give him to the bronze mannikin
so he may take him for walks at night,
and I give him to the brass mannikin
may he pay the rent for us.]

In several versions the last request, made to the *omino d'ottone* [the brass mannikin], is that the creature pay the rent for her. From these lullabies it is clear that peasants did not have much time to enjoy the arcadian landscape around them!

In several lullabies the protest expressed by mothers against their harsh life appears right at the beginning of the songs:

Nana ninana
la peina dla so mama. (Corazzini [1877] 1968: 33)

[**Nana ninana**
[you are] your mother's torment.]

Nanna eri, nanna eri
*stavo meglio quando 'un c'èri.** (Corsi 1981: 250)

[**Nanna eri, nanna eri**
I was better off when you weren't here.]

Fi la nana, fila sò
*di babèin c'a n'in vlè piò.** (Natali 1977: 12)

[Go to sleep, go to sleep
we don't want any more babies.]

Ninna su, ninna giù,
*mamma tribola un ne po' più.** (Raccolta Barbi, G00109–114)[16]

[**Ninna su, ninna giù,**
mommy suffers and cannot bear it any longer.]

Dondo dondo, dondo dondo
icchè tu fai a questo mondo?
Io lo faccio e chi ne posso
*con il mio bambino addosso.** (Currà, De Luca, Lelli, and Riga 1981: 20)

[**Dondo dondo, dondo dondo**
what are you doing in this world?
I do what I can
with my baby clinging to me.]

16. More examples can be found in Corazzini ([1877] 1968: 30–31); Currà, De Lucia, Lelli, and Riga (1981: 27–28); Giannini ([1901] 1981: 21); and Carpitella (1976: 6).

In one incipit (opening line) the protest is expressed subtly in the comparison of the father to *stoppa* [oakum], and the mother to *lino* [linen] (Raccolta Barbi, G00130). Oakum was the roughest fiber obtained from the combing of hemp; linen, in contrast, was the finest fiber used for sheets and babies' clothes. Indeed, *uomo di stoppa* was an idiomatic phrase that meant "man of no account."

The economic hardship of these rural communities may account, at times, for the behavior of those living there. Besides sending the baby to sleep and providing a safety valve for the mother's pent-up anger, lullabies also had another function, that of acculturation. If on an intimate level mothers were at times subversive, on a social level they became extremely pragmatic and traditional, preparing the children for what lay in store for them, that is, a life of hard work, poverty, and suffering. In the 57 lullabies specifically addressed to baby girls the protest is implicit: even though the mother lamented her condition in many songs, in several of these lullabies she perpetuated that condition by preparing her daughter from her first days for that same destiny (see Bonaccorsi 1956: 107 and Raccolta Barbi G00106). Maria Teresa Pacassoni, by expressing her surprise at the practicality of Tuscan and Romagnan mothers in her article entitled "Il sentimento della maternità nei canti del popolo italiano" ["Maternal feelings in the songs of the Italian people"] reveals her traditional view of family roles:

> E sorgono alle volte intorno alla culla preoccupazioni ed auguri che parrebbero più dettati dall'esperienza e praticità di un padre piuttosto che dalla sentimentalità di una madre.[*sic!*] (Pacassoni 1939: 86)

> [At times around the cradle, preoccupations and wishes arise that would seem to be dictated by the experience and practicality of a father rather than by the sentimentality of a mother.]

The baby girl was presented with two options: if she had a dowry, she could get married and lead a life full of disillusionment and hardship such as that portrayed in the songs of "La malmaritata" (Saffioti 1981: 61); or, if she did not have a dowry, she was condemned to become a spinster and look after her relatives' children. In the popular lullaby "Il bambino è della mamma,"[17] the aunt is often mentioned; and in a song from Lunigiana, specific reference is made to an anguished aunt who cries out that she wants a husband.[18] Some women, because of financial difficulty, at times may have remained unmarried against their will. Mothers, with their multiple roles – cook,[19] cleaner, dressmaker,[20] laborer, and child rearer – only could consider their children a factor in their oppression. Consequently, they imparted stoic resignation to their babies, preparing them for a harsh reality and a fixed social destiny.

The barren teachings that the baby received contained no poetic images, but often disillusionment or irony:

---

17. The following version of this lullaby and its translation are taken from the bilingual record edited by Settimelli (1972).

I' bambino è della mamma

Ninna nanna ninna nanna
i' bambino gli è della mamma
della mamma e della zia
della Vergine Maria.
Ninna nanna ninna nanna
i' bambino gli è della mamma
della mamma e della nonna
e di babbo quando torna.

["Mother's baby"

Ninna nanna ninna nanna
mother's baby
mother's baby and auntie's baby
and the Virgin Mary's too.
Ninna nanna ninna nanna
mother's baby
mother's baby and granny's baby
and daddy's too when he returns.]

18. *Ninna nanna la corba*	*Nina nana la corba*
Nina nana la corba	Big wicker basket
Santa Maria s'adorma	Holy Mary, may s/he got to to sleep
s'adorma e s'aresta	may s/he stop [crying] and go to sleep
so ma l'è anda a la festa	her/his mother has gone to thefestival
La festa de Luca	the Lucca festival
trovai na bela zucas	he finds a beautiful pumpkin
zuca e zuchei	pumpkin and zucchini
per far i canastrei	to make wicker baskets
i canastrei gen così	that is how wicker baskets are
la su zia la grida	Auntie cries that she wants
la vo trovar marì	to find a husband
con quatar anei al did.	with four rings on his fingers.
(Raccolta Barbi, G00229)	

19. See, for instance, Raccolta Barbi G00056, 45, 82, 119, and Bacci ([1891] 1978: 29).

20. See, for instance, Raccolta Barbi G00127, 182, and Giannini ([1901] 1981: 18–19).

Fa la nana e mi burdlìn,
sta cuntent che tu se' znin;
*e s'tu megn tu cresaré**
e s'tu chemp tu pianzaré. (Saffioti 1981: 42)

[Go to sleep my little child,
be happy while you are little;
if you eat you will grow
and if you live you will weep.]

[E'] contessa fa le nozze*
e con *quattro fave cotte.*
E' *contessa* fa l'invito
con *un topo arrostito,*
la bambina la vol marito. (Saffioti 1981: 78)

[[She] is a countess, for her reception
she is having a handful of broad beans.
She is a countess, for her reception
she is having a roasted mouse,
the baby girl wants a husband.]

In the first lullaby the child is told that he should be happy while he is small because if he lives to be an adult he will weep; and in the second song the fanciful allusion to a luxurious wedding is counterbalanced by a bizarre irony.

Women's destiny, whether they were married or not, was narrow; peasant family structure relegated women to a position of total subordination to the men who, even though they worked very hard, also had time to go to the inn, *l'osteria,* at night, as mentioned in "La malcontenta":

Dirindina la malcontenta,
babbo gode e mamma stenta,
babbo va all'osteria,
mamma tribola tuttavia;
babbo mangia l'erbe cotte,
mamma tribola giorno e notte;
babbo mangia e beve i' vino,
mamma tribola co i' cittino;
babbo mangia li fagioli,
mamma tribola coi figlioli;
babbo mangia 'l baccalà,
mamma tribola a tutt'andà;
babbo mangia le polpette,
mamma fa delle crocette.

Dirindina la malcontenta,
babbo gode e mamma stenta [. . .] (Currà, Vettori, and Vinci 1977: 116)

[**Dirindina** the unhappy woman,
papa enjoys himself and mama is half-starved,
papa goes to the pub and mama suffers all the time;
papa eats boiled spinach,
mama suffers day and night;
papa eats and drinks wine,
mama suffers with her little child;
papa eats beans,
mama suffers with her children;
papa eats cod,
mama suffers all the time;
papa eats rissoles,
mama stitches away.
Dirindina the unhappy woman,
papa enjoys himself and mama suffers [. . .]]]

This song, belonging to the category of "Malmaritata" songs but often used as a lullaby, clearly states the woman's discontent with a system that placed her in a position of socioeconomic dependence on a man. She not only was forced to undertake heavy home duties including the raising of the children, but also had to work in the fields.[21] In short, women were servants in a traditionally oppressive structure that gave all power and authority to men.

The most bitter destiny, perhaps, was to be abandoned after having been seduced. In this traditional social environment, seduced women almost certainly would be branded and have to endure the shame all their lives (Saffioti 1981: 31). In warning children of this danger, mothers became agents of male hegemony. They had to promote values that they may have regarded as hypocritical and unfair and that restricted women's freedom. Yet the society in which they lived offered them no alternative. In view of the heavy burden placed on peasant women, it is hardly surprising that at times they would pour out their anguish onto the babies and blame them for their arduous lives. Manifestations of this resentment are to be found in the following exclamations forming part of four lullabies, of which three are from Romagna and one from Tuscany:

21. See Raccolta Barbi G00082 and Corazzini ([1877] 1968: 30).

Ninàn ninàn babén, giglio bel fior!
*Che vo' a si néd a e' mond par dem dulor.**
Ninàn ninàn babén, giglio riel,
che vo' a si' néd a e' mond par fem daner
ninàn ninàn, babén, giglio fiurì
che vo' a si néd a e' mond par fem murì. (Saffioti 1981: 27)

[**Ninàn ninàn** baby, my beautiful white lily!
You were born to give me pain.
Ninàn ninàn baby, my royal lily,
You were born to drive me mad
Ninàn ninàn baby, my lily in bloom
You were born to be my death.]

The awareness of peasant women's sociocultural destiny rarely allowed mothers from Tuscany and Emilia-Romagna to imagine a different life for their children. Their wishes were often that the son might grow up healthy and continue in his father's occupation (Pacassoni 1939: 86; Saffioti 1981: 51, 64) and that the daughter might have enough money for a dowry enabling her to marry (Saffioti 1981: 61). In one lullaby from Romagna (Raccolta Barbi, G00100), the mother speaks of her daughter going to school to learn how to read, write, and embroider:

Ninà ninà ninola
la mimina *va a la scola**
va a la scola pr'imparé
lez e scriv e ricamé.

[**Ninà ninà ninola**
the little girl goes to school
she goes to school to learn
how to read, write, and embroider.]

This particular song is an example of the conflicting forces inherent in the message mothers passed on to their children. The instinct for conservation was strong and manifested itself in the transmission of traditional values, such as learning how to embroider. However, the message also conveyed the importance of literacy, which in itself subverted traditional ideas of a woman's role.

The coexistence of evasion and reality, subversiveness and conservation illustrates the complexity and diversity of these documents of popular culture and consequently of peasant society. The variety of motives and ways in which peasant women of different regions (and of different areas within the same region) approached the universal themes of hardship and domestic life show how popular culture changed constantly to mirror the values and structures of the society from which it originated. The fact that Emilia led the rest of Italy in developing an industrialized agriculture and that Romagna had a long anticlerical socialist tradition emerged in the lullabies of these regions.

In Tuscany alone there were versions of the lullaby illustrating the metaphorical tale of the wolf that eats the sheep. This was probably one of the most conservative songs collated: it warned babies against stepping outside their territory where they easily could fall prey to overwhelming forces.[22] Peasant mothers, enmeshed in rigid social structures, transmitted to their children conservative survival strategies to prepare them realistically for what lay ahead, thus helping them to avoid hopeless dreams and disillusionment. What was evident from these unique testimonies of peasant women was a profound and concrete consciousness of their own place in the order of things around them, which, however, they at times tried to subvert with their strong criticism.

These lullabies are invaluable as records of the lives that peasant women led in Emilia-Romagna and Tuscany during the last century and at the beginning of this century. They represent perhaps the most archaic form of popular culture and are the only documents in which women openly expressed their most intimate feelings toward motherhood and the domestic environment in which they lived. Dissatisfaction with their condition was the common theme expressed by peasant women in these lullabies, recurrent also in Spanish lullabies. Yet, despite the subversive nature of some songs, the message passed on to the children was conservative. Women's rebellious impulses seem to have been but a momentary rejection of the status quo. In a world where the only known reality was hardship, and in which severe punishment was suffered for any transgression of social norms, uneducated women had little choice but to conform. However, peasant women also instilled subversive ideas, and not just conservative messages, in successive generations. Therefore, if their dilemma was doomed from the start to remain an unresolved contradiction, one can surmise that the coexistence of two opposing forces must have produced the incentive to bring about change.

22. See, for instance, Raccolta Barbi G00105, and Saffioti (1981: 35–36).

137

Cosmology of Liberation: Black and Other Popular Madonnas at Easter Time in Italy[1]

LUCIA CHIAVOLA BIRNBAUM

Popular beliefs, according to Antonio Gramsci and Ernesto De Martino,[2] are indispensable to authentic cultural and political transformation. Folklore, for Gramsci, offers a conception of the world and life that challenges the hegemony of dominant classes. Beliefs in magic, for De Martino, have persisted over millennia in spite of imprecations invoked by Protestant Reformation theologians,[3] criticism of irrationalism by Enlightenment philosophers, and condemnations of superstition and paganism by the Catholic hierarchy. Magic, a word often pejoratively ascribed to popular religious beliefs, was an impermeable and invaluable part of the cosmology of subaltern classes in Italy for De Martino (De Martino 1986; Bo 1979; Lombardi

1. A draft of this essay entitled "Le madonne nere: religiosità popolare e movimenti sociali" was presented to the Department of Sociology, University of Padua, 11 May 1990; in another draft it has become chapter nine of *Black madonnas – Justice, Equality with Difference, and Transformation. The Case of Italy* (Boston, Northeastern University Press, February 1993). The essay is grounded on fieldwork carried out in Italy in 1988, 1989, and 1990, and personal observation of the rituals analyzed. In addition to the works cited in the notes, important bibliographical references for the subject include Lanternari (1977), Guizzardi et al. (1981), Castiglione (1981), Prandi ([1977] 1983), Gianni Gallino (ed.) (1988), Nesti (ed.) (1970), Neumann ([1963] 1974), and Adams ([1904] 1986 Penguin edition).
2. See Birnbaum ([1986] 1988). An extended analysis of the writings of Gramsci and De Martino can be found in Birnbaum, *Black madonnas*, chapter two.
3. Because this essay is included in a standardized volume, it does not follow the contemporary democratic usage of Italy and elsewhere in removing capitals from charged hegemonic words that refer to religion or politics. The publishers of the author's *Liberazione della donna* and *Black madonnas* have placed political and religious words in the lower case as a step toward the removal of hierarchies.

Satriani 1979). Often calling themselves "unedited Marxists," Italian anthropologists since the 1960s have studied Italian popular religious beliefs for their political possibilities (Tentori 1960; Carbonaro and Nesti 1975; De Martino [1959] 1987; and Cherchi and Cherchi 1987).

After I completed my study of Italian feminists (Birnbaum [1986] 1988), questions persisted regarding the woman-centered cosmology of Italian popular beliefs. Marija Gimbutas's massive archaeological evidence of the presence of a pre-Christian woman divinity in southern and eastern Europe (Gimbutas 1989; Gadon 1989) and my own study of Italian folklore support the Jungian premise that primordial memories may persist over eons of time.

For Gimbutas, the goddess-centered religion "existed for a very long time, much longer than the Indo-European and the Christian, leaving an indelible imprint on the Western psyche" (Gimbutas 1989: xiii). This prehistoric religion, extending in the historic era of Europe up to 1500 B.C., perseverated in the Christian era in European folklore that venerated "both the universe as the living body of a Goddess-Mother Creator, and all the living things within it as partaking of her divinity" (Gimbutas 1989: xiii).

Italian writers have noted the endurance of this ancient belief that is often associated with the veneration of black or dark women divinities. For Carlo Levi, "the black madonna among the grain and the animals was not the passive Mother of God, but a subterranean divinity black as the shadows of the womb of the earth, a peasant Persephone, an infernal goddess of the harvest." For peasants, wrote Levi, this black madonna was neither good nor bad; "she was much more." She withered the grain but she also nourished and protected all life and it was necessary "to adore her" (Levi [1945] 1979: 106).

The tie between the fertile earth and the prehistoric woman divinity is evident for Gimbutas "in the continuous veneration of black madonnas to this day. The color black, now commonly associated with death or evil in Christian iconography, was, in Old Europe, the color of fertility and the soil." The passionate emotions that black madonnas evoke for pilgrims the world over are related to "the blackness of these miraculous madonnas," a color that taps "profound and meaningful images and associations for devotees." The shrine of the black madonna of Czestochowa in southern Poland, notes Gimbutas, is known as the Polish Lourdes, "the holiest and most visited religious shrine in eastern Europe" (Gimbutas 1989: 144).

The political implications of black madonnas are complex and roiled by the possibility of co-optation by the Church for its own purposes; e.g., Franciscan friars turned up as papal inquisitors in the sixteenth century. Yet the radical edge of popular beliefs is visible in contemporary Italy. Throughout the 1970s on the October birthday of Saint Francis, Italians celebrated with dancing and communist posters the heretical saint who preached that the universe with all its creatures is alive (see Birnbaum [1986] 1988 for a discussion of Italian communism in the 1970s). The fervent pilgrimage to the black madonna dell'Incoronata at Foggia the last weekend of April, anthropologists have noted, is composed of the same people who, a week later, celebrate May day rituals at Cerignola, the center of Italian peasant communism (Cipriani et al. 1979).

Italy is nominally a Catholic country, but there are, as Gramsci pointed out, many Catholicisms. Taking the Church canon as her point of departure, Marina Warner has written a splendid overview of the history of the Catholic cult of the madonna, concluding that the Church image of the madonna has had a negative influence on women's self-image: the madonna, in her perfection, from the standpoint of Church doctrine, is "alone among women" (Warner 1976). Yet if one commences with popular, not papal, views of the madonna, another Mary, with different implications for women and other colonized people, emerges.

In the male-centered hierarchy of papal Catholicism (and the even more severely masculine Protestantism of the United States), the central theme of Easter is the resurrection of Jesus Christ. In popular Italian Catholic rituals of Easter, Christ's mother and other women play a significant role. Although barely mentioned in the canonical gospel (Fiorenza 1983; Pagels 1988), the Italian folklore tradition stresses Mary's human priority and prophetic implication.

Earlier, popular devotion to Mary prompted papal condemnations of "Mariolatry"; later, the Vatican promoted the pious, virginal, and resigned Mary of Michelangelo's Pietà as the correct model for women and other colonized people (Pettazzoni 1952; Delaney 1961; Warner 1976; Atkinson et al. [eds.] 1985). This was confirmed for me on Easter Sunday afternoon 1988 when I heard the bishop of Caltagirone in Sicily address a crowd that included many emigrant workers home for the holiday. The lesson of the blessed virgin, said the bishop, was *pazienza*, or patience.

This conservative version of the meaning of Mary is implicitly challenged today in folk rituals of Europe and Latin America, where popular madonnas, often black, touch deeply submerged memories, symbolize the prophetic message of Judeo-Christianity, and point to radical cultural and political change. This was evident during the successful liberation movement against authoritarian communism in Poland; the black madonna of Czestochowa was visible everywhere on Solidarity political posters. Liberation theology in Latin America, written for the most part by men (Boff 1987; Ashton 1989), has been Christocentric, bypassing the vast appeal of popular madonnas, an appeal symbolized in Latin America in the deep devotion to the black virgin of Guadalupe.

Gimbutas has located paleolithic and neolithic sites of the goddess in Europe;[4] my research finds that sanctuaries of black madonnas are located on or near areas with archaeological evidence of the presence of the primordial woman divinity. This connection, analyzed in my *Black madonnas: Justice, Equality with Difference, and Transformation. The Case of Italy*, may be suggested by noting that in Sicily sanctuaries of black madonnas of Milicia, Tindari, and Trapani are close to the paleolithic drawing of a numinous woman divinity on the Addaura cave outside Palermo. The black madonna of Siponto, the black madonna dell'Incoronata outside Foggia, and other black madonnas of the Gargano are in an area that abounds with paleolithic and neolithic signs of the prehistoric goddess.

Why, asks Ean Begg, former Dominican friar, are there only a handful of known black Christs and only a few black saints, while black madonnas are very numerous (Begg 1985)? Why are representatives of the Church defensive on the subject? This defensiveness was brought home to me when I found that black madonnas of Lucera and Montenero had been "retouched" by the Church. Subsequently I have found several cases of whitened black madonnas. Church defensiveness is strengthened by academic bastions. When the subject is brought up, someone will vouchsafe that black madonnas are "Byzantine." Dark or black madonnas of Italy often do have

4. See maps in Gimbutas 1989. Included at the end of this article is Gimbutas's map of Italy indicating paleolithic and neolithic sites of the goddess; I have circled sanctuaries of black madonnas.

Byzantine features, but this does not explain why black madonnas are believed to have "thaumaturgic" or miraculous powers. Of the two dozens or so madonnas of Italy popularly considered black, some are indisputably black, others are quite dark, and even those that have been whitened remain black in the perception of the people. Very black madonnas may be found at the national shrine (dating back to the twelfth century) at Loreto, at the fifth-century church at Siponto, at the sanctuary of l'Incoronata outside Foggia dating back to the apparition in 1,000 A.D. and today venerated by peasant communists, at the eleventh-century sanctuary for the poor at Oropa. Other madonnas that are black in the perception of the people are found at Tindari, Milicia, Bari, Trapani, Palmi, Seminara, Montenero, Bologna, Spoleto, Venice, Padua.

Leonard Moss, an American anthropologist who studied Italy's black madonnas after World War II, considered them "Christian borrowings from earlier pagan art forms that depicted Ceres, Demeter Melaina, Diana, Isis, Cybele, Artemis, or Rhea as black, the color characteristic of goddesses of the earth's fertility" (Moss and Cappanari 1982: 65, 69, 71). Moss was reminded of the black woman of the Song of Songs: "Yes, I am black! and radiant / O city women watching me / As black as Kedar's goathair tents / Or Solomon's fine tapestries" (Falk 1982: 13). This insight has been taken up by others who identify the black woman of the Song of Songs with Lilith, the first wife of Adam, who fled because she would not be beneath him (Sicuteri 1980).

"Is the Black Virgin" asks Begg, "a symbol of the hidden Church and of the underground stream?" (Begg 1985: 149). In the implicit vernacular theology of Italian Easter rituals I have observed, Jesus is accompanied by his mother, his mother's sister, and by Mary Magdalen. The son "separating" from his mother marks the beginning of Passion rituals; the mother, draped in black, concludes the Easter ritual, followed by barefoot women cloaked in black carrying candles.

In the madonna's search for her son during Easter week, she is accompanied by John the Evangelist, whose prophetic book of Revelation described a woman clothed with the sun and the stars, a woman D. H. Lawrence considered a pre-Christian goddess. On Easter Saturday, the madonna's statue carried by townsmen searches everywhere for her son, hesitating agonizingly before she enters the church. On Easter Sunday, the encounter of the mother and son [*la giunta*] takes place outside the church.

143

Heresy hovers over Italian folklore. In 1700 the Church formally limited the role of the mother in the Passion ritual to Mater Dolorosa but Italian *cantastorie* [minstrels] continued to sing, as they had for centuries, the story of Jesus and his mother, a story of a mother's search for her son, his death, and the rebirth of all life. In 1988 during Holy Week at San Biagio Platani, the community divided into two factions, *i madunnara* [devoted to the madonna] and *i signurara* [devoted to Jesus]. In the serious satire of Italians, competition between Church doctrine and popular beliefs was carried to the soccer field in a 1988 Easter game between devotees of the madonna and followers of her son (*Giornale di Sicilia* 3 March 1988)! Scenarios of Italian folk rituals, Giovanni Cammareri has pointed out (Cammareri 1988), are written by nobody and interpreted by everybody, offering a glimpse of the actual religious beliefs held by Italians who are nominally Catholic.

During the ritual of the *giunta* on Easter Sunday afternoon, men carry figures of the madonna and of Jesus through the town to the piazza in front of the church. In this denouement of Holy Week as interpreted by men, the madonna is made to drop her black cloak, seductively revealing a diaphanous blue peignoir. A local woman, observing me watch the ritual at Caltagirone, said that the *giunta* reveals religious belief crossed by "*la fantasia meridionale*" [southern imagination]. Fantasy encircling mother and son tends to push the Church to the sidelines. As Jesus and his mother neared their reunion on Easter Sunday afternoon, the statue of Saint Peter carried by townsmen was made to run hither and thither looking for some role for the Church in this heavily valenced reunion of the mother with her child.

Against a political backdrop of contemporary socialist cooperatives, Easter mysteries at Trapani ring with the sound of primordial music. An ancient wine pitcher (whose different tones depend on how much wine has been drunk), the *scacciapensieri* [mouth harp] of Jewish and Arab origin, and the *tamarreddu* [tambourine] of Greek and Roman fertility rites accompany hymns of love sung to the Sicilian earth, *brindisi* [toasts] to the sea, a lament of women waiting for their fishermen to return from the sea, and a *canto* of independent women called *fimminazzi*, who work marble.

Carnival subversion of accepted doctrine infiltrates Italian Easter rituals: women dress as Magdalen, men play Jews. In Mediterranean popular Catholicism, Holy Week is a celebra-

tion of the pagan spring solstice, the Jewish Passover, and rituals that offer a glimpse of the multilayered religious unconscious grounded on veneration of the prehistoric goddess. In
Sicily the indigenous goddess was Ibla. She was joined by religious images of women brought by Phoenicians (Canaanite
Jews), Greeks, Romans, Jews in Diaspora, Saracens, Spaniards,
Normans, crusaders, Provençal troubadours, and the Franciscan brothers of Santa Maria di Gesù. In the fifteenth century
many churches, monasteries, and convents were built on the
western Sicilian shore. Confraternities of lay brothers were
founded, some became artisan syndicates that sponsored folk
rituals enacting religious beliefs that were often "competitive
with the church" (Cammareri 1988: 81).

Heavy-handedly earlier – condemning the *processione delle Tre
Marie* [procession of the three Marys] – more subtly later,
Church and secular authorities have tried to pour water on the
conflagration of faith, flowers, and candles that turns the
churches and streets of southern Italy at Easter into theaters of
madonnas, saints, Christ, centurions, and angels. The performance is directed by the sound of *ciaccole*, clackers that cut the
air with the sharp and eery sound that determines the rhythm
of Easter processions in Mediterranean countries.

At Trapani the competition between the black madonna of
the porters and the madonna of the Church [*Madre della pietà
del popolo*] is sublimated in a ceremonial exchange. In this *incon-
tro* [encounter], representatives of artisan groups devoted to
the black madonna and lay representatives of the madonna of
the Church exchange candles. Merging, rather than competition, seems implicit in the characteristic exclamation of southern Italians – "Santamariagesù!" – and in the fused image of
mother and child of black madonnas.

The historian trying to find the meaning of southern Italian
Easter rituals is left wondering. In the Holy Week procession at
Trapani, the first float is of three figures, who are not the Trini-
ty of the Church. Jesus, placed between his mother and John
the Evangelist, is "leggermente più basso degli altri" [slightly
lower than the others] (Cammareri 1988: 81). The mother
cloaked in black begins and ends most Italian Passion rituals,
followed by a procession of women, also in black.

She eludes analysis. During Lent at San Cataldo, I noted that
priests celebrated l'Immacolata, burghers venerated the
Madonna della Mercede, artisans carved figures of the Madon-

145

na del Rosario, landowners looked to their Madonna delle Grazie, fruit growers kneeled before la Pietà, and workers prayed to the Madonna del Carmelo.

In her black manifestation the madonna taps very deep emotions. The sirocco comes up from the African desert on the Phoenician/Canaanite/African coast of Sicily at Trapani. During Easter week 1988 the hot African wind was blowing as I watched the rocking, nurturing movement of workers carrying their black madonna, a motion that resembles that of a parent rocking a child. Moved by the dirge music, in empathy with workers rocking the statue of their black woman divinity and maybe swept up by the memory of a time when the earth and all its creatures were sacred and equal, people along the route of the procession are often in tears.

After the procession, the black madonna remains all night with other women in a makeshift tent outside the church, waiting for the agony of her son's crucifixion, looking to the reunion with her son outside the church on Easter afternoon. Of the people, not of the Church, these religious beliefs seem marked by *la presenza*, described by Ernesto De Martino as oneness with a personified universe. This oneness does not lead to mysticism, but to identification with the human qualities of the madonna and her son.

Traditionally, organizers of Easter rituals in Italy have been men. When contemporary women design the rituals, religious and political implications become startling. During Easter 1988 at Pietraperzia, Sicily, women enacted their own interpretation of the story. Near the Lago di Pergusa in the center of Sicily, where the god of the underworld was said to have abducted Persephone and where her mother Demeter darkened the earth with her grief until she found her daughter and caused the flowers to bloom, women gave Easter a woman's interpretation.

In the Good Friday procession at Pietraperzia women carried a statue of Mary and a red ribbon measured the length of the dead body of her son. After Christ's death on the cross at dusk on Good Friday, women brought a tree of life into the piazza, a maypole.[5]

The players in this vernacular women's Easter ritual appear

5. *Tempo di Pasqua*, "La Settimana Santa in Sicilia. Processioni, rappresentazioni, Misteri, canti e simboli della Passione," *Giornale di Sicilia*. Supplement, 30 March 1988, p. 9.

to be the ancient earth mother goddess (symbolized by the maypole, tree of life), Mary the mother of Jesus, and women who identify with the fused mother and child of images of black madonnas. In this feminist interpretation of Christianity, pagan origins and cultural differences are celebrated. In the women-designed Good Friday ritual, women placed a small Christian cross above the multicolored globe that was supported by the pre-Christian maypole.

The political implications suggested by the ritual relate to Italian feminist emphasis on differences and a simultaneous sense of time: the old, the new, and the future. Circling the maypole, women carried streamers, each with a different woman-made lace edging, accompanied by music with ancient, old, and future notes. The ritual evoked the early Christian *ekklesia* of women (Fiorenza 1983), contemporary feminist excavation of women's silenced submerged beliefs, and the glimpse offered by the folklore of emerging theologies of liberation (Plaskow and Christ 1989).

Carrying Mary on Good Friday, the women of Pietraperzia personified the cultural theme of contemporary Italian feminists, "women are the carriers of the future." They conveyed their political message, *"Dalle donne, la forza delle donne"* [from women, the strength of women] (Italian Communist Party 1986; see also Menapace [1987] 1988). Women of Italy, insisting on their historical difference, may be prophets of different, selfmade socialisms of the third millenium (Birnbaum 1993: forthcoming).

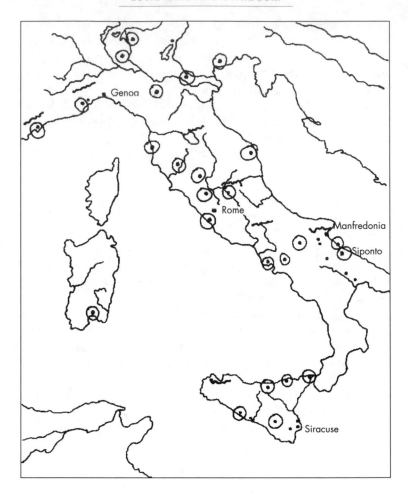

The map indicates:

— paleolithic sites of the goddess with meanders

• neolithic sites of the goddess with dots

⊙ I have circled places where I have found sanctuaries of black madonnas. Circles are often around dots, suggesting that neolithic sites of the goddess are the places sanctuaries to black madonnas have been built.

This map is reproduced from "maps" section of Marija Gimbutas, *The Language of the Goddess* (San Francisco, et al., Harper & Row, Publishers, 1989).

148

TEN

Three Generations of Women: Transformations of Female Identity Models in Italy

FRANCA BIMBI

I. Contexts of Social Change

Due to an increasing average life span, especially among women, four generations of women - and occasionally five - currently coexist in significant numbers in Italy.

The oldest, all of whom were born more than fifty years ago, are for the most part grandmothers and great-grandmothers. For their daughters, who are by now adult women between the ages of forty and fifty, these women represented a traditional model of female identity that was based on subsuming gender in a biological paradigm: a woman has the obligation to be mother and wife because her social identity is implicit in her biological ability to conceive, give birth, suckle, and feed little human beings.

However, women born after World War II have broken explicitly with their primary socialization model and have legitimized a model of female social identity that is no longer exclusively oriented toward the family. In part, they have also generalized certain types of behavior that the older generation had begun to adopt: indeed, as early as the interwar period, one may note both a trend toward less frequent pregnancies (Livi Bacci 1980) as well as individual and minority paths of emancipation through education, work, or politics.

The youngest adult women, who are now between twenty-five and forty years of age, generally regard their decision to have a child, their access to education, and their presence in the workplace as established rights. Their childhood socialization bears the marks of the conflict and the break from tradition that their mothers experienced. Moreover, the younger members of this generation have an awareness of the changes that have taken place and have a sense of their own womanhood that is free of the stigma of social inferiority regarding their male peers.

Finally, for girls the definition of the social identity of women seems to be open (Bimbi 1986a; Bimbi 1988). The meaningful spheres to which they may direct themselves (family, work, school) mainly appear to be centered on self-realization; sexual difference is seen as having positive features of social value; and equality with their male peers appears legitimized both symbolically and, to a large extent, also in law.

Thus, the current generations of women in Italian society are a significant indication of the profound changes that female identity models have undergone, and they make it possible to carry out comparative studies on the elements of continuity and discontinuity from generation to generation. The situation outlined earlier seems to be a synthesis of the continuing transformations and their trends. However, there are considerable differences in the timing of change from place to place, especially between areas of greater or lesser urbanization, and between more recent or less recent urbanization. Moreover, from one generation to the other one detects the close intertwining of modernizing processes and surviving traditional attitudes. It appears that one purpose of contemporary women's pragmatic concern with traditional types of behavior and values is to maintain the coherence of their own history by reelaborating their mothers' and grandmothers' past in their own present individual experiences and choices.

In research about the current situation of women in Italy (Barile and Zanuso 1980; Saraceno 1980; Bimbi and Pristinger 1985; Merelli, Morini et al. 1985; Giacobuzzi, Merelli et al. 1989), the simultaneous existence of processes of transformation and of surviving imbalances within the family clearly emerges. In what follows, particular reference will be made to the findings of three research projects, which concern adult married women of different generations.

The first is an oral history project, the results of which have yet to be published in their final form (Moro, Perin, and Zecchinato 1981; Bimbi, Lovisotto, and Perin 1991). The project aims to reconstruct the practices of motherhood among women born in the first thirty years of the century, focusing on sixty women (peasants and workers) from Conegliano, a town in the province of Treviso. Since the 1960s, Conegliano has been central to the region's industrialization and trade union activity. The results of this research will be used both to illustrate the social construction of patriarchy, which defines the traditional social identity of the women of this generation, and also to indicate the processes of change that are already in evidence and that will be utilized by women of future generations.

The second piece of research (Bimbi and Pristinger 1985) concerns a sample of the female population from the provinces of Verona and Padua in the Veneto region, and deals with "dual role" as the model of social identity prevalent among women born since the war. The four hundred interviewees, between the ages of twenty and fifty, amply display the dynamics of change both regarding previous generations and within their own ranks.

The findings of these two projects enable researchers to consider the formation of the processes of change, as the region in question is characterized historically by its social and cultural traditionalism: the political culture of Veneto has a Catholic matrix. In this area the decline in the number of children and the increase in the number of females at school and in the workplace have occurred considerably later than in other regions of central and northern Italy; nevertheless, these phenomena have accelerated since the war. Recently, various researchers have emphasized the aspects of secularization that have come about both in the political sphere (Bagnasco and Trigilia 1984) and to an even greater extent in the family and in everyday life (Guizzardi 1982).

The third piece of research (Bimbi and Castellano 1989) concerns ninety couples between the ages of twenty and forty with children from four towns in Emilia-Romagna. They were interviewed separately about their experiences and conceptions of parenthood. All the couples have an only child under the age of three attending a crèche. The mothers are all employed. Emilia-Romagna has, among Italian regions, one of the highest levels of female employment and school attendance (Barbagli, Capecchi, and Cobalti 1988) and one of the lowest ratios of children to women, coupled with the best facilities for children. The political milieu is predominantly socialist-communist. The results of the inquiry are interesting in that they show the interconnection between the delegitimization of the patriarchal family, the sharing and interchange in parental roles, and the imbalance in the division of work within the family. The findings indicate the continuing survival of models in the very context in which one would expect a greater linearity in the processes of change.

This research allows the examination at a conceptual level of postwar changes in female identity models, for which the term of comparison is the "grandmother" generation. By "identity model" is meant both the presentation of self in the world and the collective norms of presentation to which one adheres. The relationship between these two aspects appears to become more dynamic with the passing of time, in the sense that personal identity seems less and less rigidly defined by social role models (Berger, Berger, and Kellner 1973; Sciolla 1984). Moreover, female identity representations seem correlated both to the subjective goals of woman as agent of social change and to the structural and contextual changes in the position of women in Italy. In more recent generations the active goal-directed aspect predominates over gender definitions.

Since the interwar period and even more since World War II, certain specific and consistent trends emerge that concern women either directly or indirectly. Particularly significant in terms of demographic composition is the decline in both fertility and death rates. The data reveal the decision of women and couples to limit the size of their families. Indeed, one approaches the one-child model. Also noteworthy is the fact that the decline in the female death rate is caused, in the grandmother generation, by the virtual disappearance of death in childbirth. Equally dramatic is the virtual disappearance of neonatal deaths. Moreover, the number of people living under the same roof (Barbagli 1984) becomes fewer and fewer, with a resulting increase in the number of family units; hence woman's work for the family, for example for aged relatives, appears less "domestic" and more oriented toward creating interfamilial networks of relationships. The decline in the number of marriages shows a rather noninstitutional attitude among young people in Italy, which is counterbalanced by the low number of divorces. Finally, the figures show for the postwar period a constant and steadily increasing number of women undertaking education, including higher education, and in the workplace.

II. Mothers Given and Giving in Patriarchal Culture

The discussion begins with two examples that illustrate the "rule of the father." In the first, an elderly peasant woman from a prosperous family recalls the food-serving ritual:

> We women sat on the edge of the hearth or in a corner, ready to serve the men. If you weren't quick about it, you got into trouble. They didn't move a finger, you know. And the kids had to be fed first because the menfolk wanted to eat in peace. My father-in-law sat at the head of the table with the youngest and the eldest son on either side, then came the third son on one side and on the other side my husband. My place was in a corner. – *Regina, born 1907* (Bimbi 1986a: 385)

The above is both a description of the woman's role and an image of a society, its organization, its values, and its regulatory hierarchies. There is an evident awareness of the conflict between the female care-giving abilities and the sexual hierarchies that transformed differing abilities into social inequalities that women endured but at the same time internalized.

The second example concerns a rich middle-class family:

> They stopped me from doing it. I asked my father; I got him to come specially to the convent to see the Mother Superior. The fact that he came was quite out of the ordinary. "Your daughter would like to continue her studies." "I've already got sons to maintain our family honor. It's always a good thing to have another woman around the house. So, no permission to go on studying." – *Amelia, born 1925* (Bimbi 1986a: 386)

The latter woman, younger and richer than the former, clashed unsuccessfully as an adolescent with hierarchies similar to those present in the first scene. In the second case, the woman's place is likewise "in a corner": instead of achieving an educational qualification, she was to spend the years before her marriage in a finishing school. These episodes from two such different lives show the inner coherence of the patriarchal culture's social representation, which overrides social class and the presence or absence of extended families under the same roof (Wall, Robin, and Laslett 1983). Patriarchy, with its forms of family life in both peasant and middle-class culture, represents the form of traditional authority that defines the man's social identity and also gives content and meaning to the woman's social identity. In the give-and-take (Troeltsch 1960) between the strong, who give protection and thus dominate, and the weak, who

receive protection and thus acknowledge their social inferiority, the male role is delineated as one of responsibility for the
family as a group and toward the outside world in general, and
the female has responsibility for the internal management of
family resources and for the recognition of differing needs
(Weber 1981). In this division of roles, the man is assigned an
ethic of responsibility, the woman an ethic of "giving" (Bimbi
1987a). The woman is "given" for the marriage alliance
between families; her dowry marks the importance of the fact
that she gives herself to her new family. The gift of herself for
the purpose of reproduction is taken for granted from the
moment she marries, as is her willingness to participate in sexual intercourse: a woman is a body given for the purpose of
motherhood. This occurs independently of the will of the individual man; it depends on the social form of the matrimonial
exchange, wherein the presumption is that the body given possesses a capacity to produce children limited only by biological
factors. The distinction between social responsibility and the
gift of oneself defines sexual difference (Bimbi 1987b); hence,
it is motherhood, and not the division of work according to sex,
that determines the separation of roles into male and female.
This is evident from the interviews with the peasant women.
Although farming chores may be interchangeable, the responsibilities of motherhood are exclusive to women, even if they
are limited in part to the earliest stages in the child's life. Some
areas concern women exclusively: besides the obvious ones of
childbearing and birth, these are feeding, clothing, early
upbringing, and "doctoring." Moreover, in the tasks connected
with preparing and serving food, the specific features of the
female identity model are apparent. Around the table, at the
formalized moment of family representation, the women perform the serving ritual: they acknowledge the social superiority
of the adult males and act out the inferiority of the weak, which
is typical of the patriarchal model. However, in the overall running of the household, the women ensure that a fair share is
given to those family members who have special needs: small
children, unweaned infants, pregnant women, women who
have given birth recently or are breastfeeding, and old people
in poor health.

A considerable part of the peasant economy is traditionally a
gift economy (Mauss 1965). Even in more recent times, in tracing the history of industrialization (Pahl 1989), it has been pos-

sible to highlight the continuing importance of the economy based on give-and-take, that is, on the exchange of goods and services that have no monetary equivalent. This exchange of goods and services extends over time, and requires the acknowledgment of alliances and emphasizes individual abilities rather than abstract "services rendered." The women, from the moment of their gift of the maternal body, appear to have formed their social character within such an economy. Features such as caregiving, individualized response to needs, and responsibility toward interpersonal relationships rather than toward general principles are defined by some scholars as a "female mode of production" (Prokop 1978); others (Gilligan 1981) consider these features as aspects of woman's psychology that continue to be significant. It is interesting to note that these features are located within the gift economy, in which the traditional female identity appears defined. This applies, mutatis mutandis, also to the middle-class woman who is not allowed to study for a profession but is required instead to "professionalize" the gift of herself in motherhood (Knibiehler and Fouquet 1980). Middle-class women consequently will steer their daughters toward emancipation through education and the professions. However, for all women, be they middle-class or peasant, the way out of the patriarchal culture seems to be preeminently through the transformations of motherhood (Bimbi 1989). The processes of change may be detected even among the older women, the young women workers, and the younger peasant women. Woman's acceptance of motherhood is less and less taken for granted and the "biological" paradigm of the gift of the mother undergoes change. The younger women, particularly the women workers, speak of the emergence of a choice made by the couple about birth control. Coitus interruptus emerges as a modern means of limiting the number of pregnancies, thus replacing the period of breastfeeding and ecclesiastical injunctions to refrain from sexual intercourse for at least forty days postpartum. Coitus interruptus may be considered a modern means of limiting fertility because, even today, it is the method most widely used and has brought about a steady decline in fertility and a growing awareness of contraception. Although the practice of coitus interruptus maintains the representation of the male will as dominant in the area of sex and reproduction, it nevertheless introduces the principle that nature is not the norm to be followed. In this way, the woman's body is released from a biological obligation and becomes the subject of a social strategy shared by the couple that aims at achieving the optimal number of children. At this point the gift of oneself, in sex and in motherhood, can be presumed no longer and new rules of reciprocity will come into being in the man-woman relationship. The working-class family no longer will be able to maintain an image of male authority based on the fact of his being in paid employment; at the same time, a growing degree of privacy will give the woman increasing personal responsibility for the choice of whether or not to have children. The daughters of the women of these generations will reduce dramatically the number of children but there has also been, since the war, a change in the notion of male right over female sexuality. A woman in charge of her own fertility progressively takes charge also of the giving of herself to the man. Equality in the areas of reproduction and sex begins in the marriage bed and moves into the public sphere. In 1975, at a time when the feminist movement occupied an important role in Italian politics, a decision of the Supreme Court allowed the pill to be publicized and prescribed. However, the revolutionary decline in fertility was already well underway: it had begun at least thirty years earlier through the extremely widespread practice of coitus interruptus.

III. A Dual Role

The concept of the "dual role" (Balbo 1978), adopted in the inquiry into a sample of the female population, is useful in considering the female identity profile that has been unfolding since the war. The following discussion centers on the working identities of adult women, but at the same time is a continuation of what already has been said. Women born after World War II, albeit with numerous differences deriving from geographical context, age, and level of education, share certain common features in their social self-presentation. They have in common their refusal to consider themselves "family" women, their awareness of the necessity and the limits of emancipation through work, and their striving to reconcile various needs while maintaining their self-image as "complete" and fulfilled women, at an affective, professional, and public level. They also share a tolerance toward models of female self-fulfillment that may be radically different from their own models. "Dual role" is the thread linking all these female social images and it is the typical way of combining the work of reproduction with work in the outside world. Such a combination would seem oriented no longer toward the role of mother. Since the 1970s, dual role has developed both as an experience in the lives of women and as a representative form of female identity; this would seem to coincide with the emergence in Italy of the feminist movement (Calabrò and Grasso 1985). The postwar years of economic development, particularly since the 1960s, witnessed the establishment both of the nuclear family as a demographic model, with only two generations under the same roof and fewer and fewer children, and of generalized schooling for the young of both sexes. As a result, Italian women have greater access, and on better terms, to the job market than in the past. With fewer children, overall options become more flexible and, with higher qualifications, there is greater freedom in the choice of jobs and professions. Among the women interviewed, it is the younger, the better educated, and those who come from a more urbanized background who reveal a complete break from the image of the housewife that was a point of reference for both working-class and middle-class families until the end of the 1960s. More generally, there are now fewer women who have never been employed; there is a steady growth in the proportion of women entering the workforce and the female presence in the tertiary sector is constantly expanding. "Dual role" signifies above all the possibility for women to adopt a variety of strategies that combine work, study, family, and motherhood. Evident in these strategies is also the subjective aspect of choice that qualifies the changes made during various phases of life.

Women's presence in the work force, for example, seems characterized by a keen awareness of economic equality and no longer is determined merely by the need for a second job outside the home. All women should work; all women want, to a greater or lesser extent, to work; all women, at least at some stages of their life, do work. The figure of the middle-class woman obliged to be a lifelong housewife is tending to disappear, as is the aura of privilege surrounding women who work in traditionally male professions. However, women factory and office workers also show that they consider work and family as two areas in which they enjoy established rights and in which they decide their own participation. The questions that women would seem to ask themselves do not concern whether or not to work, but rather when to start, how to leave, and how to resume; in other words, where exactly to invest their efforts and at which particular period of their life. Consequently, in the far-from-easy task of combining her two roles, it would seem that the woman tends to look to herself in investing her energics and in making choices, which may mean giving priority at one time to motherhood, at another to work, and at yet another to education and training.

Above all, the notion of women existing in and for the family no longer appears to be recognized as an inevitable, "destined" role. The obligatory path of marriage, children, and the role of housewife has lost its legitimacy. Such a sequence of female normality used to create feelings of guilt both in women obliged to work outside the home and in those women who were conscious of the nonconformity of their individual choice. Today the family would seem to be both a sphere of professionalized family-domestic work (that is, a sort of obligation redefined in view of the combining of jobs) and a context in which choices are not predefined, but are rather the result of negotiations with the partner. In particular, the control over fertility has led to the professionalization of the job of mother both in psychological-affective terms and in its relationship with agencies of socialization outside the family. When there are two children or only one, the individual child is the object of more intense work concentrated into a shorter part of life. Women have given themselves the possibility of distinguishing between the social significance of motherhood and the desire for motherhood that is significant at the individual level. These dynamics, along with the introduction of domestic appliances and utilities such as gas and electricity, have made the home a place that is socially very different from the home of older generations. Housework is less physically taxing but includes numerous new tasks that would seem to fall to a single female figure. The division of domestic work according to sex would appear to be highly asymmetrical. Nevertheless, the home is at the center of a social web where family resources are combined and managed for the sake of the family. For the woman, who has responsibility for this, the situation holds both limitations and opportunities. Above all, even in the work of reproduction, the woman has come into contact with behavior codes of an instrumental nature, she has been involved more directly in the public sphere, and she has found herself interacting more frequently with the realities of money and public institutions. Moreover, the extended period of schooling that women have experienced has meant for those who are now adults a process of secondary socialization, which is oriented not toward the family but toward exploring their own intellectual abilities (Bimbi 1981). During the 1970s, many educated women found employment in the field of social services. With the growth of the welfare state (Ascoli 1984), therefore, even in the less highly qualified professions, women have had a massive input in terms of the relationship-directed work that is typical of the female mode of production on behalf of the family (Bianchi 1981). This is highly significant, in that it brings to light both the economic importance of the work of reproduction and of mothering, as well as the social need for caregiving (Balbo 1987), which was historically undertaken in the home.

In conclusion, through "dual role" women make explicit in the public sphere the social value of expressive abilities while simultaneously bringing to private life professional skills and instrumental abilities directed at maintaining balance within the range of their social involvements. The most significant aspect of dual role is thus to be found in the area of the transformations of female social identity models. It emerges as an open-meshed model for the combination and interaction of a type of knowledge closely linked to affective tasks (for which women are traditionally responsible within the framework of the economy and ethics of giving) and a type of knowledge characterized by its instrumental nature (which has been the traditional point of reference for male social identity). Dual role thus proposes a female image of a new kind (Saraceno 1987) but brings with it the difficulties of relating to two symbolic orders that historically are widely separated and counterposed. The women interviewed seem for the most part ambivalent toward dual role, and do not seem to look to it as a final model but rather as a way of keeping their options open regarding their own identity. In most cases it would seem more correct to speak of female identity in transition rather than of fully codified new models.

IV. Imbalances, Equality, Sexual Difference

In some ways, dual role seems to be the adult woman's "normal" social identity model that legitimizes her achievement of full equality (Walzer 1983) both in the private and the public

159

sphere; in other ways, it seems a combination of resources and bonds that go together to transform the traditional social identity and to make it possible to balance old and new self-redefinitions. The simultaneous presence of these different aspects is reflected in the experiences of younger women, who already have a family of their own, once they find themselves assuming the typically adult role of mother. In the present research into young couples with children, it was found that the women are quite at home with the notion of combining work in a family setting as mother with work in the outside world. These couples have one child, and for many of them there probably will be no more children or, at most, one more child. The couple strives toward an ideal model of equality between themselves as partners and the sharing of the responsibilities and tasks of parenting. In this context, the women concretely build their role model and their identity profile, but it is important to note that the men also find themselves in the position of redefining their identity and their familial roles within the dynamics of change. Moreover, the definitions of motherhood and fatherhood constitute the framework of primary socialization for new generations. Hence the discussion leads to an analysis of the transformations of female identity within the ambit of the dynamics of recently formed families. The research into work in the family referred to previously has revealed an objective imbalance in the division of work between the sexes regarding work in the home and the various tasks that this involves. Although this imbalance is found even in the young families, there does emerge a paternal presence, albeit limited, in work on behalf of young children. There is widespread acknowledgment of the existence of the imbalance, but the imbalance itself is not an expectation; neither the women nor the men legitimize it as a value. Moreover, all the women and all the men point to the real presence of the father, even though this would not seem to be elaborated as a model specifically referring to male identity. In terms of values, the ideal type consistently is seen as one of equality between the sexes, which would tend to make the maternal and paternal tasks the same, and would make even the subjective orientations underlying the two roles interchangeable. The young parents focus their combined efforts on home life, which, at this stage of their family life, is geared above all to the needs of the young child.

A different attitude toward work and familial authority would seem especially to distinguish self-presentations regarding the past, for which the term of reference is the family of origin. For the young mother the significance of work in the outside world would seem commensurate with the quality of her relationship with her child, and this is sought for the reciprocal satisfaction of affective needs. Moreover, for the mothers interviewed, work outside the home would seem necessary also to maintain a self separate from the family, which, at least in part, would seem to be directed at improving the emotional climate of the family. For the young father, work involves juggling economic necessities, self-recognition in a traditional area of the definition of male identity, and striving to maintain a portion of time to devote to home life, which centers on the child. The importance that the working-class or lower-middle-class father gives to home life (Ariès 1968) would seem to represent an indubitable and important reorientation of family strategies compared with the preceding generation, above all because home life is adopted explicitly as a criterion for action and as the point of convergence of maternal and paternal styles. Thus, home life emerges as the yardstick of the balances of equality and of the acceptance of imbalances. This accentuation of home life is also evident in the representation of the "modern parent," which takes the place of an image of separate maternal and paternal functions, such as was apparent in the research into the older women. In fact, the separation between the two roles is considered an image of the past, from which it is (or was) necessary to distance oneself. What is particularly rejected is the image of male authority, husband over wife, and, to a lesser extent, father over children; in short, the notion of hierarchy. The term "parent" would seem to be used with very little sexual differentiation, with the exception of some references to a maternal function, particularly regarding the biological fact of pregnancy, and with the exception of a generic reference to the child's primary processes of emotional attachment. Moreover, there emerges a task of parenting that corresponds to the parents' ideal image and that concerns the modalities of the relationship with the child, the sharing in his or her upbringing, and the negotiation of infant care tasks. This work would seem to focus on the couple and would appear to deny, conceal, or contradict, from numerous points of view, both the individuality of the parents and their sex difference. In particular the woman has the job of educating her partner, who frequently represents himself as striving to learn the maternal functions that are necessary to his new paternal profile. In this process one finds both an implicit acknowledgment of traditionally different functions and the explicit attempt to go beyond these with the aim, it seems, of achieving undifferentiated roles regarding the child. The sociological interpretation of these dynamics seems far from easy. It also must be borne in mind that what is being dealt with is a particular stage in the life both of the family and of the individuals who constitute it (Saraceno 1986). At this stage, if not at others, one detects a heightened role and representativeness of the woman in defining the arrangements of relationships within the family, which now has an additional member who prolongs the parents' generation and places them in the generational chain. However, in terms of representation, this specific significance of the female tends to be denied to achieve the goal of a paternal presence; for this purpose, the traditional resources of male social identity, such as the predominance of the instrumental aspects of his role or his symbolic significance as the decision-making and hierarchical center of the family, are neither adequate nor really necessary. In fact, this particular characteristic of the *pater familias* seems to have lost completely its capacity to define male identity and the paternal role. It is here above all that the patriarchal cultural model today reveals itself as bereft of legitimizing force. Parenthood would appear to be defined by its function of constituting the appropriate center of home life and of the shared responsibility for the child's upbringing. However, all this finds its place within the framework of the interconnectedness of the dynamics of equality, the emergence of maternal functions assigned to both parents, and the sketchy definition of relations of authority. All of these factors would seem to minimize the sex difference. The parent couple, their efforts focused on the child, either would seem to do away with the dynamics of difference or would seem to prefer not to define them, tacitly indicating that these dynamics have their real place in private interpersonal relationships, in the dyads constituted by the adult partners or by the mother-child and father-child relationship.

Nonetheless, differentiation strongly asserts itself in the division of work within the family: the further one moves away from caring for the infant, the more clearly there emerges a difference in tasks that is acknowledged even if it is not legitimized.

The division of work along sex lines, which the interviewees, especially the women, justify on pragmatic grounds, would seem the most explicit manner through which sex difference emerges, so much so that the woman often seems to defend herself from male intrusion into the tasks that she finds assigned to herself in the household.

In this area also interpretation is far from simple. On the one hand, the imbalance in domestic and family work almost seem to point to a traditional model of definition of female rather than male identity: the woman alone performs certain tasks and there is an acknowledgment that age-old habits exist that stand in the way of achieving complete equality. On the other hand, the man might well be legitimized in assuming specifically domestic tasks (unlike his father) but does not do so (often, in this, just like his father), even though he acknowledges that this "privilege" of his cannot be legitimized socially. Both the men and the women interviewed are aware that the patriarchal model has lost its legitimacy, and the men reveal this realization also through their unease in openly acknowledging their smaller involvement in domestic work. Another message that the asymmetrical organization of the family seems to suggest, when it is set alongside the content of the parents' roles, is this: through the significance of more explicit maternal functions and the limiting of more specifically female areas in the running of the house, the women seem to wish to maintain both a certain maternal pervasiveness in their style of familial relationships as well as a striving toward equality and an ever greater reciprocity in the decision-making processes.

Thus, one detects in their thinking the perception of the advantages and disadvantages that may derive from the greater or lesser importance given to sex difference in the negotiation of roles. The men seem to be searching for a paternal role that, at the present moment, is taking form through analogies with the maternal role. Therefore, the type of relationship that it is possible at present to identify between sex difference, typologies of reciprocity, patterns of equality, and contexts of imbalance might point above all to the transition toward new definitions of difference, that is, of both female and male identity models.

At this stage in their lives, there arises between the man and the woman a significant exchange that may be defined in these terms: in the man's favor there is an imbalance in the division of household tasks that is matched by an imbalance, in the woman's favor, in the expression of authority regarding maternal functions and the organization of family life. Such an exchange seems acceptable and in part clear to the two partners, but only insofar as it relates to an explicit cultural model of the nonhierarchical family. As the hierarchical family organization traditionally has had its symbolic center in the male figure of husband and father, the move away from this also may lead to the negation of possible (and even desired) specific features of male and female identity. For these reasons, there tends to emerge a representation of equality that at the social level conceals sex difference while at the same time minimizing the significant differences in specific functions that continue to exist.

However, the survival of role differentiation and even of imbalances occurs in a context of definition of the family system that has undergone profound change, both within itself and regarding the social environment. The fact that the male identity model does not take shape around the authority of husband and father, and the fact that such authority is not a point of reference for family and social organization is one of the most significant phenomena that have brought about the pluralization of directional forms within institutions. Therefore, it no longer seems possible to assign to the male gender a predominant symbolic valency of social centrality (Horkheimer 1974). This now makes it possible to give attention also to fatherhood as an experience, comparing it both with the transformations of its symbols and with the experience and representations of motherhood. In fact, the changes currently taking place do not seem to concern female identity exclusively.

Conclusions

The most striking feature of the cultural changes through which women have lived in the course of this century is their very breadth. The postwar generation above all has found itself involved in a process of reorientation of its identity models that may be compared with the changes that occur in emigration. To find oneself a foreigner, even if this is the result of a conscious distancing of oneself from the world of one's beginnings, the world of childhood and of primary socialization, has meant an initial break with the past, followed by a striving to reestablish links. The postwar period has seen the rapid acceleration of changes that previously had been adumbrated or experienced by very few women. Although the change has seemed sudden and final, it has become clear from the experiences of the older women that their unease and rebelliousness, however thwarted, have passed from one generation to the other and have constituted for the successive generation a kind of cultural capital, on which the latter have drawn to define new identity models. The younger women show that they are passing through a period of transition and adjustment that also involves male identity and that suggests open-ended change. In the long term (Braudel 1984a) the waves of change and surviving sediments intermingle. Social change seems marked by numerous discontinuities (Braudel 1984b). Not only does the past never present itself in quite the same way, but also the hypothesis of linear change seems unverified.

ELEVEN

The Women's Movement in Italy and the Events of 1968[1]

LUISA PASSERINI

Introduction

This subject is complex, and is made more so by the state of research into it. In contrast to other countries, there does not yet exist in Italy a history of the last twenty years of the women's movement. In the case of Italy, there are numerous works that consider particular aspects of the movement, but serious gaps remain in the overall picture. This state of affairs is linked to the prominence given to disciplines other than history in the intellectual debate on the Italian feminist movement; there is no doubt that philosophy, linguistics, psychoanalysis, and psychology have offered more direct approaches that serve to underpin political positions. Although Italian women historians have produced works of great interest in terms of methodology and content, they have not applied their expertise to the history of their own movement, and, above all, they have not made of their history a means of political activity. This has had both positive and negative effects. The situation may change as a result of the various initiatives under way, such as the creation of the Italian Association of Women Historians and the proposed establishing of centers for women's studies both inside and outside university institutions and, in some cases, centers linking academic and nonacademic institutions.

1. This essay, based on a paper delivered at the conference "Le culture e i luoghi del 1968," Turin 3–5 November 1988, considers research about the history of women in Emilia-Romagna undertaken by the *Centro di Documentazione, Ricerca e Iniziativa delle Donne*, Bologna, my own research on the generation of 1968 for the Italian Ministry of Education, and a research project I directed for the *Consiglio Nazionale delle Ricerche* on written and oral sources for contemporary history.

Moreover, the history of women is prey to a constant misconception in the field of historical and social disciplines. Its task is seen as that of filling the vacuum left by general histories. One hopes that there will be a strong challenge to the assumption made over recent years, at least in research practice, whereby the history of women is accorded the same status (at least at conferences and in some journals) as other specialist fields, but is ignored totally by works claiming to be general histories. This, possibly, is because male historians have failed to incorporate gender into their approach; to do so would lead to both a critique of viewpoints hitherto considered universal, and the application of gender to the study of men and to the study of the relations between men and women in their historical reality.

Within the framework outlined above, some approaches evident in past research and possible appproaches for future research will now be identified.

The Social Roots in the 1950s and 1960s

The generations of women who were to give rise to the feminist movement, in the strict sense of the term, or who were to be involved in it, were born between the end of the 1930s and the beginning of the 1950s. A study of their development therefore requires an examination of the cultural and social history of Italy beginning from the final years of the Fascist regime. Such an approach also requires a dynamic perspective on the changes in class structure over the past fifty years, with a view toward rebutting the facile cliché that claims that the women's movement is predominantly composed of middle-class women. Such labelling conceals a real diversity of social origins that would be an interesting area of research.

Existing studies have clarified two basic processes that involved these generations of women. One concerns the profound changes in everyday behavior that took place in the 1950s, to which the blanket term "informal emancipatory movements" may be applied. These included the adoption of new behavior patterns, above all regarding consumption, by very large numbers of women who were "on the move," often literally so through emigration. Suffice it here to recall Alberoni's example of the trousseau (Alberoni 1964). The changes in consumption concerned the body, the home, and transport. The changes also involved a modification of women's lifestyles and their self-presentation in everyday life: going out, walking in public, travelling, smoking, and the questioning, in part not yet translated into action, of sexual mores. In the late 1950s the direction of such questioning was toward what was broadly termed "free love."

Alongside this great process of change, there was another process, which has been defined as the marginalization of women – compared with the period of the Resistance (1943–1945) and the early years of the Republic (instituted in 1946). Some of the features of this were the reduction in the number of female factory workers, the decline in the number of women parliamentarians, and the hiatus in introducing legislation in favor of women. Simonetta Piccone Stella has pointed out that, paradoxically, there were at the same time campaigns in favor of education for women that brought Italy into step with other Western nations (Piccone Stella 1981). The overall situation was marked by a lack of channels of representation; it was left to individual women to find ways of modifying existing conditions.

In the 1960s these tendencies developed and changed, but one already could detect certain aspects that represented more specifically the adoption of responsibilities concerning gender. In most cases this was totally implicit: considered in hindsight, certain practices to be found in Catholic associations, such as group discussions akin to "consciousness raising" and the experience of leadership and social work, certainly appear so. As individual men and women recall, these practices induced both dissatisfaction and elation resulting from perceptions of gender difference. Also implicit was the general atmosphere of solidarity and conflict in the relations of peers who were forced to defend themselves from the oppression of the adult community. However, there was also the emergence of explicit behavior. Consider Simone de Beauvoir's *The Second Sex* and its publication history: it was published in France in 1949, banned by the Catholic church, and appeared in Italian only in 1961. De Beauvoir's book and the informal discussions to which it gave rise were critical stages in the lives of some women. Especially in the years around 1965–1966, this and other books, such as Betty Friedan's *The Feminine Mystique*, which came out in Italy in 1964, seem to shape new perceptions. Friedan's book reflects well the mood of the period. On the one hand, it was a critique of the American family; on the other, the book was dedicated "to Carl

Friedan and to our children – Daniel, Jonathan and Emily."
The book both denounced integration into the system and
came up with a fundamental suggestion – education. In the
case of women who had received an education but had never
taken it seriously, it suggested "an intensive concentrated reim-
mersion in, quite simply, the humanities" (Friedan [1963]
1965: 324). At this stage, it is in the area of culture that one can
understand best the questioning by women that prepared the
way for their discoveries of, and their claims to, their subjectivity.

The same characteristic is to be seen in Demau (Group for
Demystifying Authoritarianism), which generally is considered
the forerunner of women's movements in Italy. However, this is
an area open to research. In the period around 1966, Demau
initiated a critique of the type of emancipation expounded by
organizations such as the Unione Donne Italiane, and also initiated debate on what it was to call "patriarchal oppression."
Three elements of that experience are of interest here. First,
the group proposed a culture-based critique of culture (an
approach that the group Rivolta Femminile was to adopt later,
as is pointed out in Boccia 1987); that is, its first step, which
foreshadows the spirit of 1968, was to confute the dominant culture by setting it against itself – Hegel versus Hegel, Freud versus Freud. Second, it focused attention on authoritarianism,
broadly understood, and thus would later inevitably find itself
"competing" with 1968. And third, it was for certain periods of
its existence a group of both genders.

This last point is of relevance here because it is important to
begin to consider historically the question of the role played by
some men in the women's movement. Generally, the movement has considered the question symbolically – the presence
of the male gaze even when women meet among themselves –
and hence rather abstractly. However, it would be interesting to
study the role played by men from a historical and anthropological viewpoint. There are numerous pointers in this direction: some males played an important role in the early period
of the feminist movement before complete separation took
place. Demau envisaged the emancipation also of males; as late
as 1972 a book that was significant for the feminist movement,
La coscienza di sfruttata [Women's experience of exploitation]
(Abbà, Ferri, Lazzarello, Medi, Motta 1972), had a male among
its authors. This subject will be taken up again during the discussion of the feminist movement as a movement.

170

The Events of 1968

Elsewhere in this essay, an interpretation of the 1968 revolt has been proposed as the emergence of subjectivity, a long-term process in the course of which the speaking out of individuals was combined with collective action. Such an interpretation contains within it an initial hypothesis about the relationship between the 1968 revolt and female specificity. Certain facets of the movement represent a feminization in the history of Italian culture, that is, a phase that revalued aspects of Italian culture that traditionally had been relegated to the area of "darkness" and "weakness." These aspects have to do with the imaginary and the affective, with the individual and the empirical. The elements oriented toward the "dark" side were: the attention that the 1968 movement, or at least those parts of it that may be considered historically innovative, paid to the condition of real-life subjects; the fact that they were prepared to form alliances with other subjects of social change only on the basis of their own, and their interlocutors' own, political actions; and the critique of "establishment" culture. The way in which these elements were translated into action accentuated the importance of the emotional aspect (for instance, the collective falling in love with the movement's leaders, which many may recall).

A broad approach has been indicated that cannot be transferred crudely to the empirical plane, but that nevertheless has general validity in writing a cultural history that heeds such phenomena as the imaginary and the unconscious. The specific features of this history obviously are not universal and timeless: what one or two historical periods define as pertinent to the concept of "female" is not pertinent in absolute terms. One of the characteristics of 1968 that confirms in the short term this long-term interpretation was the favoring of images of androgyny, an example being the male character in Alessandra Bocchetti's film *Della conoscenza*. Clearly, when androgyny is configured in relationships in which no clear awareness of gender is achieved, it tends to be expressed in male images. However, these male images are free of machismo. Indeed, in the convergence of the image of the young male and the typically patriarchal image of the woman, there is a kind of yearning for femaleness.

The particular complexity of the events of 1968 lies in the fact that the massive emergence of female characteristics at a general level was accompanied by the widespread rejection at an empirical level, both by individuals and groups, of specific female figures, especially mothers and, in general, figures belonging to earlier generations. Thus the seeds were sown of major conflicts that were to grow in later decades.

Alongside this, there was in the area of politics – it is essential to make such distinctions to grasp the interrelatedness of the various processes – an involvement by women in the students' movement, which, quantitatively and qualitatively, was without historical precedent. New images of leadership and of other responsible roles emerged, and these, in turn, led to conflicts among women, but also brought into the open the question not only of differences but also of hierarchies among women. The full significance of this could not be recognized at the time because of the dominant ideology of egalitarianism.

In the 1968 movement, politics intermeshed with new forms of social relations (sit-ins, participation in working parties, self-management of student colleges, communal living), which were of great importance to women as experiences of escaping, albeit amidst hardships, from the "inescapable" family. In the new public arena that was being created, women had a partial, implicit experience of themselves, which, in some cases, involved conflicts among themselves. After 1968 the unease felt by women could not fail to find a voice, or, at the very least, face situations of ever greater suffering.

In this climate of radical innovation, women, some more than others, experienced together periods of elation and of humiliation, of self-recognition and of loss of direction, as they set in train profound changes. The individual likewise experienced contradictions that for the time were "put on hold"; as a part of the movement, the individual's potentialities and rights were both enhanced and negated. The alternation between democracy and authoritarianism in the operation of the movement created tensions and divisions between groups, between individuals, and within individuals.

In Italy, events reflected the different characters of different cities. One of the most interesting cases is Trent, where women had been thinking and organizing before 1968, for example, at the Collegio delle Dame di Sion. This was followed by a period of "equality," with interesting figures among the leaders: "Marianella Sclavi was like Mauro Rostagno," recalls one woman, although Marianella herself does not concur entirely with this. Finally, there emerged one of the most significant (and tormented) strands in Italian feminism: Cerchio Spezzato, comprised of radical feminism, Freudianism, and Marxism. It is not without significance that this group was to become a seminal group of the early 1970s in Milan, which was the melting pot of the national movement.

Trent represented a fusion of nascent feminist inspiration and the students' movement, of a new awareness (which was the term then preferred to "self-awareness"), and of life in communities that were run by women but generally were of mixed gender. All this was reflected in their politics (for instance, working parties on the condition of women), which led up to the events of 1968–1969. The androgynous phase, albeit in its male version, was over; a parting of the ways was imminent. One final observation is that the equality within the group that was such a strong feature in Trent and Turin, to mention two of the most important cities, was less marked in Milan and Rome, where the movement had been defined as being male-oriented. Was this really so, or are these just tricks of memory played on the minds of a few participants more than twenty years later?

The purpose of this rapid excursus was to give some notion of the strength and significance of the involvement of women and of their specificity in the events of 1968. Again, it should be emphasized that the two terms do not coincide. The significance was for women themselves, for the movement and for relations between women and men. History and the media have failed completely to do justice to this subject. Women's involvement in the events of 1968, both as subjects and as objects, was far, far greater than their involvement in the twentieth anniversary celebrations of 1988. Younger people should be fully aware that things were not as many accounts would suggest they were. Such accounts reveal that "exclusion of women," which Joan Scott has found in all political histories, the traditional stronghold of history at its most official (see Ferrante, Palazzi, Pomata 1988).

One might say, to conclude, that not only have women been expunged from the accounts and histories of 1968 but so have bodies in general. Bodies continue to have a life of sorts in photographs but history has not given them the attention they merit. Bodies and their movements and the shifts in the meanings of their acts and actions were also political statements. Although traditional forms of relations did survive, huge barriers were also moved. Types of behavior which in the previous decade had occupied "unofficial" areas of society now came

into the open. This may be seen in what, with some justification, could be termed the "sex market" where, as previously but
in a new context, love, prestige and security were bartered but
which was also an area in which people learned, experienced
themselves and others, and became receptive to issues which
only the women's movement and the homosexual movement
had specifically tackled.

The Women's Movement

The relationship between the 1968 movement and the
women's movement has many diverse strands. There is, moreover, the further complication that these issues are international phenomena. For example, women's discussion groups
formed in 1969, taking their cue from writings originating in
the American movement and written by women from the civil
rights movement, the new American Left, and the so-called
radical-bourgeois current. Among the groups that utilized
such writings were the Milanese group, which was to develop
into Anabasi; Cerchio Spezzato in Trent; and the Collettivo
delle Compagne of the Gruppo Comunicazioni Rivoluzionarie
in Turin.

In addition to the international dimension, there was another dimension, which was neither geographical nor geopolitical,
but historical. Women's movements had existed since the nineteenth century and had been relegated unjustly to the realm of
emancipationism. (One result of this reductive interpretation
was the rejection in the early 1970s of the term "feminism" by
the women's movements in Italy and France; the term has since
found acceptance again – see Marcuzzo and Rossi-Doria 1987:
7–29.) Although the history of these long-established movements, generally speaking, either had been ignored or had
been shown in a ridiculous light, as in the case of the movement for the enfranchisement of women, they still constituted a
background that was not without some importance. In the Italian context, it can be said that the Unione Donne Italiane was
seen either as a negative model or as a bequeather of political
tactics.[2]

The confluence of two approaches is thus apparent: the

2. UDI (Unione Donne Italiane), founded in 1945, was the leading women's
movement until the emergence of the new feminism after 1968. Throughout
the 1950s and 1960s it organized campaigns for equal political and social rights.
(Translator's note.)

older and more autonomous approach, which predated 1968, and the approach of the 1968 movements. The term "1968" has been used thus far to refer specifically to the students' movement, which was the starting point and the stumbling block of the broader processes that subsequently were set in motion. The argument may be extended now in two directions. What was historically new about 1968 was that it was students who rebelled, and they did so as students. Regarding the women's movement, there were two features of 1968 that gave it a broader meaning – the movements that sprang up in factories, offices, and elsewhere; and the effects of 1968 on those who were not personally involved but who experienced the resulting changes in society. The 1968 revolt, understood in this sense, was perhaps even more important to the women's movement than was 1968 in the narrow sense, with its assumption that "the girls of 1968" would, sooner or later, become feminists. (Some, in fact, never did.)

Giving the term "1968" this broader meaning, one can accept the theory that a massive example of speaking out (which was not necessarily identical with speaking sense or speaking honestly) prompted many people, in this case many women, to envisage something not only similar but better. As well as explicit continuities, there are undeniable affinities with 1968. Three are particularly important: the women's movement as a huge process of "finding the words"; the way that the women's movement achieved universality by concentrating on the particular; and the movement's use of mockery and verbal violence.

The difficulty, as with all phenomena connected to the subjective element in history, lies in being able to see events in their continuity and discontinuity. The women's movement has given preeminence to the latter and has emphasized that, despite its awareness of possible alliances against the patriarchal system, it broke away from the student and youth movements. A member of Demau wrote:

> As "1968" came to a boil, it became more and more difficult for us to communicate with one another. There were numerous differences of opinion with women who subsequently returned to independent feminism. [. . .] One part of the group disappeared because it was strongly attracted by the prospect of being politically active in the students' movement. [. . .] Many women left because they wanted to get involved in politics. (Calabrò and Grasso 1985: 215)

In *Sputiamo su Hegel,* Carla Lonzi wrote:

> In the anguish experienced by the young man in taking his place in society, there is concealed a conflict with the patriarchal model. [. . .] Without his historic ally, woman, the young man's anarchism is sheer fantasy and he yields to the call of organized mass political activity. [. . .] The young man is oppressed by the patriarchal system but in due course becomes a candidate for the role of oppressor; young men's explosive intolerance bears the mark of this inner ambiguity. (Lonzi 1970: 11 and 22)

Adumbrated in these two passages are all the problems in the relations between the students' movement on the one hand and workers' movements and Marxist ideologies on the other. Consideration of the relations between the 1968 movements and the women's movements is necessary, and a working hypothesis for further research might be expressed succinctly as follows. The women's movement, being older and concerning itself with an older contradiction, experienced periods of radical discontinuity compared with the 1968 movement, but remains indebted to it for having created a wide-ranging freedom movement that originated from its own conditions of life. Without this "jolt" to people's minds, the new feminism would have been different. Feminism benefited from 1968 and also drew elements from the atmosphere of 1968, especially the capacity to see roles, knowledge, and relationships in a political light (see Frabotta 1973: 13).

The rancorous, competitive note at times present in the women's movement regarding "students" and "young people" must be understood in the specific context of the early 1970s, that is, in the movement's bitter and frankly competitive coexistence with political groups that owed their origins in part to the events of 1968, but that were far removed from 1968 both in spirit and in action. Nonetheless, these groups were also in their way a school for other feminists; this is exemplified in the story of the movement Lotta continua, which erupted into open dissension at the 1975 Rome congress and at the Rimini congress of the following year. The successive phase of discussions, the dismantling of the old structure and the creation of a new, informal organization, was mainly the work of women.

This process, however, occurred during the second wave of Italian feminism, after the loss of the momentum of the early 1970s. (The 1968–1969 phase may be considered a prelude or prehistory, or perhaps a resumption within its longer history.)

During the first wave massive changes had taken place and, by a paradox of history, these had happened in private houses and in the meeting places of small groups. Despite this, the process that had been set in motion was to mark a turning point in relationships and attitudes. Things would never be the same again, whatever the appearances – appearances that, in a Marxian sense, kill.

What exactly had happened? Here, too, there is a discrepancy between specific events and changes in history seen also in its subjectivity, except that here the discrepancy is more marked, more dramatic, more "shocking" when compared with "factual" history. In their everyday behavior, women in numerous places began to consider themselves and other women as subjects and began to treat one another as such, and to think, speak, and study within this perspective. More explicitly than generally had happened in the past, they brought shape and consciousness to preexisting forms of cohesion and conflict among women; they recognized their own importance and enjoyed their own company and that of other women.

They thus initiated a practical and theoretical critique of Western culture, and at the same time they exposed themselves and those close to them to extraordinary changes – changes in the family, in couples, and in relationships between generations. Other less visible changes involved redefinitions of "male" and "female," or rather, of the historical versions of "male" and "female." Women also were willing, with varying degrees of conscious choice, to give up their claim on certain forms of power, first among which was motherhood. It is yet to be established to what extent and in what way the changed value attributed to motherhood or the critique of motherhood in the feminism of the early 1970s influenced both the women most deeply involved in the movement and societal behavior in general. There is no doubt that in individual cases, its influence modified or legitimized life cycles and encouraged women to postpone or reject childbearing, thus creating new kinds of relations between mothers and children.

Part of this great upheaval was the rejection by some women of certain aspects of the traditional concept of female specificity and of its images. The price paid for their search for their real identity, and hence their real identity as women, was the exclusion and supplanting of men. Nothing can be destroyed without a countereffect, of which one is conscious to a greater or lesser extent. However, what had been removed reappeared not so much within the "women's movement" in the strict sense of the term, as in the more informal and widespread movement that has been called the "women's revolt."[3]

Before examining the "women's revolt," let us turn briefly to the related subject of men in the feminist movement. It seems a small but revealing indication of women's new universalism that men appear in the analyses that women carry out, but the converse seldom occurs. Some men had a significant role in the first stage of the women's movement; they established contacts, introduced documents, and transmitted ideas. Their role, in short, was that of mediators of relationships and resources, a role that anthropology often assigns to women in nonpublic contexts. Generally connected to this role is the task of managing relationships, as well as the additional roles of love object, confidant, and emotional supporter. It is unlikely that what happened was simply a role reversal between the women and men closest to the movement, but rather was a stage in the radical changes in gender relations and in the redefinition of "male" and "female." However, this remains an unwritten chapter of one stage in the history of the women's movement.

In the early 1970s the women's movement was marked by the growth of a very large number of small groups in various cities. The groups often were called by the name of the street or private house where they met.[4] The subjects discussed in the consciousness-raising meetings and discussions were numerous: the body and the demand for a new sexuality both among women and between men and women, which represented a convergence with the freedom of sexual expression of the late 1960s; medical self-help groups, and, at a later stage, women's

3. See Albistur and Armogathe (1977). In their two-volume history of French feminism since the Middle Ages, they write:
La période la plus actuelle du féminisme est neé de la révolte idéologique de 1968. S'il n'y a pas eu de revolution dans les faits, du moins un changement s'est-il opéré dans les structures mentales. Et plus que les autres peut-être, le mouvement féministe a recueilli l'esprit qui a animé cette période: une volonté absolue de changement, un "rien ne sera plus comme avant."
[The most recent stage of feminism arose from the ideological revolt of 1968. If there was in fact no actual revolution, there was at least a change in attitudes. And, perhaps more than any other, the feminist movement inherited the animating force of the time: a determination to change things, a sense that "nothing will be as it used to be."]
4. At the end of 1974 the monthly periodical *Effe* listed more than a hundred such groups in sixty different cities.

178

health centers; and a critique of housework and traditional gender roles, which, influenced by Marxist economics, led to the suggestion, especially by the group Lotta femminista, that housewives be paid a salary. Some of their ideas on women and work were taken up again in later years and were modified by women's involvement in trade unions. There was also the subject of gender difference as it related to identity, which culminated in a critique of psychoanalysis, and here the group Psychanalyse et politique and Juliet Mitchell (Mitchell 1974) made distinctive contributions.

It is essential to point out that, in the chronological framework proposed in this essay, the dominant factors are trends; hence, the chronology will vary from place to place. In areas linked to centers where strong poles of attraction developed, the chronology will appear markedly "out of step." An example of this is the influence on cities in the region of Emilia-Romagna of groups such as Lotta femminista, and of the group that developed into the Milan Women's Bookshop group. Another example is the time span, from 1969 to the 1970s and later, during which individual female students' collectives joined the feminist movement. In addition to identifying trends and placing them in a temporal framework, it also is essential to provide historically accurate accounts of events, organized on the basis of place, relationships, or subject. For example, it would be very interesting to reconstruct exactly the positions on the subject of abortion that were held by different groups or wings of the women's movement.

The Women's Revolt

As with *intifada*, the sheer historical novelty of this revolt makes the term unique and requires that it be seen in its context and its characteristics. The term is used here to refer to the changes, both de jure and de facto, that were brought about in society as a result of the new behavior of women, both as individuals and in groups, outside the confines of the women's movement. In the 1970s there were signs of such transformations that involved men and women, and individuals and institutions, which aimed at responding to the widespread and repeatedly expressed discontent among women.

Some of the consequences of this new behavior included changes to family law, the right to abortion, equal opportunity in the workplace, and the growing number of women in the professions. Other less positive aspects should not be ignored, as they are no less a part of this process of women's full involvement in the public sphere, such as the numerous terrorists in the 1970s who were women (Guidetti Serra 1988); here, tragically, equality was achieved. This again raises the question of continuity and discontinuity, and it hardly can be fortuitous that this same question also has been at the center of an important intellectual debate on Fascism and anti-Fascism. In the case of many of the processes that began after 1968 and extended into the 1970s, one must point to two possible kinds of continuity: continuity in ideas, attitudes, and policies, of which some examples were given in the discussion of 1968 and feminism; and biographical continuity, that is, the paths that individual men and women traced in their progression through events and organizations. In addition to the continuities, the discontinuities also must be borne in mind. The two might be represented as intersecting: for instance, an individual moves from the 1968 movement to a political group, and then to feminism or terrorism. Between the first and the second step there may be clear discontinuity regarding the party of the individual's choice and yet continuity may exist between the other steps; and the same may be found between the first step and the third or between the second and the third. It is fundamental to acknowledge that the oneness of the individual is not incompatible with radical shifts in political views during the various stages of that individual's life. Conversely, it may happen that an individual, although continuing to maintain a particular political position, experiences massive changes in his or her personal life. The appropriate approach, as in studying Fascism, is to carry out a detailed study of the forms of continuity and discontinuity in relation to both the overall significance of the historical periods and the course that individual lives followed.

As for the broad sections of women who were not personally involved in movements, groups, and organizations, it is clear that in the 1970s their outlook, attitudes, and behavior underwent considerable changes. Think, for example, of the new modes of self-presentation and of self-perception among very young women and among old women, which is to say the two extremes of female solitude; or think also of the different way in which both the traditional tasks in the family and new tasks involving contacts with bureaucracy were performed (Balbo 1976). One might sum up these changes in the relationship between women and the world by saying that they represent a move "from nature to culture." What had been seen previously as naturally owing is now done by choice, even in situations where nothing seems to have changed or there seems to have been a return to the way things were before the "revolt."

Once again there was a speaking out. Things that had not been said previously or that had been only half-said now began to find open expression in relations between women and men and between women and their surrounding world. Among women themselves, the second half of the 1970s carried forward processes that reached their conclusion in the 1980s. The subject of work, both inside and outside the house, was taken up again and this led to equal opportunity and affirmative action. Another feature of these years was the dissatisfaction, both individual and collective, with activism, which represented a thorough critique of the preceding stage and cast its shadow of disorientation, devastation, and suicide over the 1980s. Nevertheless here, too, there were elements of rebirth and promise for the future.

The 1970s also need to be studied in a historical perspective, and to do this it will be necessary to take account of the new features of the 1980s: small discussion groups are being replaced by culturally active groups (research and documentation centers, bookshops, study groups) and by associations of various kinds, including associations within the institutions, which represent the professional claims of women. The affinity-based internationalism of the 1970s is being replaced by new tendencies that remain unclear but appear to base themselves more on diversity. Small groups seem to have been superseded, and there is a move in the direction of what Raffaella Lamberti has called the "politics of women citizens," which still finds room for both the small group and the individual.

By contrast, the 1970s emphasized the small group and the individual, and in this emphasis lay both its continuity and discontinuity regarding 1968. The 1970s, at least the first half, bore the same heroic mark of radical renewal. In conjunction with a move toward individual reconsideration, there was the frequent victory of destructive tendencies that already had existed in the first half of the decade, but had been held in check by opposing cohesive and positive forces. These forces, despite ideological disagreements and emotionally violent clashes, allowed a very wide range of experiments and ideas, including the concrete notion of women relating primarily to other women, which was a return to the utopia of a completely alternative sphere, with all the critical force implicit in such a choice.

It now seems possible to begin considering those years historically. Among the factors that make this possible, two in particular should be mentioned: women's recognition of the need for tolerance and democracy, both within their own organizations and in society as a whole; and women's new capacity to acknowledge their mothers, both real and symbolic, and to see their relationship with them in terms of both legacy and innovation.

Translated by David Fairservice

TWELVE

Fra Madre e Marito:
The Mother/Daughter Relationship in Dacia Maraini's
Lettere a Marina

PAULINE DAGNINO

Dacia Maraini, novelist, playwright, and poet, is one of Italy's foremost contemporary writers and a leading figure in the Italian women's movement. Her novel *Lettere a Marina* was first published in 1981 during the period in the history of the European feminist movement that marked a shift in attention from a struggle to gain entry into a predominantly male world to the exploration of the female condition and a rediscovery and creation of a women's culture based on women's experience (Kristeva 1981: 20).

The exploration of the female condition has been taken up by Dacia Maraini in her writing. Her novels published after 1975, *Donna in guerra, Storia di Piera, Lettere a Marina, Il treno per Helsinki,* and *Isolina* are concerned largely with the problems of a woman's developing awareness of herself within a male-dominated social structure. *Lettere a Marina* stands out as the only one of these novels constructed as a series of letters between women.

The name Marina in the title of this novel is similar to Maraini's own surname and provides a link with another feminist novel written in the epistolary literary tradition, *The Three Marias; New Portuguese Letters* (1971), a collaborative work by three Portuguese women, Maria Isabel Barreno, Maria Teresa Horta, and Maria Velho da Costa. In this novel three writers with the names Maria, Mariana, and Mariane write a series of letters to the imaginary Mariana, an obscure Portuguese nun whose love letters written from a convent were published

183

anonymously in French in 1669 with the title *Letters of a Portuguese Nun.*

Like *New Portuguese Letters, Lettere a Marina* is a series of love letters written between women, and is concerned with the inscription of the woman in the text. As Linda Kauffman points out, the criticism surrounding the publication of the original *Portuguese Letters* was concerned with proving the identity of the nun and the authenticity of the letters – with issues of authority and authorship, with "giving the text a father" (Kauffman 1986: 283). The writers of *New Portuguese Letters* aim to reconstruct the passion of the nun. They see their writing as a "process of restoration and recuperation: what they reinscribe is the woman in the text" (Kauffman 1986: 283).

Once the similarities have been pointed out, the differences are much easier to note. As Tzvetan Todorov observes, each contribution to a genre is not merely a repetition of what has gone before: "The work of art [. . .] always involves a transforming element" (Todorov 1977: 186). Both *New Portuguese Letters* and *Lettere a Marina* have a similar form and similar aims. The innovation in *Lettere a Marina* is that the discourse of desire is inscribed within a relationship between a mother and a daughter; the relationship between women that is the basis of the formation of the female identity.

Dacia Maraini believes that one of the reasons for the continuation of women's oppression is the absence of any representation in our patriarchal culture of a relationship between women. In her essay "Proserpina divisa fra madre e marito" [Proserpina divided between mother and husband] (Maraini 1987), she writes of the myth of Demeter and Persephone, the only story of the relationship between women to have survived in patriarchal culture. In this essay she relates the myth of Persephone, whose abduction forced her to spend her life alternating between the rich fertile kingdom of her mother and the dangerous fiery one of the bridegroom, to the perpetual situation of women, obliged to spend their lives insanely divided between the world of women and the world of men. She believes this unenviable position can be alleviated only by the reforging of the lost bonds between mother and daughter, between woman and woman. She writes, quoting Adrienne Rich:

> Il vecchio amore materno istituzionalizzato fatto di paure e di sacrifici non basta. Occorre un amore coraggioso, rifiutarsi di essere vittime [. . .] fino a che non esisterà un forte filo ininterrotto di amore,

approvazione ed esempio, da madre a figlia, da donna a donna, di generazione in generazione, le donne continueranno a vagare solitarie in un territorio ostile. (Maraini 1987: 87)

[The old institutionalized "mother love" made of fears and sacrifices is not enough. What is needed is a courageous love, the refusal on the part of women to be victims [. . .] until a strong uninterrupted line of love, approval, and example stretches from mother to daughter, from woman to woman, across the generations, women will still be wandering alone in hostile territory.]

The possibility of an important relationship between mother and daughter was the surprising discovery of Freud, whose theory of an individual identity development for both male and female, through the Oedipal conflict and adult heterosexual desire, was later challenged by his own discovery of the pre-Oedipal phase with its strong maternal attachment. This discovery of the possibility of the primacy of a mother over a husband or lover and of early childhood over maturity was for Freud like the surprise of "the discovery of the Minoan-Mycenean civilization behind the civilization of Greece."[1]

Subsequent feminist scholarship in the psychoanalytical field has sought to establish the pattern of female identity development through a study of the nature and influence of the relationship between mother and daughter. In her article "Missing Mothers/Desiring Daughters," Naomi Scheman explains that relationships are learned initially, for both male and female, from the child's original attachment to the mother. The mother is the object of the child's desire and the source of its pleasure. However, as part of taking her place in a social structure dominated by male values, the female child is required to forego what it has learned in the original attachment and replace it with an attachment to the father. Although Scheman has found, as yet, no satisfactory explanation for such a shift, she focuses on this area, believing it to be at the very center of the female problem. She comments: "The girl's attachment to her father is positively necessary in establishing her heterosexuality by breaking her attachment to her mother beyond recollection" (Scheman 1988: 69). As a result of making this shift, the female learns to repress all knowledge of her origins in a maternal tradition and to forego active desire. Her desire becomes passive and remains in fantasy, where its fulfillment

1. Sigmund Freud, "Female Sexuality" (1931), quoted in Hirsch (1981: 68).

185

requires another's fantasized activity. To thus fantasize the satisfaction of passive desire is to fantasize being the object of
another's active desire. As Scheman explains it, "[h]er desire is
more or less on demand. Like Sleeping Beauty she awakens to
the man who lays claim to her" (Scheman 1988: 71).

Dacia Maraini's novel, *Lettere a Marina*, discusses these problems of female development, the missing knowledge of origins
in the maternal and the learned passivity of female desire. The
novel takes the form of a series of letters addressed to Marina
from another woman. In these letters the writer records their
meeting, the development of the relationship and the parallel
development of her awareness of herself as woman. The personal development of the writer seems to solve the problem as
outlined by Naomi Scheman, that of the missing origins in the
maternal and the passivity of female desire.

At the beginning of the letters the writer has no knowledge
of her origins in the maternal; no knowledge of a time prior to
her entry into the male-dominated social structure when existence was governed by a relationship with another female. She
has no female genealogy and history. Hers is the universal
female experience of having the female "story" constructed and
passed on by fathers to daughters. As she writes to Marina at the
beginning of the novel, "Tu amavi una donna senza storia nata
ogni giorno dalla pancia buia del tempo nuda e nuova per te"
(Maraini 1981: 5)[2] [You loved a woman without a history a
woman born each day out of the dark belly of time completely
fresh for you]. The writer's name the reader later learns is Bianca, a name that suggests the whiteness of blank paper awaiting
the story, the carte blanche.

Absence often is marked by a gap or circle, a zero. In the letters the absence of knowledge of maternal origins is represented by the circle traced by the path of the letters from writer to
Marina. The two women share similarities. At the beginning of
the novel the writer's move to the solitary apartment is reproduced by the solitariness of Marina in her own apartment. The
two women seem to reflect each other. The projected path of
the letters between the women traces a sterile circle from writer
to reader and back to the writer, who, at the end of the novel,
takes the letters to read on the train. There is no progression:

2. All textual references are to the 1981 edition of the novel. All translations
of the passages quoted are my own.

the desire expressed in the letters is never projected to an out-side, it remains in an interior as in fantasy.

The desire of the two women is unable to reach outside because the idea of the mother, of an origin of a female tradi-tion and recipient of a female desire, is not represented in the patriarchal structure, where to desire a woman or to desire like a woman is unknown. Here female desire and a maternal tradi-tion have been channelled into the institution of motherhood. The bad mothering given to daughters by this institutionalized motherhood is expressed by Adrienne Rich:

> Few women growing up in a patriarchal society can feel mothered enough; the power of our mothers, whatever their love for us and their struggles on our behalf, is too restricted. And it is the mother through whom patriarchy early teaches the small female her proper expectations. The anxious pressure of one female on another to conform to a degrading and dispiriting role can hardly be termed "mothering," even if she does this believing it will help her daughter to survive. (Rich 1977: 246)

The roles of the two women at the beginning of the letters prevent the forging of a strong link between them based on the recognition of a common maternal origin and a desire that is active. The novel begins from the roles of mother and daughter that patriarchy has constructed for women to play. Bianca is alone and escaping from the bad relationship that these roles produce. In the opening letter she writes, "Sono qui in questo brutto appartamento finalmente sola il collo che mi fa male – lì dove hai piantato i tuoi denti di figlia" (5) [I'm here in this drab apartment alone at last my neck hurting there where like a daughter you planted your teeth]. And later, "Scappo per il tuo testardo e malandrino desiderio di farmi madre contro ogni mia voglia e madre cattiva rovinosa" (7) [I'm running away from your stubborn wicked wish to make me a mother against my every wish, a bad, destructive mother].

Bad mothering, Maraini suggests, is both a lack of knowledge about genuine female experience and a preference for a view of the world through a masculine frame. The writer's escape to the apartment is also an escape from a son. Her favoring of mas-culinity had caused a kind of internal erosion; favoring that is like having a stillborn son eternally dangling in the womb. Her experience of preferring passivity – of preferring to live her life attached to masculine activity – is presented in the novel as an emphasis on male activity. All the male characters are described

187

in terms that focus on physical fitness. The writer's father is "il mio biondo padre sfuggente atleta" (23) [my athlete father, fair and fleeing], her lover Marco, "Quel corpo di atleta quel petto largo e roccioso" (28) [that athlete's body that great rocklike chest], and her stillborn son "Aveva i muscoli di un nuotatore era un atleta" (16) [He had the muscles of a swimmer he was an athlete].

Activity for the writer of the letters is attached to masculine activity and occurs only in the interior world of memories and dreams. She remembers her childhood journeys with her father: "Mi portava con lui in montagna con lui al mare con lui nei fiumi a nuotare ad acchiappare girini con lui in motocicletta con lui in treno" (49) [He used to take me with him to the mountains with him to the seaside with him to swim in the rivers to catch tadpoles with him on the motorbike with him on the train]. She daydreams of moving with her stillborn son, "avremmo camminato insieme io gonfia e goffa con quel figlio dolcissimo e amatissimo che aveva scelto di restare eternamente chiuso dentro di me rinunciando ai giochi al mondo" (17) [we would have walked together, I swollen and ungainly, with that sweetest beloved son who had chosen to stay closed inside me for eternity giving up games, the world].

From the static position of feminine passivity the writer has had to experience movement as multiplicity and sameness. The writer's memories of movement with her father are memories of various journeys to visit his female lovers, as when she remembers being taken on his motorcycle to visit a current lover, a lady with her hair wrapped in a scarf (154). The amorous adventures of her father extend into those of the husband, Angelo, with "le sue fughe le sue avventure i suoi tradimenti le sue seduzioni la sua tenerezza la sua incostanza" (103) [his flights his adventures his betrayals his seductions his tenderness his fickleness]. It is a pattern repeated by the other male characters of the novel. The writer's first lover, Marco, made love to Bruna for eight months before he told Bianca about it. Her brother Teodoro, like her lover Damiano, is able to love two women at the same time. She is asked of Damiano: "Ma come può amare nello stesso tempo me e lei? chiedeva aggrondata. E' quello che mi ero chiesta anch'io a suo tempo con Marco con la stessa aria stupita e persa. Come si può amare due persone allo stesso tempo?" (193) [But how can he love her and me at the same time? she was asking me frowning. It is what

I too had asked myself at the time with Marco with the same stunned and lost air. How can you love two people at the same time?]

In *Lettere a Marina*, Dacia Maraini suggests that a remembered desire between women is able to recreate the conditions of the active desire present in the daughter's original attachment to the mother. As a memory, active desire exists in fantasy, in the interior space where female desire is kept repressed. In the love letter tradition the function of the letter is to recreate an absent desire. Desire can exist in a letter where distance or disinclination on the part of a lover would make it impossible (Altman 1982: 14). Writing the letters creates a distance between the desire and the act of writing. It allows a space for the recreation of the relationship. The act of remembering a past relationship between the two women through the letters becomes therapeutic. Although activity obviously was present in the past relationship between the women, their social conditioning as peripheral beings would not necessarily permit them to recognize it as such. As the writer comments in the very first letter, "bisogna che ti racconti fin dal principio la nostra storia perché te la sei dimenticata. E forse io stessa l'ho dimenticata" (5) [I have to tell you our story from the beginning because you have forgotten it. And perhaps I myself have forgotten it too]. The act of recording the relationship on the written page as it is remembered is an act of restoration.

Initially, the subject of the desire is Marina, the addressee of the letters. The ability to be active is Marina's chief characteristic. The writer records that the first thing she noticed about Marina was her feet. She recalls their first meeting: "Portavi i sandali avevi le dita dei piedi abbronzate. Che dita grassocce da bambina tozze e larghe come le foglie gonfie e spinose di un cactus ho pensato." (12) [You were wearing sandals and your toes were tanned. What plump childlike toes, I thought, short and thick like the thorny swollen leaves of a cactus.]

From an initial passive position Bianca records experiencing herself as the object of Marina's active desire. She recalls recognizing Marina's desire to possess her at their first meeting at the home of Alda and Bice. "C'era già violenza nel tuo sguardo: una volontà delicata e ritrosa allegrissima di possesso" (11) [There was already violence in your look: a fragile shy determination giddy for possession].

As the relationship develops, however, Bianca is able to initi-

189

ate the desire herself. She remembers a night they spent together at Fiammetta's house:

> Faceva freddo ma ciascuna se ne stava dalla sua parte senza toccarsi.
> Avevamo spento la luce. Tu parlavi di qualcosa che non ricordo. Io
> ti rispondevo pensando ad altro. Avevo sonno. Ero intrigata da te. E
> un pensiero vagante come un serpentello voglioso mi girava nelle
> viscere il pensiero di sedurti di cominciare io il gioco. (31–32)

> [It was cold but we each lay on our side without touching. We had
> turned out the light. You were saying something I don't remember
> what. I was replying thinking about something else. I was sleepy. But
> I was intrigued by you. And a thought wandering like a capricious
> snake twisted in the pit of my stomach the thought of seducing you
> of initiating the play myself.]

The intimacy between the two women carries with it a suggestion of incest, a term that applies to relationships that are forbidden under patriarchal law. The writer recalls how communication between women in her own family was like committing
incest. She says:

> Con mia sorella come con mia madre anche se le amo moltissimo
> non riesco a parlare. Dire qualcosa di me anche quando ero piccola
> era come fare incesto. L'intimità con loro appena aprivo un varco al
> silenzio rischiava di diventare carnale, atroce. (35)

> [With my sister as with my mother even if I love them very much I
> never manage to talk. To say something about myself even when I
> was small was like committing incest. As soon as I opened a crack in
> the silence intimacy with them ran the risk of becoming carnal, atro-
> cious.]

The prohibitions enforced by the incest taboos are precisely those
that have been designed to prevent any contamination of the family unit that privileges masculinity. Claude Lévi-Strauss describes
these taboos as existing to enforce the gift of women to others. He
comments: "The prohibition of incest is less a rule prohibiting
marriage with the mother, sister, or daughter, than a rule obliging
the mother, sister, or daughter to be given to others." [3]

The taboos, therefore, that direct the women into relationships with others work to eliminate any developing relationship
between the women themselves. As the literary critic Peggy
Kamuf sees it:

---

3. Claude Lévi-Strauss, *The Elementary Structures of Kinship* (1949), quoted in
Herman (1981: 50).

Women must circulate and must not cause to circulate. [. . .] Feminine culpability is the inevitable support of this circulation order, since a transgression of the passive, intransitive female position is structurally homologous to a transgression of the incest prohibition, and therefore the grounds for that culpability can shift: to desire the father or to desire like the father are mutually reinforcing of the feminine exclusion. (Kamuf 1982: 50)

Intimacy between the two women in *Lettere a Marina* goes past the heterosexual limits imposed by the family to expose an incestuous relationship between women.

The novel suggests that the relationship between Bianca and Marina is at the level of the mother and child symbiosis before the child has received the conditioning of culture and knowledge of the cultural taboos. Of their relationship Bianca writes:

Posso bere il tuo latte? Ti sei accucciata fra le mie braccia e hai preso a succhiarmi il seno. Era il gioco della mamma e della figlia. Dicevi che era un latte buonissimo denso e dolce e sembrava che inghiottissi davvero. Come il latte condensato Nestlè sai ma più buono dicevi. E io ti carezzavo i capelli come si carezzano a una neonata. (53)

[Can I drink your milk? You snuggled up in my arms and started sucking my breast. It was the game of mothers and daughters. You used to say it was very good milk thick and sweet and it seemed as if you really drank it down. Like Nestle's condensed milk but much better you said. And I stroked your hair just as you would stroke that of a newborn baby girl.]

Institutionalized motherhood does not allow for this kind of fluid nurturing relationship between women. Luce Irigaray describes institutionalized mothering as "smothering" when she writes: "With your milk, Mother, I swallowed ice. And here I am now, my insides frozen. And I walk with even more difficulty than you do, and I move even less" (Irigaray 1981: 60). Beyond the cultural taboos the two women experience a different kind of mother-daughter relationship. On the other side of the incest prohibition, in the area still governed by the mother-child symbiosis, the two women are beyond the identities fixed for them by the social body. In this recreated amniotic environment Bianca is able to experience her own loss of identity, the excess of her being that had never been contained by her social roles. The energizing of this previously inert part of her self is visualized in a dream as fire. As Marina interprets the dream to her:

La casa che brucia è il tuo desiderio di modificazione . . . c'è qualcosa nei tuoi rapporti famigliari che si disgrega diventa irriconosci-
bile e tu dai fuoco alla parte opaca e inerte di te in modo da essere
costretta a partire a cambiare . . . (54)

[The burning house is your wish to change . . . there is something in
your intimate relationships that is breaking up becoming unrecognizable and you set fire to that veiled inert part of yourself so that
you are forced to leave to start changing . . .]

Julia Kristeva places the fluidity of the mother-child relationship in her concept of the semiotic or mode of human development that exists prior to the social contract. As she sees it, during the formation of identity "[d]iscrete quantities of energy
traverse the body, later to be a subject, and, in the course of this
becoming, arrange themselves according to the constraints
imposed on this ever semiotizing body by the familial and social
structure" (Kristeva 1975: 21). Under these terms, the semiotic
is the place of the coexistence and that which is not identity –
identity and its excess. The receptacle or container of the semiotic Kristeva describes by the term *chora*, a term she has borrowed from Plato, which is able to indicate both the repression
of all that is not included in the social construction of identity
and the difficulty of representing what is itself prior to representation (Kristeva 1975: 21).

The closed circle traced by the passage of the letters between
the two women reproduces the Kristeva *chora*, or container of
that which is repressed by culture. The passage is sterile, without progress, because the contents have no interpretation in
the outside social group.

The relationship between the two women takes place inside
this circle, within an area that is both outside culture and yet
interior to it. Kristeva suggests that within this area a female is
able to make contact with a maternal tradition, a tradition that
was left out of the formation of her identity by the male-dominated social structure. As Josette Féral explains it: "Without a
specularization to afford her an identity and freeze her, she possesses a 'spasmodic force' (Kristeva's expression) which links
her to the mother's body and to pleasure. This is an a-symbolic
force which allows the subject to renew the bonds with what is
repressed within her, with the repressed that is always the mother" (Féral 1978: 10).

The writer of the letters records how her seduction of Marina
brought her face to face with the maternal tradition, the moth-

er, when she says she found: "Una me stessa fonda e buia che non conosco e forse non voglio conoscere. Mia madre mi guarda dall'interno di quel buio dissacrato con due occhi ciechi disperati e io sono sconvolta da una apprensione violenta che mi chiude i sensi" (32). [Myself a deep dark self that I don't know and perhaps I do not want to know. My mother looks at me from inside that desecrated darkness with two desperate blind eyes and I am thrown into confusion by a great anxiety that freezes my senses.]

Marina is the energizing force that permits Bianca to reconnect with her origins in the maternal. Bianca sees fragments of her own life represented by Marina. Thus, seeing her own representation in an exterior, she is able to see also that which has been left out of this representation. The overlapping of the two lives is represented in the novel as seduction. In another context Roland Barthes has described the overlapping of lives as the erotic practice of language, a practice that takes place "whenever the *literary* Text (the Book) transmigrates into our life, whenever another writing (the Other's writing) succeeds in writing fragments of our own daily lives."[4] In the letters, Marina acts as the text that permits Bianca to read fragments of her other experience; the excess in her socially constructed identity.

For Bianca, the situation of having her own life reflected back to her by Marina is like having Marina inside her own mind. Here she is seen performing a balancing act like Bianca herself or any woman in the male-dominated social structure, who is obliged to spend her life insanely divided between the world of women and the world of men. Bianca writes:

Sei la persona che vedo seduta pericolosamente in bilico nella mia testa. Vedo la tua faccia che si sporge; gli occhi bruni liquidi quella peluria morbida e nerissima che getta ombre sensuali sulle labbra. La cosa più antica di te: fa pensare a gonne lunghe nere di paese a dolci fatti col miele e il grano a piedi deformati dentro scarpe di cuoio duro a odore di incenso e caciocavallo al pepe qualcosa che muore senza morire . . . la madre della madre della madre della madre di mia madre che apre la porta su un fondo buio. C'è Concetta? Ora viene. (110–111)

[You are the person I see sitting dangerously balanced in my head. I see your face standing out: the brown liquid eyes that dark soft down that throws a sensuous shadow over your lips. The most

---

4. Roland Barthes, quoted in Kauffman (1986: 285).

ancient thing about you: it makes you think of long black country skirts and sweets made from honey and corn of deformed feet inside hard leather shoes of the smell of incense and caciocavallo cheese with pepper something that dies without dying . . . the mother of the mother of the mother of the mother of my mother who opens the door onto a dark bottom. Is Concetta there? She's just coming.]

Because Bianca's awareness of her maternal origins comes through Marina, Marina is portrayed as a force, one that seems to precede Bianca toward an understanding of the female condition. "Marina se riesco a finire questo maledetto romanzo lo devo a te alla tua spinosa provocazione ai tuoi piedi cactus che mi hanno preceduto sulla strada della comprensione e dell'allegria" (181) [Marina if I manage to finish this damn book I'll owe it to you and your thorny provocation your cactus feet that preceded me on the path of understanding and "jouissance"]. The activity suggested by Marina's feet is one that takes place inside, a mental activity, which, like the pain from the prick of a thorn, is located internally. Marina provides Bianca with the necessary stimulation to advance along the road of self understanding. Marina's feet are "piedi cactus" [cactus feet], Bianca is able to feel pain from those feet. She dreams, "proprio come un cactus avevi delle spine così sottili e chiare da essere invisibili. Ma sulla pelle delle dita davano più dolore di un ago" (118) [Just like a cactus you had thorns so transparent and fine they were almost invisible. But in the skin of my toes they were more painful than a needle].

As a mental force, it is appropriate that Marina makes her initial appearance in the novel as the writer's "daughter." Within the cultural system that privileges paternity, a woman's "mothering" is often her only recourse to an alternative tradition. As Naomi Scheman puts it:

The message to a woman is clear: within the systems of male privilege neither her appropriately feminine sexual identity nor her ability to assume public power is compatible with her being her mother's daughter. (What is, of course, compatible with her having been mothered is her mothering [. . .]) (Scheman 1988: 73)

Mothering, or recourse to a maternal tradition, as Maraini sees it, is the capacity to begin life out of the excess, the capacity to take a nonorigin or absence as a point of departure. Tzvetan Todorov equates living with narrating and describes narrating as a means of addressing an absence when he says:

If we consider the narrative [. . .] not as enclosing other narratives but as being enclosed by them, a curious property is revealed. Each narrative seems to have something excessive, a supplement which remains outside the closed form produced by the development of the plot. At the same time, and for this very reason, this something more, proper to the narrative, is also something less. The supplement is also a lack; in order to supply this lack created by the supplement, another narrative is necessary. (Todorov 1977: 76)

In experiencing herself also as an excess of that which is reflected back to her in the experiences of other women, Bianca is able to "mother" a whole genealogy of female relationships. She recognizes in the experiences of Rosalia, Roberta, her own mother, and others the turning away of the female from her own needs and desires and the naming of the needs and desires of others as her own. Rosalia was seduced as a child by her uncle, and now works as a waitress to support an invalid husband and four children. Bianca sees her mother as unable to shift from a favoring of masculinity, of the "gambe padrone" [master's legs] rather than the "sesso sotterraneo" [underground sex] (114); a favoring that leads to an acceptance of definition by others in the male-dominated social structure, rather than to a definition that originates from the self. In recognizing in these fragments of the lives of others parts of her own female experience, Bianca then is able to separate from them and create something new out of the excess of these experiences. She sees her mother's experience separating from her own as if she were "mothering" her own mother: "Credo che la prima figlia prima ancora di Roberta sia stata mia madre più ingenua e arresa di me alle cose come quella stella lustra e rosata che io contemplavo a lungo la notte quando non riuscivo a dormire e dicevo che era nata dal mio ventre" (77). [I think the first daughter even before Roberta was my mother more naive about things than I was like that bright rosy star I used to look at through the night when I couldn't sleep and I used to say that it was born out of my stomach.]

Female self-creation as genealogy is expressed by Hélène Cixous when she comments:

When a woman writes in nonrepression she passes on her others, her abundance of non-ego/s in a way that destroys the form of the family structure, so that it is defamilialized, can no longer be thought in terms of the attribution of roles within a social cell: what takes place is an endless circulation of desire from one body to

195

another, above and across sexual difference, outside those relations of power and regeneration constituted by the family. (Cixous 1981: 53)

At the end of the novel Bianca takes the letters to read on the train as she journeys to the house of her friend Fiammetta. Fiammetta, as her name suggests, is not dependent on definition by the social structure but creates her own life out of the excess. Her name links her to the burning house in Bianca's dream, which was interpreted as the burning of the inert part of herself. Energized from her own excess, Fiammetta was able to halt the process of the favoring of masculine activity. When Fiammetta terminated her relationship with Valerio for a relationship with a woman, Valerio fell from the window and broke both his legs.

Bianca's decision to take the letters with her to read on the train represents both her awareness of the immobility imposed on female experience by the exterior social structure, and, at the same time, a resolution to exceed this immobility. The letters never reach a destination. The sterile circle of their passage, from writer to reader and back to writer, inscribes the terms of immobility given to female experience by the social structure. Yet Bianca's decision to take the letters with her on the train gives her the opportunity of escaping this immobility.

The awareness that her experience is immobilized and the decision to escape are brought about by the close relationship between women that is remembered in the letters. This relationship recreates the conditions of the original relationship between women; conditions of fluidity and the simultaneous presence of two like bodies as it is experienced between females in pregnancy, childbirth, and lactation. In these recreated conditions female desire is activated and its passage is permitted to an exterior. From the recognition of her own likeness reflected back from an exterior by Marina, Bianca learns that she is also something more than this likeness; she learns that she has an excess that has never been represented in the exterior patriarchal social structure.

The inscription of women's excess experience establishes the female genealogy. The close relationship between the two women in *Lettere a Marina*, extended by correspondences of likeness and its excess to other women and generations of women, creates that "strong uninterrupted line of love, approval and example" (Rich 1977: 246), the forging of which often has been hampered by the cultural demands of mother-hood. Just such an extension is made by the linking of the names Marina, Maraini, Maria, and Mariana, which suggests likeness but also an excess to that likeness. Like the three Marias of the *New Portuguese Letters,* who created correspon-dence with the original Portuguese Mariana and inscribed that which had been in excess to the original manuscript, the woman in the text, in *Lettere a Marina* Maraini extends the cor-respondence one step further. Maraini's achievement in this novel is the inscription of the woman in the text in the recreat-ed conditions of female development.

THIRTEEN

Violence Against Women and the Response of Italian Institutions

TINA LAGÓSTENA BASSI[1]

I. Chronicle of Two Deaths Announced

Pierina Lopez and Bruna Odinotte met their deaths because of a failure to respond on the part of the institutions. Pierina, a forty-six-year-old factory worker, applied to the Tribunale Civile for a separation order against her husband. For more than twenty years she had endured the bullying and the physical and psychological violence that he had inflicted on her and their children. In March 1986 the presiding judge of the Rome Tribunale Civile assigned her the marital home and ordered that the husband leave within the month. The husband complied with the order but subsequently obtained from the Rome Pretore[2] an order restoring his right to reside there because his wife had not yet initiated proceedings against him. Accompanied by the police, the husband returned to the conjugal abode and stayed there undisturbed until 15 February, despite the petitions and appeals that the wife made to the court. All she was able to obtain was the confirmation of 15 February as the date by which he was to leave the house for good. However, on the morning of that day, he cut her throat with a kitchen knife and flung himself from the fourth floor.

Bruna Odinotte was fifteen when she married Mario D'Onofrio, an office worker ten years her senior. Twelve years after their marriage, Bruna died in the Villa Azzurra hospital in

---

1. *Translator's notes are in italics. Where there is no exact correspondence between the Italian and the American or British legal systems, the Italian term is retained in the text and is explained in a footnote.*

2. *The Tribunale Civile consists of three magistrates who pass judgment in civil cases that involve sums greater than five million lire . It also acts as a court of appeal for cases heard in the first instance by the Pretore. The Pretore passes judgment in civil cases involving sums of money less than five million lire .*

Terracina. Subsequent to an official complaint that her father made to the authorities, the husband was charged and tried before the Latina Corte d'Assise[3] "for having maltreated his wife with constant threats, blows, and other bodily harm that had resulted in her death." During the trial all the neighbors gave evidence against the husband and confirmed that he had been in the habit of beating his wife.

Why had the police not intervened? The reason emerges from the evidence that one of the neighbors gave at the trial: "I went to the police more than ten times but I achieved nothing." No one, in fact, helped Bruna to lodge a complaint against her husband. Degraded as a person by the violence she had suffered, Bruna sought oblivion in drink. The husband was thus able to maintain during the trial that he had hit her because she drank. According to the defense, this husband/boss[4] only committed the crime of "misuse of means of correction" but on this point the court determined that "for such an offense to be committed, it is a necessary condition that the action carried out by the accused exceed the limits of a power to correct or discipline that is actually invested in him or her regarding the injured party. A husband has no such correctional or disciplinary power over his wife." In the judgment of the court, D'Onofrio was guilty of the crime of maltreatment, but the judges in the first instance concluded that it had not been proved that Bruna's death was the result of her husband's ferocious cruelty. Four years in prison was deemed a fair sentence. However, this sentence was considered too severe by the judges of the Rome Corte d' Assise, who, in handing down their judgment on 4 November 1985, determined that a "punishment more suited to the real severity of the crime was three years' imprisonment."

It seemed appropriate to begin this short essay by telling the story of these two women killed by their husbands' violence because the cases highlight the response of the institutions or, rather, because they highlight the fact that all too often there is no response at all to the numerous women who request help to

3. *The Corte d'Assise tries crimes of violence and crimes against the state.*

4. *Here as elsewhere in her essay, the writer alludes to the title of Gavino Ledda's autobiographical novel* Padre padrone *(literally, Father/Boss), in which he describes his harsh upbringing. Thanks to the success of both the book and the film version directed by the Taviani brothers, the title has entered common Italian parlance.*

put an end to situations of extreme violence. In the tragic story of Bruna Odinotte, no one intervened because the husband's conduct was fragmented into individual episodes of blows, insults, and injuries that were actionable only on receipt of an official complaint. However, in this particular case, the judicial authorities themselves could have initiated proceedings because the husband's conduct presented a *prima facie* (self-evident) case of the more serious crime of maltreatment.

Coppi (1988) writes that the *mens rea* (criminal intent) of the crime of maltreatment is both a representation of the present and of the future and memory of the past in an encompassing awareness of the kind of life imposed on the passive party. According to jurisprudence, "the crime of maltreatment within the family is constituted by habitual conduct manifesting itself in a series of actions performed over a period of time but linked by their habituality and bound together by a single criminal intention of doing harm to the physical integrity and human dignity of the passive party."[5] Further, "the psychological element that characterizes the crime of maltreatment is a single and uniform *mens rea* that comports a serious intention to humiliate and bully the victim and that is the thread uniting the individual acts of aggression, physical or psychological, against the passive party."[6] It is precisely the fact that the psychological element is fragmented by being considered in relation to each individual act of violence that explains the reluctance of jurisprudence to recognize the crime detailed in Article 572 of the Penal Code on the grounds that the "intention to commit the specific crime in all its presuppositions and constituent elements"[7] is not present.

This attitude is exemplified well in the judgment handed down by the Foggia Corte d' Assise in the following tragic case. Pietro Candelini was charged with having caused the death of his four-year-old son and with having attempted to kill his wife, their other son, and his parents-in-law to prevent his wife from putting into effect her decision to leave the conjugal house after years of maltreatment. The court acquitted the accused on the following grounds:

5. Judgment no. 803, Corte di Cassazione, Section 6 (29 January 1983). *The Corte di Cassazione, consisting of a panel of five judges, determines if the law has been applied correctly in the decisions of lower courts.*

6. Judgment no. 1451, Corte di Cassazione, Section 6 (16 February 1983).

7. Judgment no. 2364, Corte di Cassazione, Section 6 (18 March 1983).

"As is known, Article 572 of the Penal Code punishes the person who maltreats a member of his or her family for purposes other than those of correction and discipline. The law exists in the general interest so as to protect the family against the excesses that the offender may commit within the family because his or her overbearing behavior, uncontrolled irritability, and contemptible tendency to bully result in heinous persecution and constant physical and psychological aggression, which subject the passive party to a life of particular pain and torment. It is evident, therefore, that mere quarrels and acts of loutishness do not in themselves constitute maltreatment. The male's preeminent role in the family and his authority over its other members is a normal, accepted fact and cannot in itself constitute maltreatment. Bearing firmly in mind the notion of the relativity of maltreatment, one should note further that there must be the habitual repetition of acts willed by the accused that have the sole aim of maliciously carrying out actions that physically and/or psychologically degrade the victim."

Basing its argument on the sentences regarding jurisprudence referred to earlier, the Foggia Corte d' Assise reaffirmed that "maltreatment is characterized by a plurality of acts, each of them representing an element in the series but linked by the fact of being habitual and unified by a single criminal intention of harming the physical integrity and the human dignity of the injured party." The judges found that Candelini had maltreated his wife, but that there was no *mens rea*, in that he had acted not out of hatred but out of "jealousy [. . .] which is an aspect of love." The court also found that, as Candelini's behavior was not open to the charge of maltreatment, his wife's decision to leave the conjugal dwelling along with her children to live elsewhere while awaiting a court separation order was manifestly unjust and contrary to the most basic standards of civilized behavior. Accordingly, as the injured parties had behaved "illicitly," the court allowed the mitigating circumstance of provocation. The grounds for this were that "the conduct of the wife [who had decided to put an end to the marriage] constitutes an open act of lack of respect, scorn, and insolent arrogance toward the accused. Such conduct adds a further element to an action objectively wrong in that it had no internal or external justification. Hence the angry reaction on the part of Candelini."[8] The court accordingly acquitted Candelini of the charge of maltreatment and deemed that the mitigating circumstances

8. This quotation and prior quotations from the Candelini case come from the judgment by the Foggia Corte d'Assise (30 May 1986).

outweighed the alleged aggravating circumstances. Candelini was sentenced to twelve years' imprisonment. In reviewing the case, the Bari Appeal Corte d'Assise reexamined the evidence and found Candelini guilty of the manslaughter of his son. As a result his sentence was reduced to four years in prison. To conclude this story, it should be added that the accused, who was found guilty of having killed his son to prevent his wife from leaving, had asked to be granted the mitigating circumstance that he had acted for "reasons of particular moral and social worth."[9]

Mercifully, Italian courts have not always responded so negatively. The Velletri Tribunale imposed a sentence of twelve years' imprisonment and three years' parole on a father not only for the crime of raping his daughter but also for the crime of maltreatment. Prudenzio Ricci began raping his daughter V. when she was only nine and continued raping her until, at the age of fifteen, she found the strength to rebel and to report her father. The court gave the following grounds for its findings: "[T]here is the further crime of maltreatment and here it must be emphasized that the father, by forcing his daughter from the time she was a child to have sexual relations with him, with the frequency and in the ways that have been indicated, caused in her an overwhelming trauma. Further, by continuing to abuse her sexually, by aiming at exclusive and total possession of her, by preventing her from having contacts with others, by isolating, blackmailing, and threatening her whenever this was necessary in order to maintain his absolute power over her, he caused in her enormous conflicts and reduced her life to an existence of tension and suffering. The girl wanted to confide in someone but could not as she was paralyzed by the fear both of the scandal and of upsetting her precarious relationship with her mother, who was already sorely tried by her husband's aggressive behavior. As the daughter grew up, she came to realize how monstrous such a relationship was and how crazy such an existence was, but her terror would not let her free herself from her state of submission. Obviously, in such a situation, for which her father was solely responsible, her life could be only a daily hell of constant suffering."[10]

9. Judgment by the Bari Corte d'Assise d'Appello (10 February 1987).

10. Judgment by the Velletri Tribunale (17 June 1988). *The Tribunale, consisting of three judges, passes judgment on crimes that exceed the jurisdiction of the Pretore but do not come under the jurisdiction of the Corte d'Assise.*

II. Family Violence: A Private Matter

According to figures supplied by the Italian Bureau of Statistics, the most dangerous job in the world and one that every year causes more injuries than accidents on the roads or in the workplace is not being a test driver or an acrobat or a factory worker, but being a housewife. Every day women who work at home report to hospitals with injuries requiring treatment, stitches, or a plaster cast. Why? They have fallen and bumped into a door handle, or they have tumbled down the stairs, or they have slipped on a wet bathroom floor, or they have accidentally cut themselves with a sharp knife. These are the reasons given; they are not in the least believable, and yet they are accepted by the police and doctors without further inquiry. The figures for 1986 show that in Italy there were more than 800,000 accidents in the home, of which 83.34 percent were due to people or objects falling. More than half these accidents are the result of maltreatment and violence suffered by women and children in the home. This is the violent reality to which medical institutions offer no response. Casualty staff not only pretend to believe that the "patient" has had an accident at home, even when she has cigarette burns and stab wounds, but if a woman actually says she has been beaten by her husband, she is often talked out of making a report so as "not to ruin the poor guy." Usually this is also the "response" of the police.

The response of the courts, on the rare occasions when the woman manages to lodge a complaint, is more complex. A stir was created by the unusual severity of the sentence imposed by the Pretore of Castelfranco Veneto, who jailed a violent husband for two years. What usually happens is that the Pretore imposes a fine or the minimum prison sentence, which invariably is suspended.

III. The Petition on Sexual Violence[11]

In 1978 the Women's Liberation Movement carried out a survey based on three thousand questionnaires. From the answers given it emerged that 47.5 percent of the respondents had been subjected to physical violence and 8.7 percent to torture; of these women 4.5 percent did not report this abuse because they

---

11. *Strictly speaking, the proposed changes were presented in the form of a parliamentary bill. The Italian constitution requires that such bills drafted by members of the public must be discussed if more than 50,000 people petition for it* .

considered it normal to be subjected to violence from one's husband; 4.0 percent put up with it for the sake of the children; and 18.6 percent hoped for an improvement in the situation within the family. On the basis of these figures, the Women's Liberation Movement proposed a new law relating to crimes of both sexual and domestic violence. In particular, the women proposed changes to Article 571 (misuse of the means of correction or discipline) and Article 582 (bodily harm). In addition to these proposed changes to the legislation, they requested that the penalties be made more severe and that the authorities be empowered to initiate proceedings so that women would not find themselves in the position of having to ask for their husbands to be punished by lodging a complaint. The response from parliament was once again negative. The section dealing with domestic violence was excised and locked away in a drawer. Parliament limited the discussion to the section concerning crimes of sexual violence. The only change to the law was actually in the opposite direction: proceedings against the crime of personal injuries that heal within twenty days require a complaint from the injured party.[12]

IV. A Story of Maltreatment and Rape: The Miccadei Case

Ottorino Miccadei was the father/boss of a large family (eleven children) living in Rieti. Those who saw him outside the home environment, the police, and his workmates considered him a good father and a hard worker. Things were different in the home. He beat his eleven children, he beat his wife, and, when his daughters reached the age of twelve or thirteen, he began to rape them. He raped four of them. The fourth daughter became pregnant and was thirteen when she gave birth at home; she suffered a serious hemorrhage and was taken to hospital by her mother and a neighbor. The father/boss stayed at home with the newborn infant and the youngest daughter. When the hospital doctors realized they were dealing with a birth and not a miscarriage, they enquired about the baby. Miccadei's wife returned home to fetch the baby but he was not to be found. Miccadei had killed him and buried him in the cellar. It was only after this tragedy that the wife and daughters found the strength to report the father/boss, who was brought

---

12. Law no. 698 (24 November 1981), Article 91.

to trial before the Rome Corte d'Assise and charged with "infanticide for the sake of honor, rape of his daughters, maltreatment." The prosecutor, Nicolò Amato, successfully requested that the charge be changed to first degree murder. The court allowed the request on the following grounds: "It is absurd and contradictory to maintain that the accused acted to safeguard the honor of his daughter when he himself was responsible for dishonoring her. Moreover, the safeguarding of the honor of his relatives can have no sense for a man such as he who yielded to the lowest and foulest instincts and for years desecrated and profaned this daughter and repeatedly abused sexually his other daughters as soon as they reached puberty and blossomed into womanhood."

V. Father-Daughter Rape

The figures of the Bureau of Statistics show that in 1985 there were only fifteen reported cases of crimes of sexual violence involving children. The Italian Association for the Prevention of Cruelty to Children estimates that every year between 15,000 and 20,000 children are subjected to violence of one kind or another. The most common is the rape of the daughter by the father; the victims are usually ten or eleven years old and the fathers are usually between the ages of thirty-five and forty-five. In everyday parlance, sexual violence within the family is labelled simply incest. In the present criminal code, the crime of incest is dealt with in Article 564 of Section IX (crimes against the family), subsection II (crimes against family morality). The article reads: "Whoever commits incest, in such a way that public scandal is thereby created, with an ascendant or a descendant or with a relative linked by affinity in a direct line or with a brother or a sister, is punished with one to five years' imprisonment." The punishment is more severe (from two to eight years' imprisonment) in the case of a continuing incestuous relationship, or when incest is committed by an adult with a minor. The parent found guilty of incest automatically loses his or her parental authority.

Incest is defined properly as sexual relations between two people whose relationship by birth or by marriage constitutes an absolute impediment to marriage. In the Zanardelli Code,[13]

13. *During his second term of office as minister of justice (1887–1891), Zanardelli prepared a new code that remained in force until it was replaced by the Rocco Code (see note 14).*

incest was punished on the grounds of eugenics. The Rocco Code[14] makes incest punishable only insofar as the sexual act between those related by birth (or by marriage) is carried out in such a way as to create "public scandal." Indeed, "public scandal is an objective element of punishability, and, as such, must be considered independently of the intention of the guilty."[15] Further: "[T]he public scandal that Article 564 of the Penal Code makes a necessary condition of the crime of incest must manifest itself as a feeling of profound revulsion and disgust present in a certain number of people outside the family circle of those committing incest, such a feeling arising from knowledge of the incestuous relationship through the voluntary and actual heedlessness of the incestuous parties. Public scandal does not require that such conduct, be it flaunted or imprudently revealed, be manifested directly in public, as the incestuous relationship may become apparent from other manifestations, such as its material effects and public admission."[16]

In their proposal for a new law, the women asked for the abolition of this crime, which the existing code does not punish per se but only when it gives rise to public scandal. They rejected the hypocrisy underlying the way in which this law is formulated, and stressed that, when the incestuous relationship is forced on a person, it then becomes a crime of sexual violence.

VI. Rape in Marriage

Worthy of attention, in the pathology of the family as an institution, is rape committed within marriage against the wife. This is a submerged form of violence that rarely comes into the open because of the very small number of women who report it. According to the Italian constitution (Article 29) the basis of marriage is the equality of the spouses as citizens and as persons. However, it has taken almost thirty years for this general norm to become the actual law of the land. Law 151 of 1975 did introduce, albeit tardily, laws into the civil code that aim at achieving real equality between the spouses. What is difficult, however, is to change sociocultural values and centuries-old traditions. Even today, many people see marriage as a contract whereby the husband commits himself to supporting his wife in

14. *During his period as minister of justice (1925–1932), Rocco prepared a new penal code, much of which is still in force.*
15. Judgment by the Corte di Cassazione, Section 2 (15 October 1957).
16. Judgment by the Corte di Cassazione, Section 3 (17 March 1975).

return for housework and sex. At the moment of marriage, the wife, once and for all, gives her consent to the performance of the sexual act; it follows that the wife has an obligation to this "wifely duty" whenever the husband claims it. If the woman refuses, not only does she violate her matrimonial obligations, but the husband is entitled to force her to have sex. While it is true that, in terms of jurisprudence, the husband who uses violence or threats in order to have sex with his wife commits the crime of rape, it is equally true that very few women lodge complaints against their husbands for having committed this crime. A good example is the case of a wife, K. T., who reported her husband for having on the night of 5 July 1984 "committed actions that were aimed unequivocally at achieving sexual congress without her consent, hitting her, seizing her by the neck, and tearing off her underclothes." The Rome Tribunale, in examining whether a spouse may be said to have raped his wife, decided as follows: "It has been maintained that, if the crime is committed against one's wife, it is to be considered an impossible crime, in that the marital obligation must be considered as one of the rights and duties that derive from the matrimonial relationship. Such an approach is totally erroneous and arbitrary." It is important here to note that the very language used reveals a conception of the marital relationship as a form of ownership, which is in clear contradiction not only with specific laws such as Article 143 of the civil code, but above all with the constitution, Article 29, which recognizes the rights of the family as a natural partnership based on marriage, asserts the natural and legal equality of the spouses, and declares that such equality can be subjected to limitation only if and when its implementation jeopardizes the unity of the family (see judgment no. 126 by the Constitutional Court, 19 December 1968). In the opinion of the bench, "such a state of jeopardy and the possibility of limitation are to be excluded as regards sexual relations between spouses. The sexual relationship between husband and wife can be based only on the free and spontaneous consent of both parties."[17]

In 1976 a judgment of the Supreme Court already had clarified that Article 519 of the penal code was applicable to rape within marriage, such applicability being "in keeping both with the words of the law and with an interpretation of these words,

17. Judgment by the Rome Tribunale, Section 6 (28 June 1985).

consonant not only with the penal code in force, but also with the constitutional principles of the unconditional protection of human dignity and the guaranteeing of personal freedom, which includes the freedom to do what one wills sexually with one's body; it is, moreover, in keeping with the evolution of social mores, and with legislation that aims not only at raising the marital relationship from the level of mere sexual instrumentality to the level of a spiritual and material communion between the partners, but also at creating an equal role for them both by eliminating the subordinate role of the woman who, in practice, is an adult liable to the imposition of nonvoluntary sexual acts."[18]

This approach was confirmed by Section 3 of the Corte di Cassazione in its judgment no. 10488 of 5 November 1982. The Rome Tribunale in its finding of 28 June 1985, referred to above, likewise determined that "the conduct that is the object of criminal proceedings is not the sexual act between husband and wife, but the use of violence and threats to oblige the nonconsenting partner to have sex. Such conduct impinges upon the right to sexual inviolability and constitutes the crime detailed in Article 519 of the penal code. In any case, even if the nonconsent of the partner is unjustified, this does not do away with the criminal nature of the action, and has pertinence only in terms of civil law." This is a positive response from the judges, which has met with the assent of all women.

VII. Jurisprudence Regarding Crimes of Sexual Violence

Thirty years ago, the Turin Court of Appeal determined that "marriage represents the prime aspiration of every woman. Hence, the promise of marriage, provided it be given with a minimum of seriousness, is of such determining force as to take from the woman all possibility of free decision."[19] Some years later the Florence Court of Appeal stated that "according to the ethical and social conditions predominant in present-day society, sexual intercourse before marriage is considered a sign of dissoluteness and moral disarray; it brings to the woman not only discredit but also financial harm, in that it makes it more

18. Judgment by the Corte di Cassazione, Section 3 (16 February 1976). Confirmed by judgment no. 10488, Corte di Cassazione, Section 3 (5 November 1982).

19. Judgment by the Turin Court of Appeal (13 November 1958).

difficult for her to find a husband."[20] Have these ideas been left behind? In 1981 the Siena Tribunale awarded ninety million lire in damages to a sixteen-year-old who had been raped by nine men. The court argued that "as the girl cannot find in today's society an adequate financial solution through marriage, damages must be such as to give her financial independence [. . .]." For years the approach of jurisprudence to the crime of rape was as follows: "Violence is the use of physical force in whatever measure, greater or lesser according to circumstances, that places the passive party in the condition of not being able to offer all the resistance that he or she would have desired. While it is not necessary that there be extreme violence, neither can the violence required to overcome a woman's natural reluctance be construed as irresistible violence."[21] Accordingly, the first section of the Corte di Cassazione ruled that a woman cannot defend herself against her attacker because, if she reacts by hitting him on the head with a stick and thereby causes his death, she oversteps the bounds of justifiable self-defense and must be required to pay damages.[22] A recent decision of the Corte di Cassazione[23] confirmed the sentence of the Campobasso Appeal Corte di Assise, which based its decision on the following grounds: "If, however, regardless of whether the danger was real or apparent, it may be admitted that the reaction might have exceeded to a moderately acceptable extent the limits of self-defense that the specific circumstances clearly indicated, the fact remains that she went well beyond such limits insofar as the assailant, his sexual charge in all likelihood spent after ejaculation, was manifestly and entirely inoffensive [. . . .] The prolongation of her self-defense was clearly excessive, arising from her inexcusable error in overestimating the continuation and imminence of a danger already past."[24]

VIII. The Circeo Massacre and the Simeoni Case

In 1975 three young men, Giovanni Guido, Andrea Ghira, and Angelo Izzo, abducted two seventeen-year-olds, Rosaria Lopez

20. Judgment by the Florence Court of Appeal (12 December 1962).
21. Judgment by the Siena Tribunale (21 October 1981).
22. Judgment by the Corte di Cassazione, Section 1 (20 February 1967).
23. Judgment by the Corte di Cassazione, Section 1 (2 March 1987).
24. Judgment by the Campobasso Corte d'Assise d'Appello (28 May 1986).

and Donatella Colasanti, whom they then raped and tortured in a villa in San Felice Circeo. So as to escape being reported, they then sought barbarously to massacre them. Rosaria died, whereas Donatella, presumed dead by the trio, survived and reported them. The trial was held in the Latina Corte di Assise in July 1976. The tragic story of Donatella and Rosaria heightened awareness among women, especially on the question of rape. For many people the explanation for the crime lay in the fact that all three men involved were of the extreme Right. However, in October 1976 there took place in Verona the trial of two young members of a left-wing party who had raped Cristina Simeoni, aged sixteen. In the course of the trial the girl was asked questions that were so distressing that her lawyers challenged the impartiality of the judges "as they shared the same social and cultural values as the accused." This provocative action aroused lengthy debate in broad sections of the community.

IX. Pack Rape and the Women's Movement as Coplaintiff

In March 1977 seven youths were tried for the rape of a sixteen-year-old girl called Claudia; the other nine youths involved were not identified. At this trial the Women's Liberation Movement requested for the first time permission to appear alongside the victim as coplaintiff in a rape case. The request was rejected but led to a broad debate, as a result of which representative organizations won the right to appear as coplaintiffs in defense of collective interests. This right was first recognized in October 1980 by the Lamezia Terme Tribunale.[25]

X. Trial for Rape

In June 1978 four men were tried for rape before the Latina Tribunale. The proceedings were filmed and shown on television in 1979. The documentary won the Italia Prize and was published in book form by the Einaudi publishing company. In the preface, Franca Ongaro Basaglia wrote: "[T]his trial gives us the measure of the squalor and baseness under the surface of our culture. But there is an explanation for this baseness. Women have dared to speak out and to reveal the system devised to dominate and silence them. What their silence hid is now exposed" (AA.VV. 1980: ix).

25. Judgment by the Lamezia Terme Tribunale (31 October 1980).

XI. The Story of Marinella, Raped in Piazza Navona

On the night of 7 March 1988, Marinella Cammarata was raped in the vicinity of Piazza Navona. The trial was held with all possible dispatch, and the accused were sentenced to four years and eight months' imprisonment in view of "the particular seriousness of the act committed, that is, an agreement to pack rape the victim in such numbers as to eliminate all possibility of her defending herself. The action also must be seen in the context of when and where it was committed – at night in a dark corner of a central city square. This fact undoubtedly arouses intense concern in the community." The appeal was heard on 15 November 1988. The appeal judges found that "the crime has emerged as far less serious than it was found to be in the initial trial because the violence done to the passive party was minimal, given her limited capacity to defend herself."[26] The accused were released. Marinella died three months after the appeal decision. Her death was doubtless caused by difficulties in her life, but one of these causes was the trial itself.

XII. Two Important Decisions

In conclusion, two highly significant court decisions should be mentioned. The Corte di Cassazione has declared that "in the crime of rape the victim is treated as an object, not as a subject. A human being cannot, must not be degraded to the condition of being treated as a mere body. Rape reduces a human being to a body to be possessed and it is precisely this which constitutes the criminality of the act."[27] For its part, the Constitutional Court has stated: "[O]f the crimes in the penal code, rape constitutes the most serious violation of the basic right to sexual freedom. As sexuality is one of the fundamental means of human expression, the right to do with one's sexuality what one wills is undoubtedly an absolute individual right that must be included among the individual rights protected by the constitution and considered as one of the inviolable human rights guaranteed in Article 2."[28]

Translated by David Fairservice

26. Judgment by the Rome Court of Appeal (15 November 1988).
27. Judgment by the Corte di Cassazione, Section 3 (16 November 1988).
28. Judgment no. 561, Constitutional Court (10 December 1987).

Bibliography

AA VV [multiple authors] (1980) *Un processo per stupro*. Turin: Einaudi.

ABBA, Luisa, FERRI, Gabriella, LAZZARELLO, Giorgio, MEDI, Elena, and MOTTA, Silvia (1972) *La coscienza di sfruttata*. Milan: Mazzotta.

ABRAHAM, K. [1918] (1975) "La psicanalisi delle nevrosi di guerra." In *Opere*, vol. I. Turin: Boringhieri: 96–104.

ADAMS, Henry [1904] (1986) *Mont St. Michel and Chartres*. Harmondsworth: Penguin Books.

ADY, Cecilia M. (1937) *The Bentivoglio of Bologna. A Study in Despotism.* Oxford: Oxford University Press.

ALBERONI, Francesco (1964) *Consumi e società*. Bologna: Il Mulino.

ALBISTUR, Maïté, and ARMOGATHE, Daniel (1977) *Histoire du féminisme français du Moyen Age à nos jours*. Paris: Des Femmes.

ALIGHIERI, Dante (1949–62) *The Divine Comedy, Hell, Purgatory, Paradise*, trans. Dorothy Sayers (vols. 1–3), and Barbara Reynolds (vol. 3). Harmondsworth: Penguin Classics.

——— (1964) *Dante's Purgatory*, 11th ed., trans. T. Oakey. London: Aldine House.

——— (1964) *Il Convivio*, ed. G. Busnelli and G. Vandelli, 2 vols., 2d ed. Florence: Le Monnier.

——— (1966–67) *La commedia secondo l'antica vulgata*, ed. G. Petrocchi. Milan: Rizzoli.

——— (1966) *Epistolae*, ed. P. Toynbee. 2d ed. Oxford: Clarendon Press.

——— (1968) *Vita Nuova*, ed. L. Pietrobono. 3d ed. Florence: Sansoni.

——— (1969) *La Vita Nuova*, trans. Barbara Reynolds. Harmondsworth: Penguin Classics.

——— (1978) *Opere*, ed. F. Chiappelli. Milan: Mursia.

——— (1980) *Vita Nuova*, ed. D. De Robertis. Milan-Naples: Riccardo Ricciardi.

ALINEI, M. (1982) "Rams and Billy-Goats." *Man* (n.s.) 4: 771–75.

ALTMAN GURKIN, Janet (1982) *Epistolary. Approaches to a Form*. Columbus: Ohio State University Press.

AMBROSINI, R. (1909) *Un codice autografo di Giovanni Sabadino degli Arienti*. Bologna: Zanichelli.

ARDENER, Shirley (ed.) (1975) *Perceiving Women*. London: Croom Helm.

———— (ed.) (1978) *Defining Females*. London: Croom Helm.

ARENDT, Hanna [1964] (1989) *Vita activa*. 8th ed. Milan: Bompiani.

ARIENTI, Joanne Sabadino de li (1840) *Vita del conte e senatore Andrea Bentivoglio*, ed. G. Giordani. Bologna: Tipi della Volpe.

———— (1969) *"Gynevera de le clare donne,"* ed. C. Ricci and A. Bacchi Della Lega. (*Scelta di curiosità letterarie inedite o rare*, vol. LXXXIV, dispensa CCXXIII.) Bologna: Commissione per i testi di lingua. Original edition, Bologna: Gaetano Romagnoli, 1887.

ARIES, Philippe (1968) *Padri e figli nell'Europa medievale e moderna*. Bari: Laterza.

ARNHEIM, R. (1981) "On the Nature of Photography." *Rivista di storia e critica della fotografia* 2: 2–9.

ASCOLI, Ugo (ed.) (1984) *Welfare State all'italiana*. Bari: De Donato.

ASHTON, Joan (1989) *Mother of Nations: Visions of Mary*. San Francisco: Marshall Pickering.

ATKINSON, Clarissa W., BUCHANAN, Constance H., and MILES, Margaret R. (eds.) (1987) *Immaculate and Powerful: Female in Sacred Image and Social Reality*. Boston: Crucible.

BACCI, Orazio [1891] (1978) *Ninne-nanne, cantilene, canzoni di giuochi e filastrocche che si dicono in Valdelsa*. Bologna: Forni.

BACCI LIVI, M. (1980) *Donna, fecondità e figli*. Bologna: Il Mulino.

BAGNASCO, A., and TRIGILIA, C. (eds.) (1984) *Società e politica nelle aree di piccola impresa*. Venice: Arsenale.

BAKHTIN, Mikhail (1968) *Rabelais and His World*. Cambridge, Massachusetts: M.I.T. Press.

BALBO, Laura (1976) *Stato di famiglia*. Milan: Etas Libri.

———— (1978) "La doppia presenza." *Inchiesta* 32: 3–6.

———— (ed.) (1987) *Time to Care*. Milan: Franco Angeli.

BANDETTINI, Pierfrancesco (1959–60) "The Employment of Women in Italy 1881–1951." *Comparative Studies in Society and History* 2: 369–74.

BARANSKI, Zygmunt, and VINALL, Shirley (eds.) (1991) *Women and Italy. Essays on Gender, Culture and History*. New York: St. Martin's Press.

BARBAGLI, Marzio (1984) *Sotto lo stesso tetto*. Bologna: Il Mulino.

BARBAGLI, Marzio, CAPECCHI, Vittorio, and COBALTI, Antonio (1988) *La mobilità sociale in Emilia-Romagna*. Bologna: Il Mulino.

BARBERI SQUAROTTI, Giorgio (1982) *Canto V dell'Inferno*. Naples: Loffredo.

BARGAGLI, Girolamo [1589, Siena: Bonetti] (1971) *La Pellegrina*. Florence: Olschki.

BARILE, G., and ZANUSO, L. (1980) *Lavoro femminile e condizione familiare*. Milan: Franco Angeli.

BAROLINI, Teolinda (1984) *Dante's Poets: Textuality and Truth in the Comedy*. Princeton: Princeton University Press.

BARONCHELLI GROSSON, P. (1917) *La donna della nuova Italia. Doc-*

umenti del contributo femminile alla guerra (maggio 1915–maggio 1917). Milan: Garzanti.

BARTHES, Roland (1981) *Camera lucida: Reflections on Photography*. London: Jonathan Cape.

BARWICK, Linda (1986) "The Raccolta Barbi at the Scuola Normale Superiore di Pisa." *Annali della Scuola Normale Superiore di Pisa* (classe di Lettere e Filosofia), series 3 (16): 259–98.

BASILE, Bruno (ed.) (1984) *Bentivolorum Magnificentia. Principe e cultura a Bologna nel Rinascimento*. Rome: Bulzoni.

BATESON, Gregory, and MEAD, Margaret (1942) *Balinese Character: A Photographic Analysis*. New York: Special Publications of the New York Academy of Sciences.

BEGG, Ean (1985) *The Cult of the Black Virgin*. London: Arkana.

BELLAH, Robert N. (1980) "The Five Religions of Modern Italy." In R. Bellah and P. Hammond (eds.) *Varieties of Civil Religion*. San Francisco: Harper and Row.

BELLOSI, G., MAGRINI, T., and SISTRI, A. (1980) *Romagna Vol. I* (sound recording with attached booklet). VPA 8467, Milan: Vedette Albatros.

BENJAMIN, Walter [1966] (1979) "Piccola storia della fotografia." In W. Benjamin (ed.) *L'opera d'arte nell'epoca della sua riproducibilità tecnica*. Turin: Einaudi.

BERGER, John [1973] (1985) *Ways of Seeing*. Harmondsworth: Penguin.

BERGER, P., BERGER, B., and KELLNER, H. (1973) *The Homeless Mind*. New York: Random House.

BERGIN, Thomas G. (1969) *A Diversity of Dante*. New Brunswick, New Jersey: Rutgers University Press.

BERTELLI, C., and BOLLATI, G. (1979) *Storia d'Italia, Annali 2. L'immagine fotografica 1845–1945*, 2 vols. Turin: Einaudi.

BETTERTON, R. (1985) "How Do Women Look? The Female Nude in the Work of Suzanne Valadon." *Feminist Review*, 19: 3–24.

BIANCHI, Bruna (1983) "Predisposizione, commozione o emozione? Natura e terapia della neuropsicosi di guerra (1915–1918)." *Movimento operaio e socialista* 6 (3): 383–410.

BIANCHI, M. (1981) *I servizi sociali*. Bari: De Donato.

BIMBI, Franca (1981) "Tra lavoro intellettuale e lavoro della riproduzione: percorsi delle donne e Università di massa." *Inchiesta* 49–50: 11–18.

———— (1986a) "In famiglia attraverso lo specchio. Età, generazioni, identità." In F. Bimbi and V. Capecchi (eds.) *Strutture e strategie della vita quotidiana*. Milan: Franco Angeli: 383–96.

———— (1986b) "La donna nella famiglia: dal dono materno all'orizzonte della doppia presenza." *Fare Scuola* 4: 47–58.

———— (1987a) " 'Specchio delle mie brame . . .': Immagini e riflessioni sulle trasformazioni della comunicazione." In F. Bimbi, L.

Grasso, and M. Zancan (eds.) *Al filo di Arianna. Letture della differenza sociale.* Rome: Utopia: 13–35.

—— (1987b) "Donna." In Giuseppe Zaccaria (ed.) *Lessico della politica.* Rome: Edizioni Lavoro: 201–10.

—— (1988) "Differenza, reciprocità, somiglianza. L'identità lungo il ciclo di vita." *Memoria* 22: 104–22.

—— (1989) "La maternità da 'obbligo' biologico a scelta possibile: logiche d'azione e comportamenti abortivi." In E. Quintavalla and E. Raimondi (eds.) *Aborto perché?* Milan: Feltrinelli: 128–44.

BIMBI, Franca, and PRISTINGER, Flavia (eds.) (1985) *Profili sovrapposti.* Milan: Franco Angeli.

BIMBI, Franca, and CASTELLANO, G. (1989) *Maternità e paternità.* Milan: Franco Angeli.

BIMBI, Franca, LOVISOTTO, F., and PERIN, E. (1991) *Storie di maternità.* Milan: Franco Angeli.

BIRNBAUM, Lucia Chiavola [1986] (1988) *liberazione della donna – feminism in Italy.* Middletown, Connecticut: Wesleyan University Press.

BLACKWOOD, E. (1984) "Sexuality and Gender in Certain Native American Tribes: the Case of Cross-Gender Females." *Signs* 1: 27–42.

BLAIR, Juliet (1981) "Private Parts in Public Places: the Case of Actresses." In S. Ardener (ed.) *Women and Space.* London: Croom Helm: 205–28.

BLOCH, Maurice, and BLOCH, Jean H. (1981) "Women and the Dialectics of Nature in Eighteenth-Century French Thought." In C. McCormack and M. Strathern (eds.) *Nature, Culture and Gender.* Cambridge: Cambridge University Press: 25–41.

BLOK, A. (1981) "Rams and Billy-Goats: A Key to the Mediterranean Code of Honour." *Man* (n.s.) 3: 427–40.

BO, Vincenzo (1979) *La religiosità popolare.* Assisi: Cittadella.

BOBBIO, Norberto (1980) "Pubblico-privato." In *Enciclopedia Einaudi*, vol. 11. Turin: Einaudi: 401–15.

BOCCACCIO, Giovanni (1970) *Tutte le opere di Giovanni Boccaccio*, ed. Vittore Branca. Milan: Mondadori.

BOCCIA, Maria Luisa (1987) "Per una teoria dell'autenticità. Lettura di Carla Lonzi." *Memoria* 19–20: 85–108.

BOFF, Leonardo (1987) *The Maternal Face of God: The Feminine and its Religious Expressions.* San Francisco: Harper and Row.

BOLLATI, Giulio (1983) *L'italiano.* Turin: Einaudi.

BONACCORSI, A. (1956) "Il folklore musicale in Toscana." *Lares* 3: 103–08.

BONINO, G. D. (ed.) (1978) *Il teatro italiano, II: La commedia del Cinquecento*, vol. 3. Turin: Einaudi.

BONORA, Ettore (1982) "*Inferno*, canto V." *Giornale storico della letteratura italiana* 99: 321–52.

BORGHINI, Raffaello (1578) *La donna costante.* Florence: Marescotti.

BORTOLOTTI PIERONI, Franca (1974) *Socialismo e questione femminile in Italia (1892–1922)*. Milan: Mazzotta.

———— (1978) *Femminismo e partiti politici in Italia (1919–1926)*. Rome: Editori Riuniti.

BRANDES, Stanley (1981) "Like Wounded Stags: Male Sexual Ideology in an Andalusian Town." In S. Ortner and H. Whitehead (eds.) *Sexual Meanings*. Cambridge: Cambridge University Press: 216–39.

BRAUDEL, F. (1984a) "Le responsabilità della storia." *Inchiesta* 63–64: 50–54.

———— (1984b) "Georges Gurvitch o la discontinuità del sociale." *Inchiesta* 63–64: 43–49.

BRAVO, Anna (1980) "Donne contadine e prima guerra mondiale." *Società e storia* 10: 843–62.

BRAYBON, G. (1981) *Women Workers in the First World War*. London: Croom Helm.

BROWN, P., and JORDANOVA, L. J. (1981) "Oppressive Dichotomies: the Nature/Culture Debate." In Cambridge Women's Studies Group (eds.) *Women in Society: Interdisciplinary Essays in Women's Studies*. London: Virago: 224–42.

BULLOCK, Alan (1991) *Natalia Ginzburg: Human Relationships in a Changing World*. Oxford: Berg Publishers.

BYNUM WALKER, C. (1982) *Jesus as Mother: Studies in the Spirituality of the High Middle Ages*. Berkeley: University of California Press.

———— (1984) "Women Mystics and Eucharistic Devotion in the Thirteenth Century." *Women's Studies* 1–2: 179–214.

———— (1985) "Fast, Feast and Flesh: the Religious Significance of Food to Medieval Women." *Representations* 11: 1–25.

CAESAR, Ann (1986) "Women's Writing, the Canon and the Syllabus." *Bulletin for the Society of Italian Studies* 19: 2–11.

CALABRO', Ana Rita, and GRASSO, Laura (eds.) (1985) *Dal movimento femminista al femminismo diffuso*. Milan: Franco Angeli.

CALDWELL, Lesley (1981) "Abortion in Italy." *Feminist Review* 7: 49–64.

CAMARDA, A., and PELI, S. (1980) *L'altro esercito. La classe operaia durante la prima guerra mondiale*. Milan: Feltrinelli.

CAMBON, Glauco (1961) "Dante's Francesca and the Tactics of Language." *Modern Language Quarterly* 22: 63–78.

CAMMARERI, Giovanni (1988) *La settimana santa nel trapanese: passato e presente*. Trapani: Coppola.

CAPUANA, Luigi (1879) *Giacinta*. Milan: Brigola.

CARBONARO, Antonio, and NESTI, Arnaldo (1975) *La cultura negata: caratteri e potenzialità della cultura popolare*. Rimini-Florence: Guaraldi.

CARETTI, Lanfranco (1969) "Il canto V dell'*Inferno*." In *Nuove letture dantesche*, vol. 1. Florence: Le Monnier: 105–31.

CARLI, Plinio (1950) "Dante e Francesca." *Humanitas* 5 (1): 86–91.

CARLI, Plinio, and SAINATI, Augusto (eds.) (1934) *Scrittori italiani*. 4th ed. Florence: Le Monnier.

CARPITELLA, Diego (ed.) (1976) *Musica contadina dell'Aretino, vol. 3* (sound recording with attached booklet). VPA 8288. Milano: Albatros.

CASTIGLIONE, Miriam (1981) *I professionisti dei sogni: Visioni e devozioni popolari nella cultura contadina meridionale.* Naples: Liguori.

CHANDLER, S. B. (1954) "Il *Trattato della pudicizia* di Sabadino degli Arienti." *La Bibliofilia* 56: 110–13.

CHAUCEY, G., Jr. (1982–83) "From Sexual Inversion to Homosexuality: Medicine and the Changing Conceptualization of Female Deviance." *Salmagundi* 58–59: 114–46.

CHERCHI, Placido, and CHERCHI, Maria (1987) *Ernesto De Martino.* Naples: Liguori.

CHIAPPELLI, Fredi (1990) "Il colore della menzogna nelle scenografie dell'*Inferno.*" *Lectura Dantis* 6: 3–27.

CICOGNA, Patricia, and DE LAURETIS, Teresa (eds.) (1990) *Sexual Difference. A Theory of Social-Symbolic Practice.* Bloomington: Indiana University Press.

CIONI, Raffaello [1955] (1973) *Il poema mugellano.* Florence: Libreria Editrice Fiorentina.

CIPRIANI, Roberto, RINALDI, Giovanni, and SOBRERO, Paola (1979) *Il simbolo conteso: simbolismo politico e religioso nelle culture di base meridionali.* Rome: Ianua.

CIXOUS, Hélène (1981) "Castration or Decapitation." *Signs* 1: 41–55.

CLINE HOROWITZ, Maryanne (1976) "Aristotle and Women." *Journal of the History of Biology* 9: 183–213.

COLLIER, Jane F. (1974) "Women in Politics." In M. Rosaldo and L. Lamphere (eds.) *Women, Culture and Society.* Stanford: Stanford University Press: 89–96.

COPPI, F. (1988) "Maltrattamenti." *Enciclopedia del diritto.* Milan: Giuffré.

CORAZZINI, Francesco [1877] (1968). *I componimenti minori della letteratura popolare italiana.* Milan: Edizioni del Gallo.

CORSI, G. (1981) "Sena Vetus: Ninne-nanne, preghiere, storie." *Archivio per lo studio delle tradizioni popolari* 10: 249–58.

COSSUTTA, Fabio (1977) "Francesca tra ragione e talento." *Letture classensi* 6: 111–67.

CROCE, Benedetto. *Poeti e scrittori del pieno e del tardo Rinascimento,* vols. 1–2: 1958; vol. 3: 1970. Bari: Laterza.

CURRA', A., VETTORI, G., and VINCI, R. (eds.) (1977) *Canti della protesta femminile.* Rome: Newton Compton.

CURRA', A., DE LUCIA, R., LELLI, R., and RIGA, M. (eds.) (1981) *I canti, le fiabe, le feste nella tradizione popolare: Toscana.* Rome: Lato Side Editori.

CURTIUS, Ernst R. (1953) *European Literature and the Latin Middle Ages.* New York: Pantheon Books.

DAVIDOFF, Leonore [1979] (1983) "Class and Gender in Victorian

England: The Diaries of Arthur J. Munby and Hannah Cullwick." [*Feminist Studies* 1] Reprinted in Judith Newton, Mary P. Ryan, and Judith R. Walkowitz (eds.), *Sex and Class in Women's History*. London: Routledge: 17–71.

DAVIS, J. (1980) *Antropologia delle società mediterranee. Un'analisi comparata*. Turin: Rosenberg and Sellier.

DAVIS ZEMON, Natalie (1975) "Women on Top." In N. Davis Zemon (ed.) *Society and Culture in Early Modern France*. Stanford: Stanford University Press: 124–51.

DE BENEDICTIS, Angela (1984) "Quale 'corte' per quale 'signoria'?" In B. Basile (ed.) *Bentivolorum Magnificentia*. Rome: Bulzoni: 13–33.

DEJOB, Charles (1884) *De l'influence du Concile de Trente sur la littérature et les beaux-arts chez les peuples catholiques*. Paris: Ernst Thorin.

DELANEY, John J. (ed.) (1961) *A Woman Clothed with the Sun: Eight Great Appearances of Our Lady in Modern Times*. Garden City, New York: Image Books.

DELLA TERZA, Dante (1981) "*Inferno V*: Tradition and Exegesis." *Dante Studies* 99: 49–66.

DE MARTINO, Ernesto [1959] (1987) *Sud e magia*. Milan: Feltrinelli.

DE SANCTIS, Francesco (1955) "Il canto V dell'*Inferno*." In G. Getto (ed.) *Letture dantesche*. Florence: Sansoni: 75–90.

DIBERTI LEIGH, Marcella (1988) *Veronica Franco: Donna, poetessa e cortigiana del Rinascimento*. Turin: Priuli e Verlucca.

DIONISOTTI, Carlo (1965) "La letteratura italiana nell'età del Concilio." *Il Concilio di Trento e la Riforma Tridentina: Atti del convegno storico internazionale* (Trent, 2–6 Septembre 1963). Rome: Herder: 317–43.

DOUGLASS, Carrie B. (1984) " 'Toro muerto, vaca es': An Interpretation of the Spanish Bullfight." *American Ethnologist* 2: 242–58.

DRONKE, Peter (1975) "Francesca and Héloise." *Comparative Literature* 26: 113–35.

——— (1986) *Dante and Medieval Latin Traditions*. Cambridge: Cambridge University Press.

DURAND, G. (1979) *Figures mythiques et visages de l'oeuvre*. Paris: Berg International.

ERGAS, Yasmine (1982) "1968–79: Feminism and the Italian Party System." *Comparative Politics* 14: 253–79.

ESISTERE COME DONNA. (1983) (ed. Comune di Milano) Milan: Mazzotta.

FALK, Marcia (1982) *Love Lyrics from the Bible: A translation and literary study of the Song of Songs*. Sheffield: Almond.

FERAL, Josette (1979) "Antigone or the Irony of the Tribe." *Diacritics* 3: 2–14.

FERRANTE, L., PALAZZI, M., and POMATA, G. (1988) *Ragnatele di Rapporti*. Turin: Rosenberg and Sellier.

FERRARO, GIUSEPPE (1967) *Canti popolari di Ferrara, Cento e Pontelagoscuro*. Bologna: Forni.

219

FIORENZA, Elisabeth Schüssler (1983) *In Memory of Her: A Feminist Theological Reconstruction of Christian Origins.* New York: Crossroads.

FIRTH, Raymond (1973) *Symbols Public and Private.* London: Cornell University Press.

FORCELLA, E., and MONTICONE, A. [1968] (1972) *Plotone di esecuzione. I processi della prima guerra mondiale.* Bari: Laterza.

FOSTER, Kenelm, and BOYDE, Peter (1967) *Dante's Lyric Poetry,* vol. 1. Oxford: Clarendon Press.

FOX-KELLER, Evelyn, and GRONTKOWSKI, Christine R. (1983) "The Mind's Eye." In S. Harding and B. Hintikka (eds.) *Discovering Reality.* Dordrecht: Reidel: 207–24.

FRABOTTA, Biancamaria (ed.) (1973) *Femminismo e lotta di classe in Italia, 1970–1973.* Rome: Savelli.

FRECCERO, John (1973) "Casella's Song (*Purgatorio* II, 112)." *Dante Studies* 91: 73–80.

FRESCURA, A. (1981) *Diario di un imboscato.* Milan: Mursia.

FREUD, Sigmund [1920] (1977) "Promemoria sul trattamento elettrico dei nevrotici di guerra." In *Opere*, vol. 9. Turin: Boringhieri: 167–75.

FRIEDAN, Betty [1963] (1965) *The Feminine Mystique.* Harmondsworth: Penguin Books.

FUSSELL, P. (1975) *The Great War and Modern Memory.* Oxford: Oxford University Press.

GADDA, Carlo Emilio (1931) *La Madonna dei filosofi.* Florence: Edizioni di Solaria.

—— [1934] (1973) *Il castello di Udine.* [Florence: Edizioni di Solaria.] Turin: Einaudi.

—— [1944] (1955) *L'Adalgisa.* [Florence: Le Monnier.] Turin: Einaudi.

—— [1945] (1958) "Anime e schemi." [*Il Mondo* 1 (5): 7]. Reprinted in C. E. Gadda, *I viaggi la morte.* Milan: Garzanti: 217–23.

—— [1950] (1958) "Il faut d'abord être coupable." [*Paragone*, 1, (6): 26–35]. Reprinted in C. E. Gadda, *I viaggi la morte.* Milan: Garzanti: 232–33.

—— (1955) *Giornale di guerra e di prigionia.* Turin: Einaudi.

—— (1958) *I viaggi la morte.* Milan: Garzanti.

—— (1963) *Accoppiamenti giudiziosi.* Milan: Garzanti.

—— (1964) *Le meraviglie d'Italia. Gli anni.* Turin: Einaudi.

—— (1967) *Eros e Priapo.* Milan: Garzanti.

—— (1969) *Acquainted with Grief.* (Translation of *La cognizione del dolore*) London: Peter Owen.

—— [1957] (1970a) *Quer pasticciaccio brutto de via Merulana.* Milan: Garzanti.

—— (1970b) *La meccanica.* Milan: Garzanti.

—— (1971) *Novella seconda.* Milan: Garzanti.

—— (1981) *Le bizze del capitano in congedo.* Milan: Adelphi.

—— (1983) *Racconto italiano di ignoto del novecento.* Turin: Einaudi.

——— (1984) *That Awful Mess on Via Merulana*. (Translation of *Quer pasticciaccio brutto de via Merulana*) New York: Braziller.

——— [1963] (1987) *La cognizione del dolore*. Turin: Einaudi.

GADON, Elinor W. (1989) *The Once and Future Goddess: A Symbol for Our Time*. San Francisco: Aquarian.

GALLINO GIANI, Tilde (ed.) (1988) *Le grandi madri*. Milan: Feltrinelli.

GALOPPINI, Annamaria (1980) *Il lungo viaggio verso la parità*. Bologna: Zanichelli.

GEBARA, Ivone, and BINGEMER, M. Clara (1987) *Maria madre di Dio e madre dei poveri*. Assisi: Cittadella.

GHINASSI, Ghino (1962) "Arienti, Giovanni Sabadino degli." *Dizionario biografico degli Italiani*, vol. 4. Rome: Istituto dell'Enciclopedia Italiana: 154–56.

GIACOBAZZI, D., and MERELLI, M. (1989) *I percorsi del cambiamento*. Turin: Rosenberg and Sellier.

GIANNINI, Giovanni [1901] (1981) *Canti popolari toscani*. Palermo: Edikronos.

GIBELLI, A. (1980) "Guerra e follia. Potere psichiatrico e patologia del rifiuto nella grande guerra." *Movimento operaio e socialista* 4: 441–64.

GIBSON, James J. (1962) "Observations on Active Touch." *Psychological Review* 6: 477–91.

GILBERT, Sandra (1983) "Soldier's Heart: Literary Men, Literary Women and the Great War." *Signs* 3: 422–50.

GILLIGAN, Carol (1981) *In a Different Voice*. Cambridge, Massachusetts: Harvard University Press.

GIMBUTAS, Marija (1989) *The Language of the Goddess: Unearthing the Hidden Symbols of Western Civilization*. San Francisco: Harper and Row.

GIUSEPPE PRIMOLI FOTOGRAFO EUROPEO (1982). Rome: Quater.

GIUSTI, M. E. (1986) "Notizie intorno ai canti narrativi della Raccolta Barbi." *Quaderni dell'Istituto di Linguistica dell'Università di Urbino* 4: 397–412.

GOMBRICH, E. H. (1977) *Art and Illusion*. Oxford: Phaidon.

——— (1982) *The Image and the Eye*. Oxford: Phaidon.

GORDON, B. (1984) " 'Variety': the Pleasure in Looking." In C. Vance (ed.) *Pleasure and Danger. Exploring Female Sexuality*. London: Routledge: 189–204.

GRANDGENT, Charles H., and SINGLETON, Charles H. (eds.) (1933) *La Divina Commedia di Dante Alighieri*. Cambridge, Massachusetts: Harvard University Press.

GRAVES, Robert [1961] (1984) *The White Goddess*. London: Faber and Faber.

GUARINO, Guido A. (1964) *Concerning Famous Women*. (Translation of Giovanni Boccaccio's *De mulieribus claris*) London: Allen and Unwin.

GUIDETTI SERRA, Bianca (1988) "Donne, violenza politica, armi: un'esperienza giudiziaria." *Rivista di storia contemporanea* 2: 218–45.

GUIZZARDI, Gustavo (1982) "Famiglia e secolarizzazione. La caduta di due sacralità." *Città e Regione* 4: 53–62.

GUIZZARDI, Gustavo, PRANDI, Carlo, CASTIGLIONE, Miriam, PACE, Enzo, and MOROSSI, Antonio (1981) *Chiesa e religione del popolo: Analisi di un'egemonia.* Turin: Claudiana.

HABERMAS, J. [1969] (1989) *The Structural Transformation of the Public Sphere.* Cambridge, Massachusetts: Massachusetts Institute of Technology Press.

HAMPSHIRE, S. (ed.) (1978) *Public and Private Morality.* Cambridge: Cambridge University Press.

HARDING, Sandra (1983) "Why Has the Sex/Gender System Become Visible Only Now?" In S. Harding and Merrill B. Hintikka (eds.) *Discovering Reality.* Dordrecht: Reidel: 311–24.

HARDING, Sandra, and HINTIKKA, Merrill (eds.) (1983) *Discovering Reality.* Dordrecht: Reidel.

HARRIS, O. (1981) "Households as Natural Units." In Kate Young, Carol Wolkowitz, and Roslyn McCullough (eds.) *Of Marriage and the Market.* London: Routledge Chapman and Hall: 136–55.

HATCHER, Anna, and MUSA, Mark (1968) "The Kiss: *Inferno V* and the Old French Prose *Lancelot.*" *Comparative Literature* 2: 97–109.

HAUSE, Stephen C., and KENNEY, Ann R. (1984) *Women's Suffrage and Social Politics in the French Third Republic.* Princeton: Princeton University Press.

HENLEY, N. (1985) "Psychology and Gender." *Signs* 1: 101–19.

HERLIHY, David (1985) "Did Women Have a Renaissance?: A Reconsideration." *Medievalia et Humanistica* (n.s.) 13: 1–22.

HERMAN LEWIS, Judith (1981) *Father-Daughter Incest.* Cambridge, Massachusetts: Harvard University Press.

HIGONNET, M., JENSON, J., MICHEL, S., and WEITZ, M. (1987) *Behind the Lines.* New Haven, Connecticut: Yale University Press.

HIRSCH, Marianne (1981) "A Mother's Discourse: Incorporation and Repetition in *La Princesse de Clèves.*" *Yale French Studies* 62: 67–87.

HOCKINGS, P. (ed.) (1975) *Principles of Visual Anthropology.* The Hague: Mouton.

HOLLANDER, Robert (1969) *Allegory in Dante's* Commedia. Princeton: Princeton University Press.

—— (1975) "Cato's Rebuke and Dante's *scoglio.*" *Italica* 52: 348–63.

HORKHEIMER, M. (1974) *Studi sull'autorità e la famiglia.* Turin: UTET.

IRIGARAY, Luce (1981) "And the One Doesn't Stir Without the Other." (Translated and introduced by Hélène V. Wenzel) *Signs* 1: 56–67.

—— (1982) *Passions elémentaires.* Paris: Les Editions de Minuit.

——— (1985) *This Sex Which Is Not One.* New York: Cornell University Press.

I.R.P. (Istituto di Ricerche sulla Popolazione) (1988) *Rapporto sulla situazione demografica italiana.* Rome: I.R.P.

ISNENGHI, Mario (1970) *Il mito della grande guerra.* Bari: Laterza.

——— (1977) *Giornali di trincea.* Turin: Einaudi.

——— (1978) "Alle origini del 18 aprile. Miti, riti, mass media." In M. Isnenghi and S. Lanaro (eds.) *La Democrazia Cristiana dal fascismo al 18 aprile.* Venice: Marsilio: 277–344.

——— (ed.) (1982) *Operai e contadini nella grande guerra.* Bologna: Cappelli.

ITALIAN COMMUNIST PARTY: WOMEN'S SECTION (1986) *Dalle donne la forza delle donne. Carta Itinerante. Idee, proposte, interrogativi.* Rome: Italian Communist Party.

JORDAN, Constance (1987) "Boccaccio's In-famous Women: Gender and Civic Virtue in *De mulieribus claris.*" In C. Levin and J. Watson (eds.) *Ambiguous Realities.* Detroit: Wayne State University Press: 25–47.

JUNG, Carl G. (1933) *Modern Man in Search of a Soul.* New York: Harcourt Brace.

KAMUF, Peggy (1982) *Fictions of Feminine Desire: Disclosures of Héloise.* Lincoln: University of Nebraska Press.

KAUFFMAN, Linda S. (1986) *Discourses of Desire: Gender, Genre and Epistolary Fictions.* New York: Cornell University Press.

KIRKHAM, Victoria (1989) "A Canon of Women in Dante's *Commedia.*" *Annali d'italianistica* 7: 16–41.

KNIBIEHLER, Y., and FOUQUET, C. (1980) *L'histoire des mères du moyen âge à nos jours.* Paris: Montalba.

KOLSKY, Stephen (1990) "Women through Men's Eyes: the Third Book of *Il Cortegiano.*" In Tom O'Neill (ed.) *Shared Horizons.* Dublin: Irish Academic Press: 41–91.

KRISTEVA, Julia (1975) "The Subject in Signifying Practice." *Semiotext/e* 1: 19–26.

——— (1981) "Women's Time." *Signs* 7: 187–213.

LANTERNARI, Vittorio (1977) *Crisi e ricerca d'identità.* Naples: Liguori.

"La settimana santa in Sicilia: Processioni, rappresentazioni, misteri, canti e simboli della Passione." *Giornale di Sicilia,* supplemento 30 marzo 1988: 9.

LAW TRECKER, J. (1974) "Sex, Science and Education." *American Quarterly* 4: 352–66.

LEACH, Edmund [1958] (1980) "Magical hair." [*The Journal of the Royal Anthropological Institute* 2]. Reprinted in John Middleton (ed.) *Myth and Cosmos.* Austin: Texas University Press: 77–108.

LEED, Eric J. (1979) *No Man's Land. Combat and Identity in World War I.* Cambridge: Cambridge University Press.

LEONI, D., and ZANDRA, C. (1982) "I ruoli sconvolti: donna e famiglia a Volano nel Trentino durante la guerra del Quindici." *Movimento operaio e socialista* 3: 421–38.

―――― (1986) *La grande guerra. Esperienza, memoria, immagine.* Bologna: Il Mulino.

LEOPARDI, Giacomo (1975) *Canti*, ed. Ferdinando Bandini. Milan: Garzanti.

LEVI, Carlo [1945] (1979) *Cristo si è fermato a Eboli.* Turin: Einaudi.

LEVI-STRAUSS, Claude (1953) *L'anthropologie structurale*, 2 vols. Paris: Plon.

LEVIN, Carole, and WATSON, Jeanie (eds.) (1987) *Ambiguous Realities: Women in the Middle Ages and Renaissance.* Detroit: Wayne University Press.

LEYDI, Roberto (1972) *La trasformazione socio-economica e la cultura tradizionale in Lombardia.* Milan: Quaderni della Regione Lombardia: 5–6.

LEYDI, Roberto, and MANTOVANI, Sandra (1970) *Dizionario della musica popolare europea.* Milan: Bompiani.

LISON-TOLOSANA, C. [1966] (1983) *Belmonte de los caballeros.* Princeton: Princeton University Press.

LOMAX, Alan (1956) "Nuova ipotesi sul canto folkloristico italiano nel quadro della musica popolare mondiale." *Nuovi Argomenti* 18: 109–35.

LOMBARDI SATRIANI, Luigi M. (1979) *Il silenzio, la memoria e lo sguardo.* Palermo: Sellerio di Giorgianni.

LONZI, Carla (1970) *Sputiamo su Hegel.* Rome: Scritti di Rivolta Femminile.

LORCA, Federico Garcia [1975] (1980) *Deep Song and Other Prose*, ed. and trans. C. Maurer. New York: Boyars.

LOWE, D. M. (1982) *History of Bourgeois Perception.* Chicago: Chicago University Press.

LUSSU, Emilio (1945) *Un anno sull'altipiano.* Turin: Einaudi.

LUSSU, Joyce (1986) "Il libro perogno." In J. Lussu (ed.) *Storie.* Bologna: Il Lavoro Editoriale: 219–71.

MANENTI, C. (1979) *Lyca Comerio fotografo e cineasta.* Milan: Electa.

MANZOTTI, Emilio (1984) "Astrazione e dettaglio: lettura di un passo della *Cognizione.*" *Cenobio* 4: 332–56.

MARAINI, Dacia (1981) *Lettere a Marina.* Milan: Bompiani.

―――― (1987) "Proserpina divisa fra madre e marito." In D. Maraini (ed.) *La bionda, la bruna e l'asino.* Milan: Rizzoli: 85–87.

MARCUZZO, Maria Cristina, and ROSSI-DORIA, Anna (1987) *La ricerca delle donne.* Turin: Rosenberg and Sellier.

MARINELLI, Lucrezia (1600) *La nobiltà et eccellenza delle donne co' difetti et mancamenti de gli huomini.* Venice: Ciotti Senesi.

MASSAROLI, Nino (1925) "Ninne-nanne romagnole." *Il folklore italiano* 1: 209–10.

MATHIEU, N. C. (1973) "Homme-culture et femme-nature?" *L'Homme* 3: 101–13.

MATTALIA, Daniele (1962) "Moralità e dottrina nel canto V dell'*Inferno*." *Filologia e letteratura* 8: 41–70.

MAUSS, Marcel (1965) *Teoria generale della magia e altri saggi.* Turin: Einaudi.

MAZZOTTA, Giuseppe (1979) *Dante, Poet of the Desert.* Princeton: Princeton University Press.

MELOGRANI, P. [1969] (1972) *Storia politica della grande guerra 1915–18.* Bari. Laterza.

MEMORIA FOTOGRAFICA (1908–1923). DALL'ALBUM ROMANO DI ALFREDO DE GIORGIO (12 June–13 July 1985). Rome: Palazzo Antici Mattei.

MENAPACE, Lidia [1987] (1988) *L'Economia politica della differenza sessuale.* Rome: Edizioni Felina Libri.

MERELLI, M., MORINI, M., NAVA, P., RUGGERINI, M., and VALLI, L. (1985) *Giochi d'equilibrio.* Milan: Franco Angeli.

MERRY, Bruce (1990) *Women in Modern Italian Literature. Four Studies Based on the Work of Grazia Deledda, Alba De Céspedes, Natalia Ginzburg and Dacia Maraini.* Townsville: James Cook University of North Queensland.

MINISTERO PER LE ARMI E MUNIZIONI (1918) *La donna d'Italia nelle industrie di guerra, maggio 1915–1918.* Rome: Ministero per le Armi e Munizioni.

MIRAGLIA, M. (1981) "Note per una storia della fotografia italiana (1911–1939)." In Federico Zeri (ed.) *Storia dell'arte italiana,* vol. 9. *Grafica e immagine,* part 2, "Illustrazione fotografica." Turin: Einaudi: 423–543.

MITCHELL, Juliet (1974) *Psychoanalysis and Feminism.* London: Allen Lane.

MODERATA FONTE (1988) *Il merito delle donne,* ed. Adriana Chemello. Venice: Eidos.

MOEBIUS, P. J. (1978) *L'inferiorità mentale della donna.* Turin: Einaudi.

MOLETA, Vincent (1980) *Guinizelli in Dante.* Rome: Edizioni di storia e letteratura.

MONTANO, Rocco (1956) *Suggerimenti per una lettura di Dante.* Naples: Conte.

MORO, A. M., PERIN, E., and ZECCHINATO, O. (1981) "Percorsi della maternità in due generazioni di donne." Honors thesis. University of Padua, Italy.

MOSCATI, Dodi (ed.) (1975) *Ti converrà mangiare i' pan pentito* (sound recording with attached booklet). LPP 291. Turin: Fonit/Cetra.

MOSS, Leonard W., and CAPPANARI, Stephen C. (1982) "In Quest of the Black Virgin: She is Black Because She is Black." In James J. Preston (ed.) *Mother Worship.* Chapel Hill: University of North Carolina Press: 65–71.

225

MULVEY, Laura (1974) "Visual Pleasure and Narrative Cinema." *Screen* 3: 6–18.

MUSA, Mark (1971) *Dante's* Inferno. Bloomington: Indiana University Press.

——— (trans.) (1985) *Petrarch: Selections from the* Canzoniere *and Other Works.* Oxford: Oxford University Press.

NATALI, P. (ed.) (1977) *Cultura e tradizione in Emilia-Romagna*, vol. 3 (sound recording with attached booklet).

NEISSER, U., and KERR, N. (1973) "Spatial and Mnemonic Properties of Visual Images." *Cognitive Psychology* 5: 138–50.

NEISSER, U. (1981) *Conoscenza e realtà.* Bologna: Il Mulino.

NESTI, Arnaldo (ed.) (1970) *L'altra chiesa in Italia.* Milan: Mondadori.

NEUMANN, Erich [1963] (1974) *The Great Mother: An Analysis of the Archetype.* Princeton: Routledge.

NEWTON, Esther (1979) *Mother Camp. Female Impersonators in America.* Chicago: Chicago University Press.

——— (1984) "The Mythic Mannish Lesbian: Radclyffe Hall and the New Woman." *Signs* 4: 557–75.

NOAKES, Susan (1983) "The Double Misreading of Paolo and Francesca." *Philological Quarterly* 62: 221–39.

ODDI, Sforza Degli (1578) *L'erofilomachia, ovvero il duello d'amore e d'amicizia.* Venice: Sessa.

——— (1978) "L'erofilomachia." In G. D. Bonino (ed.) *Il teatro italiano, II: La commedia del Cinquecento*, vol. 3. Turin: Einaudi: 3–131.

O'GRADY, Deidre (1987) "Women Damned, Penitent and Beatified in the *Divine Comedy.*" In Eric Haywood (ed.) *Dante Readings.* Dublin: Irish Academic Press: 73–106.

OLTRE LA POSA. IMMAGINI DI DONNA NEGLI ARCHIVI ALINARI (1984), ed. Libreria delle donne di Firenze. Florence: Alinari.

ORTNER, Sherry, and WHITEHEAD, Harriet (1982) *Sexual Meanings. The Cultural Construction of Gender and Sexuality.* Cambridge: Cambridge University Press.

OVID (1955) *The Metamorphoses*, trans. Mary M. Innes. Harmondsworth: Penguin Classics.

PACASSONI, Maria Teresa (1939) "Il sentimento della maternità nei canti del popolo italiano." *Lares* 10: 83–101.

PAGELS, Elaine H. (1988) *Adam, Eve and the Serpent.* New York: Vintage Books.

PAGLIARO, Antonio (1967) *Ulisse. Ricerche semantiche sulla* Divina Commedia. 2d ed. Messina-Florence: D'Anna.

PAHL, R. (ed.) (1989) *On Work: Historical, Comparative and Theoretical Approaches.* Oxford: Basil Blackwell.

PALAZZESCHI, Aldo (1920) *Due imperi . . . mancati.* Florence: Vallecchi.

PAPARELLI, Gioacchino (1979) "Reinterpretazione di Francesca." *Letture classensi* 7: 29–50.

PASOLINI, Pier Paolo (1960) *La poesia popolare*. Milan: Garzanti.

PAVESE, Cesare [1941] (1968) *Paesi tuoi*. Turin: Einaudi.

—— [1950. Turin: Einaudi] (1978) *La luna e i falò*. 9th ed. Milan: Mondadori.

—— [1951. Turin: Einaudi] (1981) *Collezione di poesia*. 8th ed. Turin: Einaudi.

PELI, Santo (1983) "Composizione di classe e conflittualità. Alcune considerazioni a partire dal caso ligure." In G. Procacci (ed.) *Stato e classe operaia in Italia durante la prima guerra mondiale*. Milan: Franco Angeli: 230–43.

PERELLA, Nicholas J. (1969) *The Kiss Sacred and Profane*. Berkeley: University of California Press.

PERISTIANY, J. G. (ed.) (1966) *Honour and Shame. The Values of Mediterranean Society*. Chicago: Chicago University Press.

PETRARCA, Francesco (1972) *Canzoniere*, ed. Gianfranco Contini and Daniele Ponchiroli. 4th ed. Turin: Einaudi.

PETTAZZONI, Raffaele (1952) *Italia religiosa*. Bari: Laterza.

PIANTA, Bruno (1982) *Cultura popolare*. Milan: Garzanti.

PICCONE STELLA, Simonetta (1981) "Crescere negli anni 50." *Memoria* 1–2: 9–35.

PITT-RIVERS, J. (1977) *The Fate of Schechem*. Cambridge: Cambridge University Press.

PLASKOW, Judith, and CHRIST, Carol P. (1989) *Weaving the Visions: New Patterns in Feminist Spirituality*. San Francisco: Harper and Row.

POGGIOLI, Renato (1957) "Tragedy or Romance? A Reading of the Paolo and Francesca Episode in Dante's *Inferno*." *Publication of the Modern Language Association of America* 72: 313–58.

POMATA, Gianna (1979) *In scienza e coscienza*. Florence: La Nuova Italia.

—— (1983) "La storia delle donne: una questione di confine." In Giovanni De Luna, Peppino Ortoleva, Marco Revelli, and Nicola Tranfaglia (eds.) *Gli strumenti della ricerca* (vol. 2: *Questioni di metodo*). Florence: La Nuova Italia: 1434–69.

POPOLIZIO, Stephen (1980) "Literary Reminiscences and the Act of Reading in *Inferno* V." *Dante Studies* 98: 19–33.

PORTA, Giambattista Della (1591) *La Penelope*. Naples: Mattio Cancer.

—— (1726) *Delle commedie di Giovanbattista de la Porta Napoletano*, ed. Gennaro Muzio. Naples: Gennaro Muzio.

PORTER, Mary C., and VENNING, Corey (1976) "Catholicism and Women's Role in Italy and Ireland." In Lynne Iglitzin and Ruth Ross (eds.) *Women in the World. A Comparative Study*. Santa Barbara: Clio Books: 81–103.

POSANI, R. (1968) *La grande guerra*. Florence: La Nuova Italia.

PRANDI, Carlo (1977) *Religione, arte e classi subalterne: ceramiche devozionali in Emilia Romagna*. Rome: Atesa.

—— (1983) *La religione popolare fra potere e tradizione: per una sociologia della tradizione religiosa*. Milan: Franco Angeli.

227

PRESTON, James J. (ed.) (1982) *Mother Worship: Theme and Variations.* Chapel Hill: University of North Carolina Press.

PROCACCI, Giovanna (ed.) (1983) *Stato e classe operaia in Italia durante la prima guerra mondiale.* Milan: Franco Angeli.

PROKOP, U. (1978) *Realtà e desiderio. L'ambivalenza femminile.* Milan: Feltrinelli.

QUAGLIO, Antonio Enzo (1973) *Al di là di Francesca e Laura.* Padua: Liviana Editrice.

RADCLIFF-UMSTEAD, Douglas (ed.) (1978) *Human Sexuality in the Middle Ages and Renaissance.* Pittsburgh: University of Pittsburgh Press.

REITER, Rayna R. (1975) "Men and Women in the South of France: Public and Private Domains." In R. R. Reiter (ed.) *Toward an Anthropology of Women.* New York: Monthly Review Press: 252–82.

—— (ed.) (1975) *Toward an Anthropology of Women.* New York: Monthly Review Press.

REVELLI, Nuto (1985) *L'anello forte.* Turin: Einaudi.

RICH, Adrienne (1977) *Of Woman Born.* New York: Norton.

RODONDI, Raffaella (1982) "Un inedito di C. E. Gadda – *Cinema (Secondo Tempo)*." *Strumenti critici* 49: 275–93.

ROSA', Rosa (1981) "Le donne del Posdomani." In Rosa', R. (ed.) *Una donna con tre anime. Romanzo futurista.* Milan: Edizioni delle Donne: 122–26.

ROSALDO, Michelle, and LAMPHERE, Louise (eds.) (1974) *Women, Culture and Society.* Stanford: Stanford University Press.

ROSE, Mary Beth (ed.) (1986) *Women in the Middle Ages and the Renaissance.* Syracuse: Syracuse University Press.

ROSSI, Ida (1896) "Ninne-nanne del Cosentino." *Archivio per lo studio delle tradizioni popolari* 15: 79–81.

ROSSI, Joseph, and GALPIN, Alfred (eds. and trans.) (1957) *De Sanctis on Dante.* Madison: University of Wisconsin Press.

RUBIN, Gayle (1975) "The Traffic of Women: Notes on the Political Economy of Sex." In R. R. Reiter (ed.) *Toward an Anthropology of Women.* New York: Monthly Review Press: 157–210.

RUESCH, J., and KEES, W. (1961) *Non-Verbal Communication.* Berkeley: California University Press.

RUSSO, Vittorio (1965) "*Tristitia* e *misericordia* nel canto V dell'*Inferno*." In V. Russo, (ed.) *Lezioni e studi sull'Inferno di Dante.* Naples: Liguori: 87–106.

RUTTER, Itala C. (1990) "Feminist Theory as Practice: Italian Feminism and the Work of Teresa De Lauretis and Dacia Maraini." *Women's Studies International Forum* 13: 565–75.

RYAN, Lawrence V. (1976) " 'Stornei, gru, colombe': The Bird Images in *Inferno V*." *Dante Studies* 94: 25–45.

SAFFIOTI, Tito (1978) *Enciclopedia della canzone popolare e della nuova canzone politica.* Milan: Teti.

_____ (ed.) (1981) *Ninne-nanne: condizione femminile, paura e gioco verbale nella tradizione popolare*. Milan: Emme.

SALOME', Lou Andreas (1985) *L'erotismo. L'uomo come donna*. Milan: La Tartaruga.

SANDAY, Peggy R. (1974) "Female Status in the Public Domain." In M. Rosaldo and L. Lamphere (eds.) *Women, Culture and Society*. Stanford: Stanford University Press: 189–206.

SANGA, Glauco (ed.) (1978) *Il linguaggio del canto popolare*. Milan: Giunti/Marzocco.

SARACENO, Chiara (1980) *Il lavoro maldiviso*. Bari: De Donato

——— (1984) "Shifts in Public and Private Boundaries: Women as Mothers and Service Workers in Italian Daycare." *Feminist Studies* 10: 7–29.

——— (ed.) (1986) *Età e corso della vita*. Bologna: Il Mulino.

——— (1987) *Pluralità e mutamento*. Milan: Franco Angeli.

SCHEMAN, Naomi (1988) "Missing Mothers/Desiring Daughters: Framing the Sight of Women." *Critical Inquiry* 15: 62–89.

SCHNEIDER, J. (1971) "Of Vigilance and Virgins: Honor, Shame and Access to Resources in Mediterranean Society." *Ethnology* 1: 1–24.

SCIOLLA, L. (ed.) (1984) *Identità*. Turin: Rosenberg and Sellier.

SCOTT, Joan W. (1983) "Women in History. The Modern Period." *Past and Present* 101: 141–57.

——— (1988) *Gender and the Politics of History*. New York: Columbia University Press.

SCOTT, John A. (1979) "Dante's Francesca and the Poet's Attitude towards Courtly Literature." *Reading Medieval Studies* 5: 4–20.

SERGIACOMO, Lucilla (1988) *Le donne dell'ingegnere*. Pescara: Medium.

SERAO, Matilde (1991) *The Conquest of Rome*, ed. Ann Caesar. London: Pickering and Chatto.

SETTIMELLI, Leoncarlo (1972) *Cittadini e contadini, Urbanites and Country Folk: Canzoni del folklore toscano, Folksongs from Tuscany*. VPA 8135. Milan: Vedette Records.

SHANKLAND, Hugh (1975) "Dante 'Aliger'." *The Modern Language Review* 4: 765–85.

——— (1977) "Dante *Aliger* and Ulysses." *Italian Studies* 32: 21–40.

SHAPIRO, Maryanne (1975) *Woman Earthly and Divine in the Comedy of Dante*. Lexington: University of Kentucky Press.

SHOAF, R. A. (1975) "Dante's *colombi* and the Figuralism of Hope in the *Divine Comedy*." *Dante Studies* 93: 27–59.

SICUTERI, Roberto (1980) *Lilith. La luna nera*. Rome: Astrolabio.

SILTANEN, J., and STANTWORTH, M. (1984a) *Women and the Public Sphere*. London: Hutchinson.

——— (eds.) (1984b) "The Politics of Private Woman and Public Man." *Theory and Society* 1: 91–118.

SINGLETON, Charles (1967) *Journey to Beatrice*. Cambridge, Massachusetts: Harvard University Press.

SONTAG, Susan (1978) *Sulla fotografia.* Turin: Einaudi.

SPERBER, Dan (1981) *Per una teoria del simbolismo. Una ricerca antropologica.* Turin: Einaudi.

——— (1985) "Anthropology and Psychology: Towards an Epidemiology of Representations." *Man* (n.s.) 1: 73–89.

SPITZER, Leo (1976) *Lettere di prigionieri di guerra italiani 1915–1918.* Turin: Boringhieri.

STATO MAGGIORE DELL'ESERCITO (1978) *L'esercito italiano nella prima guerra mondiale. Immagini.* Rome: Stato Maggiore dell'Esercito, Ufficio Storico.

STEFANATI, Gianni (1986) *Fòra la pórta d'Asia: repertori di tradizione orale a Pieve di Cento.* Padua: Interbooks.

STRANIERO, Michele L. (1981) "Il rito, l'incanto: funzione apparente e funzione reale della ninna nanna." In Tito Saffioti (ed.) *Ninne-Nanne.* Milan: Emme: 89–99.

SWAIN WARD, Elisabeth (1986) " 'My Excellent and Most Singular Lord': Marriage in a Noble Family of Fifteenth-Century Italy." *Journal of Medieval and Renaissance Studies* 16: 171–95.

SWING, T. K. (1962) *The Fragile Leaves of the Sibyl: Dante's Master Plan.* Westminster, Maryland: Newman Press.

TARCHETTI, Igino Ugo (1869) *Fosca.* Milan: Treves.

TAYLOR, Karla (1983) "A Text and Its Afterlife: Dante and Chaucer." *Comparative Literature* 35: 1–20.

TENTORI, Tullio (1960) *Antropologia culturale.* Rome: Editrice Studium.

TESTAFERRI, Ada (ed.) (1989) *Donna-Women in Italian Culture.* Toronto: University of Toronto Italian Studies.

TODOROV, Tzvetan (1977) *The Poetics of Prose.* Oxford: Basil Blackwell.

TORRETTA, Laura (1902–1903) "Il *Liber de claris mulieribus* di Giovanni Boccaccio." *Giornale Storico della Letteratura Italiana* 39 (1902): 252–92; 40 (1903): 35–65.

TOURING CLUB ITALIANO (1965) *La nostra guerra 1915–1918 nel Cinquantennio.* Milan: Touring Club Italiano.

TRECKER, J. Law (1974) "Sex, Science and Education." *American Quarterly* 4: 352–66.

TRICHTENBERG, A. (1985) "Albums of War: On Reading Civil War Photographs." *Representations* 9: 1–32.

TROELTSCH, E. (1960) *Le dottrine sociali delle chiese e dei gruppi cristiani.* Florence: La Nuova Italia.

URETTINI, Luigi, and GUARNIERI, Silvio (1985) *Il giovane Comisso e le sue lettere a casa (1914–1920).* Abano Terme: Francisci.

VECCHI GALLI, Paola (1984) "Il Ms. 165 della Biblioteca Universitaria di Bologna (con inediti di Sabadino degli Arienti)." In Bruno Basile (ed.) *Bentivolorum Magnificentia.* Rome: Bulzoni: 223–53.

VERGA, Giovanni (1882) *Il marito di Elena.* Milan: Treves.

VIRGIL (1985) *The Aeneid*, trans. Robert Fitzgerald. Harmondsworth: Penguin Classics.

VITALI, Giulio (1908) "Donne italiane a Congresso." *La rassegna nazionale XLVII,* 12 June 1908: 306–14.

WALL, Richard, ROBIN, Jean, and LASLETT, Peter (eds.) (1983) *Family Forms in Historic Europe.* Cambridge: Cambridge University Press.

WALZER, M. (1983) *Spheres of Justice: A Defence of Pluralism and Equality.* Oxford: Basil Blackwell.

WARNER, Marina (1976) *Alone of All Her Sex: Cult of the Virgin Mary.* New York: Picador Books.

WEBER, M. (1981) *Economia e società.* Milan: Comunità.

WILLIAMS, J. (1972) *Battleground. The Home Fronts: Britain, France and Germany, 1915–1918.* Chicago: Chicago University Press.

Notes on Contributors

Margaret Baker is senior lecturer in Italian at Flinders University, Adelaide. Her main areas of interest are Renaissance and twentieth-century literature, particularly Italo Calvino and Carlo Emilio Gadda.

Franca Bimbi is *professore associato* (senior lecturer) in sociology at the University of Padua. Her main research interest is the sociology of the family. She is the author of several monographs and articles on women in the family and in the Italian workforce. She has been involved in the Italian feminist movement since the early 1970s.

Lucia Chiavola Birnbaum is former assistant professor of history at San Francisco State University. She has written on European and American history and is the author of the monograph *Liberazione della donna – feminism in Italy*.

Piera Carroli is an Italian-born scholar affiliated with Flinders University, Adelaide. She successfully completed an M.A. thesis on the Italian writer Alba De Céspedes.

Diana Cavuoto is lecturer in Italian at Flinders University, Adelaide. Her main fields of research are Dante and eighteenth-century Dante criticism. She currently is completing a Ph.D. dissertation on women in Dante's *Comedy*.

Mirna Cicioni is senior lecturer in Italian at La Trobe University, Melbourne. She convened the conferences entitled "Women in Italian Culture" (30 June–2 July 1989, and 3–5 July 1992), and teaches a course on women in twentieth-century Italy.

Flavia Coassin is assistant lecturer in Italian at La Trobe University, Melbourne. She has completed a Ph.D. dissertation on Dante's poetic theories and their application in the *Comedy*.

Pauline Dagnino has completed a Ph.D. dissertation on the contemporary feminist writer Dacia Maraini at the University of Auckland, New Zealand.

Paola di Cori is *ricercatrice* (research fellow) in contemporary history at the University of Urbino. She has written extensively on nineteenth- and twentieth-century Italian history and on modern and contemporary women's history. She was one of the founding editors of the women's history journal *Memoria*. She has been active in the Italian women's movement since the early 1970s.

Stephen D. Kolsky is senior lecturer in Italian at the University of Melbourne. He has published widely in the field of Italian Renaissance studies, particularly on Isabella d'Este and on Castiglione's view of women.

Tina Lagostena Bassi is one of the leading Italian feminist lawyers. She has been active in the Italian women's movement since the early 1970s and has made important contributions to the reform of Italian laws on abortion, domestic and sexual violence, and drug addiction.

Walter Musolino is assistant lecturer in Italian at La Trobe University, Melbourne. He currently is working on a Ph.D. dissertation on female characters in the fiction of Cesare Pavese. His other research interest is modern and contemporary Italian poetry.

Luisa Passerini is *professore associato* (senior lecturer) in history at Turin University. She has published widely on oral history, particularly on Turin during the Fascist period. Her monograph *Fascism in Popular Memory: The Cultural Experience of the Turin Working Class* appeared in English in 1987.

Nicole Prunster is lecturer in Italian at La Trobe University, Melbourne. Her major field of research is the Italian theater of the sixteenth century, with particular reference to the Counter Reformation.

Index

Since this is a collection of essays rather than a monograph, entries covering such broad areas as "Italy," "Italian literature," "Italian history," and "Italian society," have not been included in the Index.